SAGE was founded in 1965 by Sara Miller McCune to support the dissemination of usable knowledge by publishing innovative and high-quality research and teaching content. Today, we publish over 900 journals, including those of more than 400 learned societies, more than 800 new books per year, and a growing range of library products including archives, data, case studies, reports, and video. SAGE remains majority-owned by our founder, and after Sara's lifetime will become owned by a charitable trust that secures our continued independence.

Los Angeles | London | New Delhi | Singapore | Washington DC | Melbourne

JAMMU AND KASHMIR

JAMMU AND KASHMIR

1990 AND BEYOND

COMPETITIVE POLITICS IN THE SHADOW OF SEPARATISM

REKHA CHOWDHARY

SAGE SERIES ON POLITICS IN INDIAN STATES–II

SERIES EDITORS
SUHAS PALSHIKAR
RAJESHWARI DESHPANDE

SAGE

Los Angeles | London | New Delhi
Singapore | Washington DC | Melbourne

First published in 2019 by

SAGE Publications India Pvt Ltd
B1/I-1 Mohan Cooperative Industrial Area
Mathura Road, New Delhi 110 044, India
www.sagepub.in

SAGE Publications Inc
2455 Teller Road
Thousand Oaks, California 91320, USA

SAGE Publications Ltd
1 Oliver's Yard, 55 City Road
London EC1Y 1SP, United Kingdom

SAGE Publications Asia-Pacific Pte Ltd
18 Cross Street #10-10/11/12
China Square Central
Singapore 048423

Published by Vivek Mehra for SAGE Publications India Pvt Ltd, typeset in 10.5/13 pts Berkeley by Zaza Eunice, Hosur, Tamil Nadu, India.

Library of Congress Cataloging-in-Publication Data

Name: Chowdhary, Rekha, author.
Title: Jammu and Kashmir: 1990 and beyond: competitive politics in the shadow of separatism/Rekha Chowdhary.
Description: New Delhi, India: SAGE Publications India, 2019. | Series: Series on politics in indian states; v.II | Includes bibliographical references and index.
Identifiers: LCCN 2018052202| ISBN 9789353282318 (print: alk. paper) | ISBN 9789353282325 (e pub 2.0) | ISBN 9789353282332 (e book)
Subjects: LCSH: Jammu and Kashmir (India)—Politics and government—21st century. | Jammu and Kashmir (India)—History—Autonomy and independence movements. | Insurgency—India—Jammu and Kashmir.
Classification: LCC DS485.K27 C493 2019 | DDC 954/.6053—dc23 LC record available at https://lccn.loc.gov/2018052202

ISBN: 978-93-532-8231-8 (HB)

SAGE Team: Abhijit Baroi, Guneet Kaur, Syeda Aina Rahat Ali and Rajinder Kaur

CONTENTS

LIST OF TABLES

LIST OF ABBREVIATIONS

ADDC	Additional District Development Commissioner
AFSPA	Armed Forces (Special Powers) Act
AICSCSTO	All India Confederation of SC/ST Organizations
APHC	All Party Hurriyat Conference
CCC	Coalition Coordination Committee
CM	Chief Minister
CMP	Common Minimum Programme
CSDS	Centre for the Study of Developing Societies
CSR	child sex ratio
CVHDC	Chenab Valley Hill Development Council
DAA	Disturbed Area Act
ETOs	Excise and Taxation Officers
HUM	Harkat-ul-Mujahideen
JKAH	Jammu and Kashmir Jamiat-e-Ahlihadees
JKAL	Jammu and Kashmir Awami League
JKDFP	Jammu and Kashmir Democratic Freedom Party
JKDPN	Jammu and Kashmir Democratic Party Nationalist
JKHCBA	Jammu and Kashmir High Court Bar Association
JKPP	Jammu and Kashmir Panthers Party
JMM	Jammu Mukti Morcha
JSM	Jammu State Morcha
LBA	Ladakh Buddhist Association
LeT	Lashkar-e-Toiba
LMA	Ladakh Muslim Association
LoC	Line of Control

LUTF	Ladakh Union Territory Front
MUF	Muslim United Front
NC	National Conference
NEFA	North-East Frontier Agency (NEFA)
NWFP	North-West Frontier Province
PoK	Pakistan-occupied Kashmir
PRC	permanent resident certificate
RTI	Right to Information
SAC	State Accountability Commission
SASB	Shri Amarnath Shrine Board
SAYSS	Shri Amarnath Yatra Sangharsh Samiti
SCs	Scheduled Castes
SECC	Socio Economic and Caste Census
SIC	State Information Commission
SKEWPY	Sher-i-Kashmir Employment and Welfare Programme for Youth
SOGs	Special Operation Groups
STs	Scheduled Tribes
UN	United Nations
UT	Union Territory

SERIES NOTE

The *SAGE Series* on *Politics in Indian States* aims at developing comprehensive, contemporary political histories of Indian states looking at the past two and a half decades. The series will consist of volumes covering important trends in the politics of major states of India. Each volume, devoted to one particular state, would situate the politics of that state in the larger socio-historical context and present a detailed analysis of the significant patterns of competitive politics in the state with a focus on framework of party competition, rise of new social forces, role of leadership and the context of regional political economy. Going beyond state-specificity, each volume would also attempt to situate the politics of the state in the larger all-India context.

Besides analysing the state-specific trends in party politics that have led to the rise of many state parties, these volumes would also carefully look at the social bases of parties and their electoral fortunes in the backdrop of fluctuations in voter choices during elections of past quarter of a century, making use of the rich data archives of Lokniti.

The unfolding dynamics of politics since the 1990s, which manifested at the state level at slightly different moments and sometimes even preceded the 1990s, have forcefully brought back the states in the consciousness of students of Indian politics. It has led to a renewed interest among sociologists and economists about the political processes at the state level and their interconnections with socio-economic developments in India. At the same time, there is a glaring absence of detailed documentations of the state-specific political processes during the past two decades. The series will address this gap in the literature on Indian politics. The series will also propel more informed cross-state comparisons as a starting point to truly grasp 'all-India' politics.

INTRODUCTION

The volume titled *Jammu and Kashmir: 1990 and Beyond—Competitive Politics in the Shadow of Separatism* has been designed around the politics of this state as it evolved in the post-1980s period. The period assumes importance not only in the context of metamorphosis that the state underwent due to the onset of militancy and separatism but also because of major shifts in the competitive politics. The armed militancy accompanied by massive popular separatist surge in the early 1990s resulted in the near-total collapse of the democratic politics in Kashmir. The ascendancy of the separatism and the prevailing violence during next one decade or so made it difficult for the democratic political space to regain itself. Although formal attempts were made with the 1996 Assembly election to restore the political processes, however, it was not before the 2002 Assembly election that democratic space could find some ground. For next one decade or so, there was a constant expansion of this space.

What has been peculiar about the expansion of democratic space in Kashmir is that it had been taking place in the larger context of separatism. Without challenging the relevance of separatist politics around the larger issue related to conflict and its resolution, the political actors in the democratic space had restricted their role mainly to the 'politics of governance'. It is in the distinction between the two spheres of politics (the democratic sphere of 'politics of governance' and the separatist sphere of 'politics of conflict resolution') that one can find much explanation as to how the democratic space which had been delegitimized in the post-1989 period became so vibrant after 2002 that even the separatists had to acknowledged its reality.

Separatism, meanwhile, continued to assert itself, and even while there have been aggressive competitive elections with huge voter turnouts, the popular separatist sentiments have often been expressed on the streets of Kashmir. Some of the massive agitations that took place during the 2008–2010 period, and more recently in 2016, have reflected the intensity of the separatist sentiments on the ground.

The parallel existence of the democratic and separatist spheres of politics and the way the two had intersected and impacted each other in the period after 1990s make Kashmir a unique study. Both the spheres are interesting for the purpose of analysis as in each case there have been significant internal shifts. Separatist politics has changed its course from the militancy to the post-militancy stage and has, over the years, become much more inward looking and intense.

Interesting shifts have also been reflected in the domain of democratic politics. To begin with, significant changes have taken place in the nature of party competition. The 2002 elections marked the end of the era of hegemonic politics of the National Conference (NC) and ushered the state into the phase of intensely competitive politics with a number of political parties having a stake in power. The fragmented verdicts in each election and coalition politics have been the logical corollaries of the aggressively competitive electoral politics of the state.

Changes meanwhile have also taken place in the regional balance of power. With the decline of the hegemonic base of the NC, the regional politics of Kashmir has become fragmented between two or more parties. As a consequence, unlike the earlier situation when governments were formed by a party which captured most of the seats of Kashmir region without having to depend on other regions, a new situation has evolved in which there is a regional parity. Every coalition government since 2002 is a combination of regional partners—with one party having its stronghold in Kashmir region and the other in Jammu region.

It is in this context of fundamental shifts that have taken place in the last two and a half decades in the politics of Jammu and Kashmir that this book has been designed. The state has caught sufficient attention of the academics and journalists, and a plethora of work has been produced, especially after the outbreak of militancy. While much of this work is historical in nature, going back to the roots of conflict, there have been quite a few studies that have been dealing with the situation as it evolved in the later years of the 1980s and during the early years of armed militancy. Some of these studies have gone deep into the intricate political question and have made serious conceptual and theoretical interventions around the themes of identity, ethnicity, nationalism and democracy.

While these studies have been very useful in understanding the complex questions of conflict politics, the internal political processes, as these have taken shape during the last two and a half decades, have not been analysed in detail. There is virtually no discussion on the internal dynamics of militancy and separatism, transition from militancy to post-militancy phase of separatism, the collapse and restoration of democratic space, linkage between separatism and democratic politics, regional and subregional complexities, and the like.

This volume aims to fill this important gap in the understanding of the politics of Jammu and Kashmir state. Although the particular situation of conflict as well as its constitutional specificity (special constitutional status under Article 370) makes this state quite distinct from other Indian states, yet the patterns of competitive politics, especially the nature of party and electoral politics, leadership trends, governance as well as the socio-economic issues, are comparable to other states. It is in this dual context of specificity as well its location in the broader trends of state politics of India that the present volume is located. The basic questions that it seeks to address fall in four categories: those related to the specificity of the structural and institutional dimension of the state politics; those related with the implication of the conflict situation, particularly the resistance/separatist politics; those related with democratic political space; and those related with the convergence/overlap between the separatist and democratic spaces. Within the confines of these categories, there is a detailed analysis of the broad trends pertaining to the post-1989 politics of separatism and its changing nature through the last two and a half decades; the electoral politics that include focus on the changing party system and leadership shifts; the regional politics that not merely refers to the patterns of regional and subregional politics but also focuses on interregional relations; and the social demography, socio-economic developments and emerging issues around gender, caste and religion-based assertions. More specific attention is paid to the changing response of people towards the 'politics of governance' and reconciliation of this politics with the 'separatist sentiments'. Since the space for politics of 'governance' was gradually extending, there is also a comparative performance analysis of various governments since the restoration of electoral politics in 1996.

The present volume is divided into nine chapters. The first two chapters lay down the setting for the succeeding chapters. Of these two chapters, the first one titled 'The Background to the State Politics of Jammu and Kashmir: The Context of Conflict' provides a basic understanding of the conflict situation, particularly from the internal perspective, and focuses on 'Kashmir Valley' as the theatre of conflict. Referring to the initial process of harmonization of the Kashmiri identity politics with the Indian nationalist project, it makes a detailed analysis of the fundamental principles underlying such a process of harmonization and the rupture that developed in the Delhi–Kashmir relationship in the later period. It particularly deals with the process of de-institutionalization of the democratic structures, the non-participatory nature of the competitive politics and excessive intrusion by the Centre in the state politics on the one hand and the emergence of the separatist space under the banner of the Plebiscite Front and its legitimization on the other. Tracking the history of conflict and democratic politics till 1989, the chapter goes on to focus on the period of 1975–1982 when the separatist political space was briefly pushed to the background and there was ascendance of the democratic political space. This space, however, was so extremely manipulated in the period after the death of Sheik'h Abdullah that it led not only to the failure of democratic processes per se but also to the total collapse of the authority of the state. The chapter on the whole lays down the background in which there was onset of militancy and separatism in the Kashmir Valley in the post-1989 period.

The second chapter titled 'State of Jammu and Kashmir: Internal Complexity' takes the discussion beyond the Kashmir Valley and highlights the complex reality of the state both from the perspective of the social composition and multiplicity of political perspectives. While locating the centrality of the conflict situation in Kashmir's identity politics, the chapter focuses on various other manifestations of the identity politics. More particularly, it refers to the political divergence that exists within the state and the resultant tensions that such divergence generates in the context of interregional and subregional relations. Dismissing the notions of homogenized or singular nature of political expressions, it also seeks to demolish the idea that all political differences within the state can be reduced to religious divide between 'Muslim Kashmir' and 'Hindu Jammu' and 'Buddhist Ladakh'. The chapter, therefore, explores the complex social and political reality of these two other regions of the state and brings to the focus the 'regional' factor in the identity politics of the state. It also seeks to highlight the multiple contexts of marginalization and assertions that somehow tend to generally remain hidden due to the focus only on the conflict politics as it manifests in Kashmir. Therefore, besides the regional and subregional identity politics, the chapter focuses on the issues of caste, tribe and gender.

Chapter 3 focuses on the politics of separatism in Kashmir and details the nature of separatism through three major phases from 1989 to 2010. The peculiarity of the first phase of separatism was the centrality of militancy and its linkage with the popular separatist response. It was during this phase that there was a total rejection of the democratic politics and the masses of Kashmir were swayed by the slogan of *azadi*. Militancy that had received the full support of people enjoyed legitimacy in this phase. By the end of the 1990s, the separatism had already entered its second phase when militancy had been delegitimized to a large extent. It was during this phase that the peace process was initiated and democratic politics was revived. However, the extension of democratic space did not take place at the cost of separatist politics. It continued to assert itself in one form or the other. Such assertion was clearly reflected during the third phase of post-militancy separatism when there was a clear decline of militancy. The massive separatist agitations—as in 2008 and 2010—clearly marked the continued existence and assertion of separatism.

Chapter 4 titled 'The Exodus of Kashmiri Pandits' deals with the very tricky issue emanating from the context of conflict when almost the whole Kashmiri Pandit community that formed a minuscule minority in otherwise predominantly Muslim Kashmir left the valley. Such an exodus has resulted in challenging the very concept of 'Kashmiriyat' reflecting the syncretic Kashmiri tradition and the cultural continuity between the Kashmiri Pandits and Muslims. The chapter details the historical background of the intercommunity relations and the nature of political divide that existed between the two communities. It then goes on to discuss the situation in which the exodus took place and analyses the question of their return.

Chapter 5 focuses on the nature of democratic space as it started extending in Kashmir after the 1996 Assembly election. This space had totally vanished in the wake of the violence unleashed by militancy and militarization in the post-1989 period. With the decline of militancy and installation of NC government after the 1996 Assembly election, this space was restored to some extent, but it did not gain legitimacy till 2002. It was with the 2002 Assembly election that a paradigm change was brought about in Kashmir's party politics, so much so that the democratic space started getting extended and entrenched. The newly floated People's Democratic Party (PDP) strategically locating itself in the conflict politics, through its call for 'healing touch' and bringing to the mainstream the political agenda that was exclusively in the separatist domain so far, succeeded in invigorating the democratic political space and making it extensively competitive. Every election since 2002 became intensely competitive adding to the credibility of the democratic process. However, what was peculiar about this process was that the extension of democratic space did not take place at the cost of separatism. The period between 2002 and 2014 actually saw a parallel existence of the mainstream 'politics of governance' and the separatist 'politics of conflict resolution' with the two overlapping with each other. While separatism continued to assert itself, as reflected from the upsurge in 2008–2010 and more recently in 2016, the democratic space also extended itself as has been reflected through the keenly contested and participatory 2008 and 2014 Assembly elections.

Chapter 6 titled 'Competitive Politics in Jammu and Kashmir' focuses on party and electoral politics and analyses the nature of shift from single-party dominance to intensely competitive party politics since 2002. After analysing the implications of the dominant and hegemonic role of the single party particularly for the conflict-ridden Kashmir Valley in the pre-2002 period, the chapter goes on to discuss the nature and implications of shift in the party politics since 2002. The focus here is placed not only on the new pattern of electoral politics due to the multiplicity of parties and fragmented verdicts but also on the nature of power sharing—with greater regional balance and visibility of regions other than Kashmir, particularly Jammu region, in the power politics. Much of the credibility of the electoral politics in Kashmir region, the chapter argues, is mainly due to the changed nature of party politics.

Chapter 7 titled 'Governance in Jammu and Kashmir' focuses on the problematic area of governance in the state. Locating the background of the governance issues in the state in the pre-militancy period, the chapter goes on to analyse the problems of governance during the various phases of militancy and separatism. Governance, as the chapter reflects, was the most knotty issue during the 1996–2002 period, since much of the energy of the NC government was used in rebuilding the infrastructure damaged during the earlier period of militancy. The high level of violence and the lack of legitimacy of this government were also the critical issues because of which this government could not deliver much on the ground. It was in the post-2002 period that due to the higher level of legitimacy of the elected government there was a better linkage between the government and the people, and the successive governments could pay better attention to governance as such. Mufti-led government that was installed in 2002 in fact could respond to the conflict and militarization-related problems faced by the people in general. However, the coalitions that were formed since 2002 faced their own kinds of problems: of coalition partners being pushed in different directions and often struck in various kinds of political controversies. Chapter 7 on the whole shows that though there has been a better regional balance in the process of power sharing and governance; however, the basic issues particularly those related to employment and corruption have continued to remain unaddressed. The chapter highlights the implications of the conflict situation on the process of governance and particularly reflects on the lack of institutionalization as the major problem in this process. The chapter also focuses on economic backwardness as being the major issue confronted by the state.

Chapter 8 titled 'Interregional Relations and Politics of Jammu and Ladakh Since 1990' focuses on the regional dimensions of politics and extends the discussion around the politics of diversity and political divergence in the post-1990 period. The political divergence that exists between Kashmir region on the one hand and Jammu and Ladakh regions on the other came to be much more sharply focused during the period of militancy and in both the regions there was resurgence of regional sentiments and articulation of the demand for regional autonomy. The politics of 'trifurcation' was also meanwhile highlighted in the urban centres, particularly of Jammu region. The chapter goes on to explore as to how the unaddressed problem of the ideological and political divide among the three regions has resulted in interregional tensions. These tensions came out more openly during the 2008 Amarnath land row when the two major regions of the state, namely Jammu and Ladakh, were placed in a confrontationist situation.

Chapter 9 titled 'Democracy and Politics of Separatism in Kashmir: 2014 and After' locates the politics of the state since 2014 vis-à-vis three major phenomena: the Assembly election, the BJP–PDP coalition government and the ascendancy of separatism in post-2014 period. The 2014 Assembly election that was intensely competitive and highly participatory in many ways reflected as to how the democratic politics had come to be entrenched, despite the 2008 and 2010 separatist resurgence. Continuing with the recent tradition of the fragmented verdicts, it not only marked the further decline of the NC but also registered the rise of BJP, which swept the Jammu region. The election threw up a peculiar situation in which the two ideologically opposite parties emerged as the major claimants of power. The coming together of these two parties—BJP being the dominant party in Jammu region and PDP being the dominant party in Kashmir region—threw its own kind of challenges. This has been one of the most difficult coalition governments that has seen more political controversies than any other earlier coalition. The chapter delineates the implications that this coalition government has had on the process of governance. The third phenomenon that has been discussed in this chapter relates to the resurgence of the separatist wave since 2014. This separatist wave that engulfed the whole valley—particularly the south of Kashmir, the bastion of the PDP—has once more problematized the politics of Kashmir.

The Background to the State Politics of Jammu and Kashmir

The Context of Conflict

1

THE KASHMIR CONFLICT: EXTERNAL DIMENSION

While discussing the competitive politics of the state of Jammu and Kashmir (J&K), it is important to refer to the conflict situation in which the state has been embroiled for the last seven decades. The conflict situation has impacted the politics of the state in a variety of ways. Apart from the uncertainties that it has created and turbulence that it has resulted in, the conflict situation has also directed and shaped the politics of the state. Whether it is in the areas of democratic institution building, the dynamics of the federal relations or economic and development processes, the import of the conflict situation can be clearly seen. Even in other areas, including the intrastate political processes, interregional and intercommunity relations, social movements and various layers of identity politics, one can see the imprint of the conflict in the background.

The conflict situation is quite layered and complex and is comprised of both the external and internal dimensions. The external dimension of conflict is marked by the centrality of the 'Kashmir question' in India–Pakistan relations and is manifested in the continued hostilities between the two countries and the volatility of borders, competitive claims and maximalist position of the two countries, and the division of the state into the Indian and Pakistan administered parts around the Line of Control (LoC).

The seeds of conflict can be traced to the very moment of Accession which took place on 26 October 1947, much after the deadline of 15 August 1947, in abnormal conditions when the state was facing tribal invasion, on the one hand, and internal rebellion, on the other. Indecisiveness on the part of the ruler on the question of accession created a state of political uncertainty that was compounded by the external pressures and internal turbulence. Although ruled by a Hindu ruler, this predominantly Muslim-majority state was claimed by Pakistan because of demographic reasons and also because of its geographical location as well as its strategic importance. This claim was, however, clearly rejected not only by India but also by the Kashmir's popular leadership and the National Conference (NC). This organization, right from the time of its inception, was engaged in a sustained anti-feudal and anti-monarchical movement in Kashmir[1] (Bamzai 1973; Bazaz 2002; Chowdhary and Kumar 2002).

Sheikh Abdullah, the charismatic and popular leader of Kashmir, though ambivalent about his position on the question of accession, had unequivocally dismissed the idea of Pakistan as the Muslim homeland for Kashmiris. However, notwithstanding such a position of Sheikh and other Kashmiri leaders, the state was invaded by the Pak-supported tribals from the then North-West Frontier Province (NWFP). This invasion coincided with a local rebellion of Muslims of Poonch against the Dogra ruler in Jammu region. These developments resulted in a full-fledged war between India

[1] The anti-feudal movement that had started taking a concrete shape in the early years of the decade of 1930s had gone through various phases. Initially, it had taken a religious route and was based on the construction of 'Muslim identity' and assertion of unity of Muslims across the two major regions of the state. The All Jammu and Kashmir Muslim Conference was a manifestation of this identity politics. By the late 1930s, the direction of the movement was changed drastically as radical economic goals assumed centrality and the Muslim Conference was converted into the All Jammu and Kashmir National Conference (Chowdhary 2016).

and Pakistan that lasted till January 1948. Although the Dogra ruler acceded the state to India in this situation of turbulence, a large part of the state came under the control of Pakistan with a ceasefire line lying between the two parts of the state (Bose 2003; Dasgupta 2015; Whitehead 2007).

By 1948, Kashmir conflict had attained most of its attributes and had already assumed a complex character. Pakistan's contestation of the accession of the state with India, its control over around one-third part of the state, the military hostilities between India and Pakistan—all these had provided the external dimension of the conflict. The conflict by this time had also attained an international character since India had approached the United Nations (UN) terming Pakistan as an aggressor, and it was on the UN's intervention that the ceasefire could take place and the Ceasefire Line, which was later on termed the LoC, be drawn.

The external dimension of conflict, particularly the hostilities between India and Pakistan, has had implications of serious nature for this state. These hostilities often have resulted in full-fledged wars between the two countries (the 1965 war, the 1971 war and the Kargil War of 1999). However, it is not only during the war time, but even in the 'normal' times when no such war has been declared, that the borders have generally remained volatile. With the exception of a brief period after the formalization of the 2003 ceasefire agreement between India and Pakistan, the guns never fell silent and the life of people living near the borders has continued to be adversely affected. These people since 1947 have been living lives of uncertainties, experiencing the horrors of war on a day-to-day basis and constantly facing the problems of displacements and rehabilitation. The situation faced by the state has also resulted in hosts of 'refugees' (the Pakistan-occupied Kashmir or PoK refugees, the West Pakistan refugees and Chhamb refugees) whose rehabilitation is still an issue and even seven decades after their displacement, they are still waiting to get duly settled and compensated for the loss that they suffered because of Partition. In addition to these people, there are a large number of families which were divided between the two sides of the LoC and have been unable to interact with each other due to the stringent border regimes

(Banerjee and Roy Choudhury 2011; Chowdhary 2012; Manchanda and Husain 2013).

In the more recent decades, the external dimension of conflict, apart from wars and border skirmishes, has been reflected in the very phenomenon of militancy. Although rooted in the internal political situation, the militancy has been sustained mainly because of the explicit support by Pakistan. Apart from violence unleashed during this period, militancy had the implications of impacting the society, politics and economy in a variety of ways.

INTERNAL DIMENSIONS OF CONFLICT: THE DELHI–KASHMIR RELATIONSHIP

Initial Harmony between Indian and Kashmiri Nationalism

The external dimension of the conflict, which in itself is quite complex, is compounded by the fact that there is an internal dimension of conflict. The logic of the internal dimension of conflict is defined by the New Delhi–Kashmir relationship and one can see its manifestation in various forms ranging from the discourse of autonomy to the discourse of 'plebiscite' and 'azadi'.[2]

The story of internal conflict is best told with reference to a period (1947–1953) in which there was harmonization of Kashmiri identity politics with the Indian nationalist project. This was a period when the NC and its charismatic leader, Sheikh Abdullah, were convinced that the association of the state, especially of Kashmir, with India was the best option available not only because of 'kinship' of ideals between the Kashmiri and the Indian nationalist leaders but also because of the pragmatic reasons for preserving the 'Kashmiri regional identity' and for pursuing the 'radical land reforms'.

[2] Although following two different points of reference, the two kinds of politics get linked at some point. In fact, the roots of 'azadi' politics can be traced in the failure of 'autonomy politics'.

The concept of 'kinship of ideals' was used by Sheikh Abdullah to express the ideological similarity between the goals of the political movement led by the NC and the national movement led by the Indian National Congress. The political position of the Congress was quite close to the ideological goals that the NC had chalked before itself—the restructuring of the state's economy, especially the land reforms and abolition of monarchy. What appealed to the Kashmiri leaders was the empathy that the leadership of the Congress showed to the aspirations of the people of the princely states and the role that it played in organizing the All India States People's Conference[3] (Chowdhary 2016).

For an organization that had emerged after shedding the religious character of the political movement and had reframed its political objectives as reconstructing the polity and economy so as to benefit the mass of the peasantry, artisans and the working classes, Pakistan was no option at all. Described by Abdullah as a 'landlord-ridden state with many feudal privileges intact', it had no possibilities of economic changes that the Kashmiris were looking for (Abdullah 1951, 106). There was an apprehension that Kashmiri identity might be endangered in Pakistan as it might be subsumed by larger religion-based identity. India, in the opinion of Sheikh Abdullah, was a different case. The leadership of the national movement had committed itself to agrarian reforms. In any case, India appealed to the political sensibilities of Kashmiri leadership for a number of other reasons. There was the promise of democracy and accommodation of social and political differences and a secular nature of the Indian State that matched the plural character of the Kashmiri society.

On the whole, it was the 'politics of land reforms' that resolved the issue of accession for Kashmiris. The aggressive approach of the NC towards these reforms in the post-Accession period, in fact, was met with approval of Kashmiris. In a short period between 1948 and 1950, the NC government legislated some of the most radical land

[3] The association of the Kashmiri leadership with the All India States People's Conference was very strong. Sheikh Abdullah was elected as its vice-president and also its president.

reform laws. It was because of these legislations that privileges of parasitic classes (including Jagirdars, Muafidars and Mukkarrees) were abolished. A large number of tenants were freed from the exploitative system of tenancy and the rate of rent was rationalized. There was also scaling down of the debts and numerous distressed peasants were given relief by Debt Conciliation Boards. However, the most effective were the reforms related to ceiling and redistribution. The ceiling limit which was fixed at 22.75 acres helped the state to acquire a large part of the land, which was earlier in the hands of the big landowners and was redistributed to the landless cultivators. What was the most peculiar part of this legislation was that unlike the rest of India, the landowners who surrendered their surplus land were not paid any compensation. Similarly, the cultivators to whom the land was transferred did not have to make any payment for it. Just by a few strokes of law, the class of intermediaries was abolished, the exploitative basis of tenancy was done away with and land security was provided to the tenant. Most significantly, the concentration of land in a few hands was dealt with stringently (Aslam 1977; Beg 1995; Ladejinsky 1952; Thorner 1953).

All this was possible only because of the special constitutional status of the state that NC had succeeded in negotiating. Although many other states also went for land reforms, the rigour that underlay the reforms pursued by this state could not be matched. With the state being insulated, especially in the effect of Fundamental Right to Property, there was more leverage for the government to give a stringent form to the land reforms.

These radical policies while helping the party build linkages with the rural peasantry were also helpful in endorsing Kashmir's bond with India. With most of the landless tillers having become owners of the land overnight (without paying for the land they got) and freed of the burden of the debt, they were overwhelmed by the political developments. And as Wolf Ladejinsky during his field trip in the immediate post-land reform period observed, there was so much goodwill that Sheikh had earned because of the land reform legislations that his decision to endorse accession with India had full support of the people (Ladejinsky 1952, 180).

Despite Pakistan claiming the state of J&K on the basis of religious affiliations of the majority of the people of the state, the Kashmiris were quite happy with the developments. The Maharaja's decision to accede to India in the background of 'tribal invasion' and local rebellion in some areas of Jammu region did not invoke negative response. On the contrary, Indian intervention was eulogized by Sheikh Abdullah later in the UN.

On his own part, Sheikh as the undisputed leader of Kashmir started with a positive orientation towards India. His speeches during the initial post-Accession period reflected his state of mind where he expressed his complete satisfaction with the direction that the relationship of the state with India had been taking. The fact that India had opted for a model of asymmetrical federalism in which J&K was treated differently in the application of the Constitution of India was a matter of great satisfaction for him and he expressed this satisfaction in explicit terms in his opening remarks to the Constituent Assembly of J&K.

> We are proud to have our bonds with India, the goodwill of those people and government is available to us in unstinted and abundant measure. The Constitution of India has provided for a federal union and in the distribution of sovereign powers has treated us differently from other constituent units. With the exception of the items grouped under Defence, Foreign Affairs and Communications in the instrument of Accession, we have complete freedom to frame our Constitution in the manner we like.... (Abdullah 1951, 86)

It was the ideal of secular democracy which led to Sheikh's appreciation for India. It was his regard for the secular basis of the Indian Constitution that he felt that Kashmiris, by rejecting the two-nation theory, would be comfortably placed in India. His faith in secular democracy reflects in the following sentences:

> The real character of a State is revealed in its Constitution. The Indian Constitution has set before the country the goal of secular democracy based upon justice, freedom and equality for all without distinction. This is the bedrock of modern democracy. This should meet the argument that the Muslims of Kashmir cannot have security in India, where the large majority of the population are Hindus. Any unnatural cleavage between religious

> groups is the legacy of Imperialism, and no modern State can afford to encourage artificial division if it is to achieve progress and prosperity. The Indian Constitution has amply and finally repudiated the concept of a religious State, which is a throwback to medievalism, by guaranteeing the equality of rights of all citizens irrespective of their religion, colour, caste and class. (Abdullah 1951, 104)

Rather than the conflictual relationship, the initial New Delhi–Kashmir relationship was based on principles of harmony and mutual appreciation. Kashmiris on the whole were quite positively inclined towards India. Such positive inclination was, therefore, clearly reflected in Sheikh Abdullah's opening remarks in the Constituent Assembly of the state. He expressed his full confidence in the federal framework of the Constitution, especially its asymmetrical nature, and the way the state was given a special treatment. In his understanding the Constitution of India not only provided an opportunity for the state to take its own political direction but also provided a very good model of federal cooperation. To quote him:

> You are no doubt aware of the scope of our present constitutional ties with India.... In order to live and prosper as good partners in a common endeavour for the advancement of our peoples, I would advise that, while safeguarding our autonomy to the fullest extent so as to enable us to have the liberty to build our country according to the best tradition and genius of our people, we may also by suitable constitutional arrangements with the union establish our right, seek and compel Federal co-operation and assistance in this great task as well as offer our fullest co-operation and assistance to the union. (Abdullah 1951, 86)

Association with India, therefore, rather than thwarting the goals of Kashmiri nationalism, was seen as a source of support through which most of its goals could be fulfilled. This is the way Sheikh located Kashmir in its relationship with India during the early post-Accession period:

> The position today, as heretofore, is that our State is a constituent unit of the Indian Union and the relationship is based on the same terms as were laid down in the Instrument of Accession. The State has transferred three subjects of Defence, Foreign Affairs and Communications, and for the residuary powers inherent in it, it has complete freedom to exercise an autonomous position.

> I am fully convinced that this position, consistent with the principles of democracy, could be secured for the State only through a continued association with India, where the large majority of the people are striving to democratize their mode of economic and political development. The support given to our decisions by the Indian people is an effective guarantee that we shall have the fullest opportunities of adopting progressive policies for the benefit of the masses. (Abdullah 1952)

Interestingly, this was the time when the external context of conflict was assuming more intricate forms. The fall-out of the tribal invasion and the local rebellion in Poonch was that the state stood divided between the Indian and Pakistani administered areas. Around one-third of the princely state, falling mostly in Jammu division, came under the control of Pakistan. The efforts to liberate the areas under the control of the tribals and Pakistani forces resulted in a full-fledged war that continued up to early 1948 till a ceasefire as per the terms laid down by the UN was agreed upon. India had earlier approached the UN against Pakistan's aggression in Kashmir.

However, despite the intricacy of the external dimension, the internal situation vis-à-vis the state of J&K was quite peaceful. In Kashmir particularly, a favourable environment existed vis-à-vis the ongoing developments. In fact, as Sheikh stated in the UN, Kashmiris were quite happy allying with India in the light of the danger that Pakistan posed through its tribals.[4]

There were certainly a few voices in Kashmir which had the pro-Pakistan orientation and favoured the state's accession to Pakistan. The Muslim Conference led by Mirwaiz Yusuf Shah and G. M. Karra, for instance, represented this politics. However, these voices existed on the margins of Kashmir's politics. The NC, meanwhile, was a mass party, and Sheikh Abdullah was the most popular leader and represented the dominant stream of Kashmir's politics.

[4] Underlining that it was the situation of distress in which Pakistan had placed the people in the state and India not only offered to help but also offered placing the question of accession before people once the situation was normalized. In his opinion, the Prime Minister of India was under no obligation to add the proviso, but he did it (Abdullah 1948).

Sheikh was the most staunch defender of the state's accession to India in the international fora. With Sheikh at the helm of affairs in Kashmir, India had a very strong moral case in Kashmir which it lost after Sheikh was removed from power and was incarcerated for a very long period.

Negotiability of the State Government and the Politics of Autonomy

One factor that contributed to the harmony between the state and the Centre in the initial period was that the NC was able to pursue its political goals that it had chalked out during the pre-Accession period, and it had succeeded not only in negotiating autonomy for the state but also in pursuing radical land reforms and other policies that favoured the mass of Kashmiris.

In his speeches in the early post-Accession period, Sheikh Abdullah emphasized the freedom that the state enjoyed in negotiating its own constitutional status and in going ahead with the process of dismantling the feudal agrarian structure.

While becoming part of the Indian Union, the state of J&K was not obligated to be governed by the Constitution of India or to follow the pattern of Centre–state relations as was defined by the Indian Constitution. On the contrary, it was given the freedom to negotiate as to which provisions of the Constitution, other than Article 1 and Article 370, could be extended to this state. It could thereby opt for its own pattern of Centre–state relations. The negotiability of the state in these matters was inbuilt in Article 370. Thus, while it was mentioned in Article 370 that Articles other than the two mentioned above would not apply to the state, the mechanism by which other provisions could be extended to the state was also provided in this Article. What was significant in the mechanism was the consent of the state.

Although there were other states which have been dealt with special constitutional provisions, J&K was however the only state which was provided with a whole arrangement for an altogether different scheme of federal relations. This was the only state for which the division of power as contained in the Seventh Schedule of the Constitution of India was not applicable and which had the privilege of drafting its own constitution.[5]

The application of the Centre–state relations was limited to those matters which were agreed upon in the Instrument of Accession and for any other further extension, the concurrence of the state government was essential. Article 370 (1) (b) (i) clearly provided that the power of Parliament to make laws for the state shall be limited to:

> Those matters in the Union List and the Concurrent List which, in consultation with the Government of the State, are declared by the President to correspond to matters specified in the Instrument of Accession governing the accession of the State to the Dominion of India as the matters with respect to which the Dominion Legislature may make laws for that State.

However, it also provided for further application of other matters to the state only with the concurrence of the state government.[6]

That negotiability of the state was a major principle in the relationship between the Centre and this state was clearly reflected in the later

[5] As per Article 370 of the Indian Constitution which provides for the relationship of the state with the Union of India, the application of the Indian Constitution was limited to only two Articles: Article 1 and Article 370. Following the signing of the Instrument of Accession, the state had joined the Union of India and this position was reaffirmed by the application of Article 1. This Article after mentioning that India is a Union of States specifies that 'states and territories thereof shall be as specified in the First Schedule of the Constitution' and that territories of India, among others, 'shall comprise the territories of the states'.

[6] While restricting the applicability of the Constitution of India to the state and limiting the power of the Parliament to legislate for the state, Article 370 was not static. But, on the other hand, provided the mechanism of further extension of both the application of the Constitution of India and the Parliament's power—however, with the concurrence of the state. The state government therefore was empowered to negotiate and keep the initiative as well as the final decision to itself. The Article clearly specified the role of the Constituent Assembly of the state which had to approve all such extensions to the state. The presumption was that with the making of the state constitution, the scheme of the Centre–state relations will be finalized, and it will be clear as to which provisions of the Indian Constitution were applicable to the state and for which matters the state constitution would be applicable. With such a clarification, the purpose of Article 370 as a temporary and transitory provision would have been fulfilled.

developments. Whatever constitutional extension took place in the initial years followed the agreed position of the state and the Centre.

In 1950, the Constitution of India (Application to Jammu and Kashmir) Order, 1950, was issued by the President of India with two Schedules. By the first Schedule, the power of the Parliament to legislate for the state was elaborated in accordance with the matters already specified in the Instrument of Accession. Certain items from within the Union List of the Seventh Schedule to the Indian Constitution were specified on which the Union Parliament could make laws for this state. The second Schedule listed those provisions of the Indian Constitution which were to be applicable to the state, besides Article 1 and Article 370.[7]

As A. S. Anand has argued, the Constitutional Order of 1950 in effect had gone beyond the Instrument of Accession. In his words, 'the powers of the Union Parliament with regard to this State were extended beyond what was originally surrendered in the Instrument of Accession' (Anand 2013, 102). However, since this followed a process of long negotiation, there was not much issue about this.

Negotiability of the state continued through the later years. With the formation of the Constituent Assembly in 1951 the question of Centre–state relations was more clearly confronted and the scope of the Constitution of the state was debated.[8] The Constituent Assembly

[7] Other than Parts III, IV, XIV and XVIII, which were not made applicable to the state, provisions from other Parts of the Constitution with exceptions and modifications were extended to the state. To quote A. S. Anand, '... It is evident that the powers of the Union Parliament with regard to this State were extended beyond what was originally surrendered in the Instrument of Accession' (Anand 2013, 102).

[8] While drafting the Constitution of the state was the major task before the Constituent Assembly of the state, it was also assigned with two other tasks: to decide the 'future of the royal dynasty' and to give a final verdict on the issue of 'compensation to the landowners' whose land had been acquired following the radical land reform legislations. On 19 August 1952, the Constituent Assembly–cum-Legislative Assembly passed a resolution abolishing monarchy (Diwan 1953). Similarly, a resolution was introduced and later adopted to the effect that no compensation be granted to landlords. The resolution stated that 'both on principle and policy the payment of compensation to the expropriated proprietors is not desirable' (Jammu and Kashmir Constituent Assembly, n.d., 337).

(which also served as the first Legislative Assembly) was 'elected' in 1951.[9] Although the Constitution of the state was to deal with matters that were related to the process of state's governance, however, it was also tasked with the responsibility of further defining the relationship between the Centre and the state.[10] One can imagine that with the culmination of the formulation of the state's Constitution, the state's relationship with the Centre—beyond the Instrument of Accession and beyond the Constitutional Order of 1950—could have been clearly defined.

For formalizing this process, negotiations were already on between the state government and the Centre, which later culminated in Delhi Agreement of 1952. This Agreement clearly specified the matters in which the provisions of the Indian Constitution would be extended and the matters which would form the content of the state Constitution.

As per this Agreement, important questions related to residuary power, citizenship, state flag, etc., were resolved. It was resolved that while for other states of India the residuary power was vested in the Centre, in case of J&K this was to remain vested in the state. It was also resolved that the persons who are domiciles of the state were to be regarded as the citizens of India. However, the state legislature was to be given the power to make laws for conferring special rights and privileges to the state subjects. On the issue of state and national flags, it was agreed that the state flag would continue to be recognized. However, the Union flag will have supreme place in the state.

Consensus was also reached about the provisions related to the Parliament, President and Supreme Court. As regards the provisions related to the President of India, it was agreed that Articles 52–62 should be extended to the state. It was also agreed that the power of the

[9] Since the only opposition party that existed in the state at the time had boycotted the election, the NC was able to win 100 per cent of the seats without any competition. All but two seats were returned unopposed. It was in 1957 that the Constitution of the state came into force.

[10] As per the preamble of the state Constitution, one of the major purposes of the Constitution is to 'further define the existing relationship of the State with the Union of India as an integral part thereof'.

President to grant reprieve and commuting of death sentence would be extended to the state. With regard to the Supreme Court, it was decided to have only appellate jurisdiction. On the issue of conduct of election to the Houses of Parliament, the application of Article 324 to the state was agreed to.

As regards the state government, it was agreed that 'the Head of the State shall be the person recognized by the President of the Union on the recommendation of the Legislature of the State' and that 'he shall hold office during the pleasure of president'. While in other states the Head of the state was the nominee of the President (Centre), in case of this state, the Head of the state was to be elected by both Houses of the State Legislature.

There were certain issues which were tricky and a clear-cut agreement could not be reached. On the issue of Fundamental Rights, it was agreed that these rights have to be extended to the citizens belonging to the state but no agreement could be reached as to whether the chapter of Fundamental Rights as contained in the Constitution of India should be extended or should it form a part of the state Constitution. According to Sheikh Abdullah, 'it was agreed, however, that the Fundamental Rights, which are contained in the Constitution of India could not be conferred on the residents of J&K State in their entirety' keeping in view the specific context of the political movement and the ideological goals as enshrined in the New Kashmir Manifesto. 'The need for providing suitable modifications, amendments and exceptions as the case may be in the Fundamental Rights Chapter of the Indian Constitution in order to harmonize those provisions with the pattern of our principles was admitted' (Abdullah cited in J&K Government 2000, 47–59).

On the issue of Emergency powers, while it was agreed that Articles 356 and 360 would not be extended to the state, there were different opinions on the extension of Article 352. While the Government of India believed that extension of this Article was necessary in the interest of the security of the state, the state representatives 'indicated that they were averse to internal disturbance being referred to in this connection as even petty internal disorder might be considered sufficient for application of Article 352'. Hence it was decided to add a proviso to the Article 352 that application of this Article would be 'at the request or with the concurrence of the Government of the state'. However, further discussion on application of Articles 353, 354, 358 and 359 was required (J&K Government 2000, 47–59).

Agreement over the issue of financial integration could also not be reached. While the need for some sort of financial arrangement between the state and the Union was recognized, however, it was felt that the matter needed further examination.

This process of negotiation, however, was halted with the removal of Sheikh Abdullah from power in 1953. The official Indian narrative that was defined by the need to maintain the 'autonomy' of the state so as to respond to the sensitivities of the state government in this process was drastically changed. Rather than the 'autonomy' it was the idiom of 'integration' that reigned supreme thereafter. All the constitutional and political developments in this later period were aimed at bringing the state constitutionally at par with other states of India. The process started with the Constitutional Order of 1954 which was a comprehensive order that went beyond the Instrument of Accession and extended the power of the Dominion legislature to make laws on almost all the matters contained in the Union List. While much of the Constitutional Order of 1954 followed the spirit of the Delhi Agreement reached between Sheikh Abdullah and the Central Government on the question of extension of the scope of Article 370, yet there were many matters which went beyond this Agreement.[11] By more than 40 constitutional orders issued from time to time, various provisions of the Indian Constitution were extended to the state. Among the provisions that were extended to the state included those related to customs, central excise, civil aviation, posts

[11] For instance, Article 3 that related to the alteration of areas, boundaries and names of existing states was extended, though with a proviso of requiring the consent of the state legislature of the state, was not part of Delhi Agreement. Similarly, Part III of the Indian Constitution containing the Fundamental Rights was made applicable for the state. This matter had remained unresolved during the Delhi Agreement. After agreeing in principle that the Fundamental Rights were to be made available for the citizens in the state, it was to be decided whether these would emanate from Indian constitution or state constitution (Chowdhary 2016).

and telegraphs; extension of All India Services; functions of the office of Comptroller and Auditor General; extension of jurisdiction of Supreme Court and Election Commission of India; and direct election to Lok Sabha (Bamzai 2016). Changes were also brought about by the 6th Amendment of the state Constitution. Not only the nomenclature of 'Prime Minister' and 'Sadar-e-Riyasat' were changed to Chief Minister (CM) and Governor, but the very specificity about the institution of the Head of State was changed. Until this amendment was passed, the Sadar-e-Riyasat was not the nominee of the Centre and was elected by the state legislature. This had a great symbolic value for autonomous status of the state since there was no agent of the Centre in the state in the form of a governor nominated by the President. However, with this amendment, Sadar-e-Riyasat was replaced by Governor. No more was the office filled in through the state legislature, but on the contrary was appointed by the President of India.[12]

THE RUPTURE

The removal of Sheikh Abdullah from the centrality of Kashmir's politics in 1953 brought about a tectonic shift in the direction of the state's politics. Being the architect of people's politics, he was no ordinary leader. He had a stature which was much taller than the other leaders of Kashmir, and after the land reforms he was virtually seen as a messiah by a large number of rural masses. When a leader of such a stature was arrested and an alternative government and leadership was imposed on people, it created the first kind of ruptures at many levels—rupture of people with the democratic politics, rupture of the state with the Indian leadership, rupture of Kashmiri nationalism from the Indian nationalism, and even rupture within Kashmir's politics. Kashmir's politics changed its nature and the harmony that was to be seen between the Kashmiri identity politics and Indian nationalist

[12] The situation as it existed in the late 1990s was that 260 out of the 395 Articles of the Constitution were extended to the state. In terms of the Parliament's lawmaking power, 94 out of the 97 entries of the Union List and 26 out of the 47 entries of the Concurrent List have been extended to the state. Out of the 12 Schedules, 7 are applicable to the state (J&K Government 2000).

project was dissipated to a large extent. Rather than taking the same direction, the goals of the two were now defined in a rather conflictual manner.

Removal of Sheikh Abdullah in 1953, seen retrospectively, was not an ordinary event. It was a deep psychological moment which has gone into the collective memory of Kashmir as the first major betrayal by the Indian State.[13] The roots of political alienation of Kashmiris towards the Indian State go back to this moment itself. This started a phase of discontent which lasted throughout the period of Sheikh's incarceration[14] (Bhattacharjea 2008; Bose 2003; Qasim 1992).

This discontent took the form of the first phase of separatism in Kashmir. Sheikh, who—in the pre-1953 period—was the most important agent for legitimizing Kashmir's relationship with India, now questioned the finality of accession and demanded *rai shumari* (plebiscite). This demand took a more organized form in 1955 when the Plebiscite Front was launched by the colleagues and supporters of Sheikh Abdullah (Fazili 1982; Qasim 1992; Wani 1996).

Like the NC earlier, the Plebiscite Front became a major force for political mobilization of Kashmiris. In fact, this newly floated organization was no different from the NC of the pre-1947 period, since much of its cadre was comprised of those people who were earlier part of the NC and had now shifted their sides to the Plebiscite Front. The official NC also existed, but it was now a much more truncated body, with not only its popular base shifting to the Plebiscite Front but it also losing much of its legitimacy. For the next two decades, the demand for 'plebiscite' became the commonsensical demand of Kashmiris and

[13] After the arrest of Sheikh Abdullah, the situation was quite precarious in Kashmir. Mir Qasim in his memoirs (Qasim 1992, 69–71) has described the situation in which Bakshi Ghulam Mohammed, Sheikh's successor, and his other colleagues were faced with angry crowds immediately after his arrest. The anger of people towards the new regime, as he recounts, remained in the psyche of people for such a long time that despite its pro-people policies, the Kashmiris did not forgive them.

[14] The accumulated discontent in Kashmir came out in open in early 1960 around the issue of the loss of the Holy Relic from Hazratbal Shrine in Srinagar. This became an occasion of massive public protests leading almost to the collapse of the state authority. The Government of India was forced to intervene and send senior Congress leader Lal Bahadur Shastri to handle the situation.

Sheikh's politics of interrogating the Indian claim on this state became the popular politics of Kashmir. Generations of Kashmiris got mobilized and politicized into this politics, and rather than the competitive electoral politics, it was this politics that became the 'mainstreamed' politics of common Kashmiris. While the governments were being installed, the chief ministers appointed or removed, 'elections' being held—this politics of plebiscite continued to sustain itself. Whenever Sheikh Abdullah would be released from the jail, he would attract huge crowds and in popular imagination he was growing taller by each day.

In the situation that evolved, Kashmir stood divided and pulled in two different directions of politics—in one direction there was resistance politics that had the mass base, and in the other direction there was the formal, government-level politics. Being perpetually in crisis, this second level of government politics did not engage the Kashmiris and operated more or less in a superficial manner. As a consequence, there developed many distortions in this politics.

Of the many distortions that creeped into the mainstream politics of governance, the most crucial one related to the 'democratic deficit'. While democracy was gradually taking roots in the rest of India, in Kashmir, whatever little base it had in the pre-1953 phase was eroded in the post-1953 period. The NC particularly lost its essential character. With Sheikh Abdullah moving away, and its mass base shifting to the Plebiscite Front, it lost its moral basis. The party still had stalwart leaders such as Bakshi Ghulam Mohammed, G. M. Sadiq and Mir Qasim, but these leaders did not have the charisma of Sheikh and could not compete with his tall stature. Also, these leaders were seen as 'betrayers' not only of Sheikh but of the Kashmir cause. Bakshi, who replaced Sheikh as the leader of the party in 1953, particularly faced the tremendous pressure not only of fighting the tag of being a 'stooge' of the Government of India, but also of proving as good a leader as Sheikh. Constantly facing the crisis of legitimacy, he and others who followed him used all sorts of manipulative strategies to keep themselves in control (Puri 1968; Qasim 1992).

Bereft of the ground support, the party heavily depended on the Central Government for its survival and therefore allowed itself to be influenced by the politics and policies of the Indian National Congress, the ruling party at the Centre. The intervention of the Congress in the internal politics of the NC was so strong that it gradually lost its autonomy. By the beginning of the decade of the 1960s, the difference between the NC and the Congress was obviated and it was almost seen as a branch of the Congress.[15] It was the result of the 'Congressization' of the NC that it was ultimately dissolved and merged with the Congress in 1965.

The deinstitutionalization of the NC was a major blow to the democratic politics of the state. This was a fully evolved party with an organizational structure evolved up to the village level, a mass base and a vast network of its cadre. Being a key mediating structure, this party could have played a very useful role in democratizing the politics of the state. However, as this party was itself compromised, rather than contributing to the democratic processes, it added to the culture of undemocratic practices that had overtaken the politics of the state after 1953 (Bhattacharjea 1994, 14).

Bakshi Ghulam Mohammed, who succeeded Sheikh after 1953 and remained at the helm of affairs for the next one decade, introduced a few unhealthy practices. Apart from the fact that the structures of accountability were almost totally missing, there was a disproportionate influence of the family of Bakshi on the politics of the state. Bakshi Rashid, brother of Bakshi Ghulam Mohammed, operated a 'Peace Brigade' which was in reality an organization of goons who had the major job of intimidating and threatening the political opponents of Bakshi (Puri 1968, 229).

What remained a gross problem during this time was the total delegitimization of the electoral process. Apart from intimidation of the candidates seeking to contest election, it was through the phenomenon of uncontested returns that the ruling party was able to capture most

[15] An evidence to the fact can be put forth with reference to Bakshi's ouster from the power in 1962 via the Kamraj Plan which was purely the plan of the Congress party that sought to rejuvenate the cadre and organization of the party by seeking resignation from Congress CMs and cabinet minister in the Central Government. Bakshi, despite the fact that he did not hold the primary membership of the Congress party, offered his resignation which was accepted by the Congress leadership and he was replaced by Shamsuddin.

of the seats of the Legislative Assembly from Kashmir. Thus, out of the total 42 seats, as many as 35 Assembly seats in 1957 and 32 seats in 1962 were returned uncontested. The phenomenon of uncontested returns was so institutionalized that it continued even after Bakshi was succeeded by Ghulam Mohammed Sadiq, who had a reputation of being a more seasoned politician. As many as 22 out of the 42 seats were returned uncontested during 1967 Assembly election. It was mainly because of these uncontested returns that the NC was able to capture all the seats of the Assembly in Kashmir. Whatever minimum was the number of other candidates or parties within the Assembly, that came from Jammu region (Chowdhary et al. 2007).

The electoral process was so openly farcical that it was noticed by the then leading commentators of the time, who critiqued it strongly. Referring to the huge numbers of uncontested returns during the 1957 Assembly election, the *Hindustan Times* editorial thus raised a question: 'How then did Bakshi Ghulam Mohammed achieve this happy state of affairs in Kashmir? Is it that the policies of his government are so universally accepted that we might as well replace in his domain the process of election by the process of acclamation?...' (*Hindustan Times* 12 February 1962, cited in Singh 1982, 65–66). Also interesting is the comment made by B. Shiva Rao about the 1962 Assembly election:

> Taking all the state legislative assemblies, there were 23,838 nominations for 3,487 seats. Of these nominations, 426 were rejected on technical grounds—a little under 2 per cent. But in Jammu and Kashmir, 126 papers were rejected out of 461 nominations which was nearly 30 per cent. The same result is reflected in the number of uncontested returns.... The all-India figures for all twenty assemblies were 3,487 seats, with 34 uncontested ones (22 from Jammu and Kashmir).... It is unnecessary to comment on these figures, except to point out that the Chief Minister Mr. Sadiq's party strength without these 22 uncontested seats would drop to 38 in a House of 75. (*The Tribune* 7 February 1968)

Manoeuvred electoral process had severe implications for a trouble-torn state like J&K. Since most of the seats of the Legislative Assembly were filled in without a contest, there was virtually no engagement of ordinary Kashmiris with the electoral process. The 'elected' legislators who had been mostly returned unopposed, meanwhile, had no connection with the people. In sum, the process rather than linking the people with the processes of democratic governance was further alienating them. Added to this was the fact that the leaders were being replaced mainly through the intervention of the Centre. Sheikh Abdullah was not the last leader to be replaced at the instance of the Central Government, but there were others to follow. Bakshi Ghulam Mohammed, as noted above, was replaced in 1962 under the Kamraj Plan; Shamsuddin was replaced by G. M. Sadiq. The change of leadership rather than following the logic of ground-level politics of the party emanated from some logic of the 'national interest'. It was in pursuance of the same logic that in 1975 Mir Qasim was asked to step down in favour of Sheikh Abdullah. All this created a deep-rooted impression in Kashmir that decisions about government formation in the state were taken at the Central level and neither the popularity of the leader nor the choice of the people did matter in that context. In the end, all this led to serious questions about the state's relationship with the Centre. Not only was democracy seen to be greatly compromised, but doubts were expressed about the political autonomy of the state.

In the situation in which the separatist psyche was taking deep roots via the political discourse of Plebiscite Front and constant interrogation of the State by Sheikh Abdullah, the absence of democratic space was a major problem. A vibrant competitive political space might have contributed to not only providing the possibility of channelling the popular discontent in democratic direction, but also in building the stakes of the common people in democratic governance. However, this was not possible since the whole of the mainstream politics was under the hegemony of a single party with no democratic means of expression of dissent and opposition.[16] Until 1965, it was the NC, and after

[16] Two national political parties, namely the Indian National Congress and the Communist Party of India, that could have some base here, had earlier taken a conscious decision to not stand in opposition to NC. Both these parties saw the NC as an ideologically compatible party and therefore felt comfortable operating through it rather than against it. The communists had started influencing the cadre of the NC right at the time when it operated in its earlier avatar as the Muslim Conference in the 1930s. It was under the influence of this party that the NC had adopted the radical socialist goals and had adopted the New Kashmir Manifesto. This document that had taken the language and form of a communist document was prepared by Freda Bedi and B. P. S. Bedi who were active Indian communists. The Congress was

its dissolution, it was the Congress which completely monopolized the democratic political space in Kashmir, not only filling most of the Assembly seats but also controlling the competitive politics per se.

That the democratic space be fully monopolized by the ruling party and that there be no opposition to it was a part of the national policy on Kashmir. With the accession of the state being challenged externally by Pakistan and internally by the Plebiscite Front, the national government put all its eggs in the basket of the ruling party and saw in it all the scope of the defence of the Indian case. In the kind of precarious political balance that existed in Kashmir, the Central leadership felt that any critique to this party would amount to destabilizing it and in the process helping the anti-national forces in the state. Hence, it overlooked all undemocratic tendencies within this party and allowed it to operate in an unbridled manner. So long as the local leaders were able to control and silence the voices critical to accession, everything was fine in the state. It was in this process of dependence of the Central Government on a single party that a tradition for tolerating and overlooking all democratic flaws on the part of the state leadership was evolved.

It was for this reason that all such opportunities for a democratic opposition evolving in the state were sidelined by the Central Government. Nehru, for instance, pressurized the leaders of the Democratic National Conference, formed by a breakaway group of NC in 1957, to join back the parent party with the argument that the 'nationalist forces' in Kashmir should not be divided and should be on the same side of politics. It was with the same logic that the effort made by the Socialist Party to start a branch in Kashmir was termed 'opposed to the national interest' by the Central leadership (Bose 2003, 72).

With one party monopolizing the mainstream politics, there was no space left for the expression of any genuine dissent or opposition to this party's politics or policies. The only space that was available was in the sphere of resistance politics. The Plebiscite Front therefore not only offered the space for resistance to the Indian State, but also for

---

also meanwhile influencing the NC, but it sought to intervene in the NC's politics in the post-1953 period in a more aggressive manner.

opposition to the issues related to governance. The Plebiscite Front leaders, particularly Mirza Afzal Beg, were in the forefront critiquing the government policies.

As the democratic space was totally stifled, the roots of the separatist politics were deeply entrenched in Kashmir during the 1953–1975 period. With formal governmental politics lacking legitimacy and credibility, on the one hand, and the democratic space not engaging the mass of Kashmiris, on the other, the next few generations of Kashmiris got emotionally involved in the 'plebiscite' politics. The continued popularity of Sheikh Abdullah and the Plebiscite Front generated a political psyche in Kashmir that not only developed a deep-rooted distrust of the Central Government, but also sought to question the finality of the Indian claim on Kashmir. Irrespective of the direction that the formal governmental politics was taking and irrespective of the processes of constitutional integration, there was greater disconnect taking place between the Kashmiris and the Indian national politics. The deinstitutionalization of the NC, its overwhelming intrusion by the Congress party and finally its merger with this latter party—all this further distanced the Kashmiris not only from the Congress but from the Central Government per se. In the decades of the 1960s and the early 1970s, there was formidable anger against the Congress in Kashmir. In response to a boycott call, the Congress members were socially ostracized and were not even allowed to use the local graveyard (Qasim 1992, 107). This anger, however, did not remain limited to the Congress but was soon to be extended to the Central Government as a whole and also towards the Indian State.

The process of constitutional integration, similarly, remained an alienated process. Although most of these changes were brought in with the consent of the state governments of the time, the lack of legitimacy of those governments and the constant critique by the leaders of Plebiscite Front, particularly Mirza Afzal Beg, generated a negative response towards this process. In common Kashmiri parlance, this was not only a deviation from the original terms of negotiated relations between the Centre and this state, but a major 'breach of trust'.

The political developments of the 1953–1975 period provide important insights into the present context of conflict. Although the politics of 'azadi' was to manifest quite late in the post-1989 period, the psyche of separatism was created during this period. The psyche that evolved during this period was based on interrogation and contestation of the Indian State. While the finality of accession was questioned, the legitimacy of the mainstream politics and its implications for common people were also contested. Meanwhile, there was a response against the intrusive role of the Central Government (Puri 1968).

Return of Sheikh Abdullah to Power Politics: An Opportunity Lost

Despite a psyche of separatism being evolved in the 1953–1975 period, an opportunity to resolve the internal context of conflict was provided in 1975 when Sheikh Abdullah shifted the base of his politics from the mode of resistance to power politics. However, as the later developments, particularly of 1983–1987 period, proved, this opportunity was completely lost and the state was pushed into an aggressive phase of separatism.

Following the Indo-Pak war in 1971 and the Shimla Accord, Sheikh Abdullah was reconciled to the idea of accepting the futility of the demand of plebiscite and building bridges with the Government of India. Following the talks between Mirza Afzal Beg representing him and G. Parthasarathy representing the Government of India, his return to power politics was facilitated following a formal Accord. As per the Accord, while the formal status of the state being the 'constituent unit of the Union of India' was reiterated, the continued relevance of Article 370 was also emphasized (The Kashmir Accord 1974).[17] While the possibility of altering or repealing alternations and modifications in any provision of the Indian Constitution that had been applied to the state with such adaptations and modifications was inbuilt in the

[17] It was also stated that:

> The residuary powers of legislation shall remain with the State; however, Parliament will continue to have power to make laws relating to the prevention of activities directed towards disclaiming, questioning or disrupting the sovereignty and territorial integrity of India or bring about secession of a part of the territory of India from the Union or causing insult to the Indian National Flag, the Indian National Anthem and the Constitution. (The Kashmir Accord 1974)

Accord,[18] the state government was given the option of reviewing the laws made by the Parliament and extended to the state after 1953.[19]

Mobilized into the politics of contestation, the masses of Kashmir were confused with the changing of tract by their leader, yet they followed him—at least the majority of them did. There were some young people who were disgruntled with Sheikh and, rejecting his leadership, took upon themselves the mantle of separatist politics. Many of them joined underground outfits, mostly sponsored by Pakistan. A few of them took to the overground politics and remained severe critics of Sheikh.[20] However, due to his tall stature, Sheikh continued to remain central to Kashmir's politics. And with him steering the power politics,

[18] As per Point 3 of the Accord:

> Where any provision of the Constitution of India had been applied to the State of Jammu and Kashmir with adaptations and modifications, such adaptations and modifications can be altered or repealed by an order of the President under Article 370, each individual proposal in this behalf being considered on its merits, but provisions of the Constitution of India already applied to the State of Jammu and Kashmir without adaptation or modification are unalterable. (The Kashmir Accord 1974)

[19] As per Point 4 of the Accord:

> With a view to assuring freedom to the State of Jammu and Kashmir to have its own legislation on matters like welfare measures, cultural matters, social security, personal law and procedural laws, in a manner suited to the special conditions in the State, it is agreed that the State Government can review the laws made by Parliament or extended to the State after 1953 on any matter relatable to the Concurrent List and may decide which of them, in its opinion, needs amendment or repeal. Thereafter, appropriate steps may be taken under Article 254 of the Constitution of India. The grant of President's assent to such legislation would be sympathetically considered. The same approach would be adopted in regard to laws to be made by Parliament in future under the Proviso to clause 2 of the Article. The State Government shall be consulted regarding the application of any such law to the State and the views of the State Government shall receive the fullest consideration. (The Kashmir Accord 1974)

[20] A. G. Noorani has noted as to how the shift in Sheikh's position led to some unrest in Kashmir and the emergence of some organizations whose direction of politics was rooted in the resistance to the Indian State. Referring to the talks between the Government of India and Mirza Afzal Beg, he notes that 'tension in Srinagar was palpable in 1974 as reports of the parleys came in. The rift led to the birth of Jammu and Kashmir People's League on October 13, 1974, with Qureshi as its chairman.' He further notes:

> The People's League marked a watershed. Its founders shot into prominence later—Sheikh Abdul Aziz, Musaddiq Adil, Bashir Ahmed Tota, Azam Inquilabi, Abdul Hamid Wani alias S. Hamid, who was president of the Young Men's League, and Shabbir Shah, its general Secretary.... The League was stoutly opposed to the 1975 accord. (Noorani 2000)

this politics gained legitimacy and the separatist politics was pushed to the margins.

What helped gain the legitimacy of the mainstream power politics during this period was the continued assertion of Sheikh Abdullah vis-à-vis the Central Government, however, in a different mode. Rather than interrogating the finality of accession and demanding self-determination, Sheikh's politics now revolved around questioning the intrusive role of the Centre and asserting political autonomy of the state vis-à-vis the powers that be in New Delhi. Much of the vacuum created by the dissolution of Plebiscite Front, and its demand for Plebiscite, was therefore filled in by the aggressive politics of Kashmiri identity and much of the anti-State discontent was transformed into his anti-Centre and anti-Congress politics.

Although the Congress had made way for Sheikh Abdullah to rejoin power politics and provided his newly revived NC with outside support in 1975, the party continued to nurture its ambitions of regaining power in the state. From the beginning there was pressure on Sheikh Abdullah to either merge the NC with the Congress or to have an electoral alliance with it. On getting no positive response from Sheikh the Congress withdrew its support in March 1977, plunging the Sheikh government into a crisis. Following the mid-term election, the NC swept the polls winning as many as 39 out of 42 Assembly constituencies.[21]

The 1977 Assembly election was intensely competitive. Although the Janata Party, which was the ruling party in the Centre at that time, was also in fray, the real competition was between the NC and the Congress. In the situation in which the Congress was seen to have betrayed Sheikh Abdullah, there was a strong sense of identification with the NC and therefore an intensified sense of involvement in the electoral process as well. For the common Kashmiris, this keenly contested election was the first such real opportunity for engaging with the process of government formation and electing a party and leader of their own choice. For the satisfaction that this election generated

[21] Only two seats were won by the Janata Party and one by Jamaat-e-Islami.

at the ground level, it came to have the reputation of being the most 'free and fair' election of the state (Chowdhary et al. 2007).

The space that was so created for the democratic politics remained intact for almost a decade. In the constant struggle that he was involved in challenging the authority of the Centre and asserting his own position vis-à-vis Indira Gandhi, the popular support remained with Sheikh. It is a different matter that scepticism against Sheikh was also developing and as Victoria Schofield has noted, the educated class was not ready to accept the 1974 Accord as the resolution of Kashmir issue. For this class there were no dividends of this Accord as Sheikh failed to get any concession even of symbolic nature to offer to the people (Schofield 2003, 125). Confronted with the Central Government's position that it is rather difficult to reverse the motion of the clock and revert to the pre-1953 constitutional autonomy, he got only some minimal kinds of concessions, like the possibility of review of central legislations; but even on this count, he could not deliver. The Committee that was constituted to suggest revision was internally divided and came up with two altogether contradictory reports.

However, for the masses of Kashmir, Sheikh still represented the tradition of Kashmiri identity politics and they followed him throughout his lifetime, and after his death, they continued to identify with the politics of the NC, as was reflected during the 1983 Assembly election. This election, like the 1977 Assembly election, also gained the reputation of a credible election both because of the aggressive electioneering both by the Congress and the NC and also because of the involvement of common Kashmiris in it. Despite the personal stakes of Indira Gandhi in this election, the NC now led by Farooq Abdullah had a landslide victory. Conceding only two seats to the Congress, it could win most of other Assembly seats of the Valley (38/42). The massive mandate for the NC was not only because of the sympathy factor that operated in favour of Farooq Abdullah because of the recent death of Sheikh, but it was because of the direction of politics that Farooq was taking at that time. With Sheikh away from the scene, the Congress had increased its pressure on the NC to merge or ally with it during the 1983 Assembly election, but Farooq had stood his ground and took the decision to go alone even at the cost of earning the fury of

Indira Gandhi. The 1983 Assembly election was therefore a very bitterly contested election between the NC and the Congress. Invoking the issues of Kashmiri identity and autonomy, Farooq had raised the emotions of Kashmiris. Antagonizing the Congress leadership, Farooq had to pay the price when a few months after the elections, defections within the NC were engineered and the NC government was toppled and replaced by a government of defectors with the outside support of the Congress (Punjabi 1992).

The removal of the Farooq Abdullah government did not bode well with the democratic environment of Kashmir. It generated afresh an identity crisis. This episode, though linked with the declining fortune of the Congress party and its desperation to keep as many states in its kitty as possible, had the impact of sharpening the Kashmiri identity politics vis-à-vis the Central Government, on the one hand, and alienating the Kashmiris from the Indian state, on the other. Although the engineered defections within the ruling NC in 1984 was a part of the strategy of the Congress and was replicated in Andhra Pradesh and Karnataka as well, in Kashmir, it had different implications. That, despite the massive mandate in favour of the NC, Farooq's government could be so easily replaced was seen as an affront to the people's choices. This not only had the impact of devaluating the whole electoral process but also of questioning the very relevance of democratic processes in Kashmir. More importantly, this had the impact of reviving the earlier wounds. Farooq's dismissal in 1984 was seen as a repeat of 1953 when Sheikh Abdullah was removed from power and incarcerated for a long time. The general refrain vis-à-vis the electoral politics in Kashmir thereafter has been that election is a farcical exercise—governments are actually 'made' or 'unmade' in Delhi without any reference to the mandate of the people (Sinha 1996).

The situation could still have been handled if Farooq had continued with his aggressive political mode of linking the Kashmiri identity politics with the ongoing anti-Congress politics of opposition parties at the national level. Soon after being deposed from power, he joined the opposition conclaves being organized and hosted one in Kashmir. The anti-Congress stance of these opposition conclaves served the Kashmiri identity politics quite well and also helped sustain it within the democratic political space. However, the shift in Farooq's stance and his decision to enter into an alliance with the Congress in 1986 led to a major blow to such efforts. With his declaration that it is difficult to survive in power without being on the right side of the ruling party in the Centre, the common Kashmiris were convinced that they had no role to play in electing their own government and it is the will of the Centre rather than the choice of the voter that matters (Widmalm 2002, 71–77).

The 1986 Rajiv–Farooq Accord went a long way in exacerbating the crisis in Kashmir. For a decade or so, the NC had channelled the Kashmiri identity politics in the democratic direction via the aggressive Centre–State mode. The abrupt shift in its politics led to a total political vacuum that came to be filled initially by the radical Jamaat-e-Islami politics and later by a hardcore separatist politics. Jamaat had been in existence in Kashmir since long, but could not make a space in the electoral politics in the presence of the NC, which throughout remained the first choice of the people. The lack of popularity and even the resentment against this party was reflected in 1979 when following the hanging of Zulfikar Ali Bhutto, the party members and sympathizers had to face the fury of Kashmiris, and their houses and business establishments were attacked (Shah 2014).[22] However, in 1986 when Jamaat organized the Muslim United Front (MUF), it emerged as an extremely popular organization. Taking advantage of the popular resentment against the NC, the MUF sought to redefine the Kashmiri identity politics in the mould of Jamaat's politics and brought the question of both 'religion' and 'self-determination' to the centre of the democratic politics.

The 1987 Assembly election provided the last straw for the total breakdown of the democratic space. There were widespread perceptions about manoeuvring and the elections in the end were seen to be

[22] Suhail A. Shah notes, 'The arson and loot continued for three days and spilled over to every Jama'at household in Kashmir, particularly the Islamabad district.' He further notes, 'The property destroyed was estimated at nearly Rupees 40 Crore with 1245 residential houses set ablaze, 466 of them looted, 513 granaries burnt, 338 shops gutted, 70 apple orchards destroyed, 509 cowsheds blazed down and 24 Jama'at offices destroyed' (Shah 2014).

totally farcical. Despite its popularity, in a fair assessment MUF could not have won more than 10–15 seats in the Assembly. However, it could win only four seats, and its defeat in some constituencies where it had greater chances of winning led to the delegitimization of the whole electoral process. What further spoiled the situation was the way the NC–Congress government handled the protests following the elections. Not only were these protests forcefully suppressed, but the MUF leaders and supporters were also jailed and mistreated. It was in the wake of this situation that the seeds of militancy and separatism were sown.

To Conclude

To conclude, one can say that though militancy and separatism erupted in the post-1987 period, the roots of such a situation lay in the 1953–1975 period. It was during this period that a mass political psyche of contestation of the Indian State took roots and the discourse of resistance acquired centrality in Kashmir's politics. The failure of democratic politics and the intrusive politics of the Central Government led to accumulation of discontent, which found its expression in the separatist politics. The insecurity and the manipulative politics of the successors of Sheikh Abdullah in the NC added to the discontent. Apart from derailing the democratic politics, their corrupt practices generated resentment among the common people. Over time there were other beneficiaries of the system whose opportunism aggravated the context of conflict. Right from the beginning, the Centre had sought to fill in the democratic gap through the politics of concessions, subsidiaries, and financial and developmental benefits. These policies not only distorted the nature of economy and diluted the logic of economic development as pursued by the Sheikh Abdullah government, but also had implications for the state's relationship with India. Not only did the state become perpetually dependent on the Centre, but the vested interest of the political and economic elites became linked with the perpetuation of conflict.

The shift in Sheikh's politics in 1975 widened the democratic space in Kashmir and provided an opportunity for articulation and expression of discontent. However, due to the fragility of the state leadership and the intrusive politics of the Centre, the state was plunged again into the separatist politics after the 1987 Assembly election.

References

Abdullah, Sheikh. 'Excerpts of Sheikh Abdullah February 5, 1948, Speech in the UN Security Council'.

http://www.satp.org/satporgtp/countries/india/states/jandk/documents/papers/excerpts_of_sheikh_abdullah's_february_5_1948_speech.htm (accessed on 5 September 2018).

———. 1951, 5 November. 'Statement of Sheikh Abdullah in the Constituent Assembly of Jammu and Kashmir'. *Jammu and Kashmir Constituent Assembly Official Report: Assembly Debate*, Part I, Vol. 1 (1951–1955): 82–110.

———. 1952, 2 September. 'Sheikh Abdullah's Broadcast'. *The Statesman*.

Anand, A. S. 2013. *The Constitution of Jammu and Kashmir: Its Development and Comments*. New Delhi: Universal Law Publishing.

Aslam, Mohammad. 1977, November. 'Land Reforms in Jammu and Kashmir'. *Social Scientist* 6 (4): 59–64.

Bazaz, Premnath. 2002. *Inside Kashmir*. Srinagar: Gulshan Publishers.

Bamzai, Sandeep. 2016. 'Autonomy vs. Integration: Eternal Kashmir Debate', ORF Special Report No. 26, Dep 23. http://www.orfonline.org/research/autonomy-vs-integration-kashmir/ (accessed on 24 August 2018).

Bamzai, Prithvi Nath Kaul. 1973. *A History of Kashmir: Political, Social, Cultural, from the Earliest Times to the Present Day*. Metropolitan Book Company.

Banerjee, Paula, and Anasua Basu Roy Choudhury. 2011. *Women in Indian Borderlands*. New Delhi: SAGE Publications.

Bazaz, Prem Nath. 1954. *The History of Struggle for Freedom in Kashmir: Cultural and Political, from the Earliest Times to the Present Day*. Kashmir Publishing Company.

Beg, Mirza Afzal. 1995. 'Land Reforms in Jammu and Kashmir'. In *The Story of Kashmir: Yesterday and Today*, Vol. 2, edited by Verinder Grover, 406–410. New Delhi: Deep & Deep Publications.

Bhattacharjea, Ajit. 1994. *Kashmir: The Wounded Valley*. South Asia Books.

Bhattacharjea, Ajit. 2008. *Tragic Hero of Kashmir: Sheikh Mohammad Abdullah*. New Delhi: Roli Books.

Bose, Sumantra. 2003. *Kashmir: Roots of Conflict: Paths to Peace*. Cambridge, MA: Harvard University Press.

Chowdhary, Rekha. 2012. *Border and People: An Interface*. New Delhi: Centre for Dialogue and Reconciliation.

———. 2016. *Jammu and Kashmir: Politics of Identity and Separatism*. New Delhi: Routledge.

Chowdhary, Rekha and Ashutosh Kumar. 2002. 'Ideology and Politics of National Conference', in Arun K. Jana and Bhupen Sarmah, *Class, Ideology & Political Parties in India*. South Asian Publishers.

Dasgupta, C. 2015. *War and Diplomacy in Kashmir: 1947–48*. New Delhi: SAGE Publications.

Diwan, Paras. 1953, July. 'Kashmir and the Indian Union: the Legal Position'. *International and Comparative Law Quarterly* 2 (3): 333–353.

Fazili, Manzoor. 1982. *Kashmir: Government and Politics*. Srinagar: Gulshan Publishers.

J&K Government. 2000. *Report of the State Autonomy Committee*. Srinagar and Jammu: General Administration Department.

Jammu and Kashmir Constituent Assembly. n.d. *Official Report: Assembly Debate*, Part I, Vol. 1 (1951–1955), 260–345.

Ladejinsky, Wolf. 1952. 'Land Reform Observations in Kashmir'. In *Agrarian Reforms as Unfinished Business*, edited by L. J. Walinksy. Oxford, UK: Oxford University Press.

Manchanda, Rita, and Sahba Husain. 2013, 3 August. 'Unequal Citizens'. *Economic & Political Weekly* 48 (31), 131–136.

Noorani, A. G. 2000, 30 September–13 October. 'Jammu and Kashmir: Contours of Militancy'. *Frontline* 17 (20). http://www.kashmirlibrary.org/kashmir_timeline/kashmir_files/militancy_noorani.htmm (accessed on 1 November 2017).

Punjabi, Riyaz. 1992. 'Kashmir: The Bruised Identity'. In *Perspectives on Kashmir*, edited by Raju C. Thomas. Boulder, CO: Westview Press.

Puri, Balraj. 1968. 'Jammu and Kashmir'. In *State Politics in India*, edited by Myron Weinter. Princeton, NJ: Princeton University Press.

Qasim, Mir. 1992. *My Life and Times*. New Delhi: Allied Publishers.

Schofield, Victoria. 2003. *Kashmir in Conflict: India, Pakistan and the Unending War*. London: I.B. Tauris.

Singh, Balbir. 1982. *State Politics in India: Explorations in Political Processes in Jammu and Kashmir*. New Delhi: Macmillan.

Sinha, Aditya. 1996. *Farooq Abdullah, Kashmir's Prodigal Son: A Biography*. New Delhi: UBS Publishers.

Shah, Suhail A. 2014, 14 April. 'Black April'. *Kashmir Life*. http://kashmirlife.net/black-april-58004/ (accessed on 21 October 2017).

Thorner, Daniel. 1953, 12 September. 'The Kashmir Land Reforms: Some Personal Impressions'. *The Economic Weekly* 5 (37): 999–1002.

The Kashmir Accord. 1974. 'Jammu and Kashmir Documents'. http://www.jammu-kashmir.com/documents/kashmiraccord.html (accessed on 24 August 2018).

Wani, Gull Mohd. 1996. *Kashmir: From Autonomy to Azadi*. Srinagar: Valley Book House.

Widmalm, Sten. 2002. *Kashmir in Comparative Perspective: Democracy and Violent Separatism in India*. London: Routledge.

Whitehead, Andrew. 2007. *A Mission in Kashmir*. New Delhi: Penguin.

State of Jammu and Kashmir

Internal Complexity

2

While discussing the background to the state politics of J&K, it is important to focus on the internal complexity of the state. Much of the available literature on the state focuses on the Kashmir conflict and exhausts the understanding of the state from that perspective. For many, the terms 'Kashmir' and 'State of Jammu and Kashmir' remain synonyms and one barely gets to have an idea about the other two regions of the state. The social and political reality of Jammu and Ladakh regions does not necessarily echo that of Kashmir region, and on many points these regions diverge politically. Besides the Kashmiri identity politics that remains the core of Kashmir conflict, there are other competing identities which operate in parallel as well as in opposite directions.

The multiple identity politics influences the direction of the politics. The internal dynamics of the state politics—the political aspirations, demands, pressures and tensions—all emanate from the way these identities interact with each other. To get a complete picture of the politics of the state in its entirety, therefore, it is important to refer to the social diversity and political divergence within the state and to focus on multiple identity politics.

NATURE OF DIVERSITY

Religious Diversity

The state of J&K is a highly diverse society.[1] What is peculiar about its diversity is that it exists at multiple levels. Thus, while at one level

[1] The Anthropological Survey of India recognized as many as 111 ethnic communities in J&K. Some of the prominent communities included Bakarwal, Balti, Brokpa, Chibalis, Dogras, Gujjars and Hanjis (Bhat and Mathur 2011, 588).

there is religious diversity, at another level there are regional, cultural and linguistic diversities. There are also tribal and caste-based diversities. These multi-layered diversities so cut across and overlap each other that these create a complex pattern of identities, termed as 'mosaic' by Balraj Puri (2001).

At the first layer lies the religious diversity. Although this is a Muslim-majority state, it hosts all the three major religions of South Asia: Hindus, Muslims and Buddhists. Muslims form more than two-thirds (68.31%) of the total population. Hindus are 28.43 per cent. Buddhists who are concentrated in Ladakh's Leh district form 0.89 per cent of the state population. Around 1.87 per cent people are Sikhs and 0.28 per cent are Christians (see Table 2.1).

The above mapping of religious composition however does not reflect the complexity either of the religious composition or its socio-cultural diversity. Each of the three regions of the state has its own peculiarities and its demographic patterns. Of all the regions, it is the Kashmir region which is comparatively more homogenous. Here, with the exception of a small minuscule minority of Hindus, all others are Muslims. As per the 2011 Census, the percentage of Muslims to the total population of the region is 96.40 per cent. While 2.45 per cent of the total population is that of Kashmiri Hindus, Sikhs are a minuscule minority having their presence in few pockets of the Valley.

As one can see from Table 2.2 reflecting the demography of Kashmir, most of the districts have around 95–99 per cent Muslim population. The highest percentage of Hindu population is in Kupwara district which has around 4.26 per cent Hindu population, followed by Srinagar and Baramulla districts which have only 3.43 per cent and 3.03 per cent Hindu population, respectively.

Table 2.1 *Demography of the State (in Percentage)*

Muslims	*Hindus*	*Sikhs*	*Christians*	*Buddhists*	*Jains*	*Others*	*Religion not Stated*
68.31	28.43	1.87	0.28	0.89	0.01	0.01	0.16

Source: Census of India (2011).

Table 2.2 *District-wise Religious Demography in Kashmir Region (in Percentage)*

District	*Muslim*	*Hindu*	*Others*
Kupwara	94.52	4.26	1.22
Badgam	97.65	1.34	1.01
Baramulla	95.15	3.03	1.82
Bandipora	97.39	2.15	0.46
Srinagar	95.19	3.43	1.38
Ganderbal	97.69	1.88	0.43
Pulwama	96.48	2.46	1.06
Shopian	98.51	1.17	0.32
Anantnag	97.98	1.22	0.80
Kulgam	98.49	1.00	0.51
Kashmir Region	96.40	2.45	1.15

Source: Census of India (2011).

The demography of the Hindu population has been adversely affected by the mass exodus of the Kashmiri Pandits from the Valley after the onset of militancy in 1990 but even with the Kashmiri Pandit population intact as in pre-militancy period, Muslims were predominant in the Valley.[2] As per the 1981 census, the percentage of Muslims in Kashmir Valley was 94.96.[3]

[2] The Muslims were 94.41 per cent of the Valley's population as per 1961 census and 94 per cent as per 1971 census. After the exodus of Kashmiri Pandits, their percentage increased to 97.16 per cent as per 2001 census. (Due to militancy no census could be conducted in the state in 1991.)

[3] Interesting information has been revealed by the 2011 census regarding the Hindu population of Kashmir. As per the age distribution data of various religious communities, the Hindu population is largely comprised of adult males. The percentage of females and children is proportionately very small. Thus while the total Hindu population in the Valley is 1,68,333, the female population within this number is only 15,764. There are only 4,986 children of the 0–6 years range. Instead of almost half the Hindu population, the women are only 9.34 per cent of the total Hindu population. The percentage of children is only 2.95 (Centre for Policy Studies 2016).

Despite their relatively small number, the Kashmiri Pandits were dispersed in the whole region. Although there were certain localities, for example Habbakadal, Rainawari and Karan Nagar in Srinagar, which were known as Pandit localities, however, they were visible even in remote corners of the Valley. After 1990, the number of Kashmiri Pandits who continued to stay in Kashmir significantly declined to the extent of being almost non-existent.

Muslims of the Valley are largely Sunni. Besides the ethnically Kashmiri Sunnis, the non-Kashmiri groups such as the Gujjars, Pathans and Paharis settled in the peripheries of the Valley are also Sunnis (Rao 1999, 12). There are no officially available figures of the Sunni–Shia population of Kashmir, but it is generally presumed that the Sunnis form around 90 per cent of the total Muslim population of Kashmir. Walter Lawrence, in fact, gave the figure of Shias as only 5 per cent (Lawrence 1895, 284). Shias are largely located in a few pockets of the Valley, for instance in Badgam, Srinagar, Bandipora and Baramulla districts.

A large number of the Kashmiri Muslims are converts who trace their lineage to the Kashmiri Pandits and have family names which are same as those of Pandits. However, there are also Muslims who have come from outside. These include the Arabs, Mughals and Pathans.

Ladakh and Jammu regions are religiously plural societies. Ladakh has a presence of both Muslims and Buddhists. It also has Hindu population. As per 2011 census, 48.40 per cent of the population is Muslim and 39.65 per cent Buddhists. Around 12 per cent of the people in the region have been identified as Hindus (see Table 2.3).[4]

Of the two districts of this region, Leh has a majority of Buddhists (66.39%) and Kargil has a majority of Muslims (76.87%). However,

[4] There are two interesting facts about the Hindus in Ladakh. First, as compared to the 2001 census, the percentage of Hindus has almost doubled (from 6% to 12%). However, the second fact is that most of the Hindus are adult males and the number and percentage of Hindu women and children are very small. Among the total Hindu population of 33,223, only 1,280 (less than 4%) are women (Centre for Policy Studies 2016).

Table 2.3 *Demography of Ladakh by Districts (in Percentage)*

	Muslim	Buddhist	Hindu
Leh	14.26	66.39	17.14
Kargil	76.87	14.21	7.34
Ladakh	48.40	39.65	12.11

Source: Census of India (2011).

although the Buddhist population is dominant in Leh, Muslims have a sizeable presence at 14.27 per cent. Kargil similarly has 14.21 per cent Buddhist population. Muslims of Leh and Kargil, however, are internally differentiated with strong sectarian identities. While the Kargil Muslims are Shias, the Muslims of Leh are Sunnis and have some Kashmiri linkage. Referring to the distinction between the Shias and Sunnis of Ladakh, van Beek thus notes, 'Traditionally, a careful distinction has been made between the Shias, who were deemed to be "indigenous", and the "alien" Sunnis. The Shias, regardless of place of residence or origin, are commonly called "Baltis", while the Sunnis are referred to as "Khache", emphasizing their links to Kashmir' (van Beek 1998).

Of all the regions, the Jammu region is the most complex one in terms of the patterns of religious demography (see Table 2.4). Though it has a two-thirds Hindu majority, however, 6 of the 10 districts of the region have a large number of Muslims. These include the districts of Poonch, Ramban, Rajouri, Kishtwar, Doda and Reasi. Only four districts, namely Udhampur, Samba, Kathua and Jammu, are predominantly Hindu in their composition. Poonch has as high a percentage of Muslims at 90.44 per cent. While Ramban has 70.67 per cent Muslim population, Rajouri has 62.71 per cent Muslims. The districts of Kishtwar, Doda and Reasi have mixed population though with Muslims being in majority. While the Muslim population of Kishtwar is 57.74 per cent, the Hindus are 40.71 per cent; in Doda, the Muslim population is 53.81 per cent and Hindu population is 45.76 per cent. Although Reasi has almost an even population, Muslims have a slight edge with 49.66 per cent population, while the Hindus are 48.90 per cent.

Table 2.4 *Demographic Pattern of Jammu Region (in Percentage)*

District	Hindus	Muslims	Others
Doda	45.76	53.81	0.43
Ramban	28.55	70.67	0.78
Kishtwar	40.71	57.74	1.55
Udhampur	88.11	10.76	1.13
Reasi	48.90	49.66	1.44
Jammu	84.26	7.02	8.72
Samba	86.33	7.19	6.48
Poonch	6.83	90.44	2.73
Rajouri	34.53	62.71	2.76
Kathua	87.61	10.42	1.97
Total Jammu Region	62.55	33.45	4.0

Source: Census of India (2011).

Cultural–Linguistic Diversities

The religious identity does not exhaust all social differentiations. Religion, though an important marker of identity in the state, is neither exclusive nor a single unified identity. It is internally differentiated and at many points is cut across by regional, cultural, ethnic and caste identities. There are a number of regional–cultural markers of identity of which three are most prominent: Kashmiri, Dogra and Ladakhi identities.[5] All of these three identities extend beyond religious boundaries and are region-specific. What is particular about these identities is that each one of these is internally inclusive. Thus, Kashmiri identity that is based on linguistic, cultural and ethnic factors and draws its historical roots about 5,000 years back is a shared identity of Kashmiri-speaking Muslims and Pandits located in Kashmir.

[5] These are also based on the three predominant languages of the state, namely Kashmiri, Dogri and Balti. The Constitution of the state recognizes eight regional languages: Kashmiri, Dogri, Balti, Dardi, Punjabi, Pahari, Ladakhi and Gojri. However, Urdu as per Section 145 of the state Constitution is the official language of the state and English continues to be used for all official purposes of the state.

Before their migration, the Kashmiri Pandits—though a minuscule minority—formed an essential part of Kashmiri identity, not only because of their spread all over the Valley but also because of the influence they enjoyed in the Kashmiri society. Most of the teachers, doctors, revenue officials and petty bureaucrats of the Valley before 1990 came from this community and were quite integrally linked with the lives of the Muslims (Chowdhary 2016, 124–125).

Like the Kashmiri identity, the Dogra identity is also inclusive of the Hindus and Muslims and has its spread over the districts of Jammu, Kathua, Reasi, Samba, Udhampur and parts of Ramban and Rajouri. The hallmark of this identity is the Dogra culture and the Dogri language. Dogras have linguistic–cultural affinity with the people of Himachal Pradesh, particularly Chamba.

Ladakhi identity represents the Ladakhi-speaking people who are either Buddhists or Muslims. Ladakhis, irrespective of their religious affiliations, see themselves as a distinct identity different from Kashmiris on the one hand and Dogras on the other.

Other than these, there are two other cultural–linguistic identities which extend beyond the regional boundaries. These are the Gujjars and Paharis, who are located both in the Jammu and the Kashmir regions. Gujjars in the state, though they are all Muslims, define themselves to be a distinct community and claim to be the third largest community of the state after Kashmiris and Dogras. Comprising nomadic, semi-nomadic and settled communities, the Gujjars are the Gojri-speaking endogamous tribals. According to Puri:

> Gojri is exclusively the language of the Gujjars, all of whom are Muslims. But as a community, the Gujjars have at least as much, if not more, emotional and ethnic affinity with the Hindus, Muslims and Sikhs of the neighbouring States of Himachal Pradesh, Punjab, Haryana, Rajasthan and Uttar Pradesh as they could possibly have with their co-religionists in the State. (Puri 2001)

They are spread all over the Jammu region, though concentrated in the twin districts of Poonch and Rajouri, and in Kashmir they live in the upper reaches of the hilly areas as well as in the border areas.

The Paharis are a mixed group of hill people who are located in the outer areas of Kashmir, particularly in Uri, Boniyar, Keran and Karna and in Poonch–Rajouri districts of Jammu region. Speaking variant forms of Pahari language, the Paharis share a linguistic–cultural affinity across the border in Pakistan-administered Kashmir. While the Paharis in Kashmir and those across the LoC are Muslims, in the Jammu region they are a mix of Muslims, Hindus and Sikhs. Many of the Hindu and Sikh Paharis have migrated from across the LoC and have been relocated in various parts of the Jammu district.

Region as Marker of Identity

Since the linguistic–cultural identities overlap with the regional identities, it becomes important to discuss the regional identities. Region forms not only an important marker of sociocultural identity but also becomes the basis of political specificities within the state. Each of the three regions of the state, namely Kashmir, Jammu and Ladakh, is not only seen as socially and culturally distinct but also as a full-fledged political unit having a direction of its own politics. Rather than the unified and integrated identity of the state therefore, it is the regional identity that remains marked within the state.

The regional identity is defined by historical specificity, cultural uniqueness and even geographical peculiarities. The three regions are quite distinct in terms of the nature of their geography, terrain and climatic conditions. While Kashmir Valley is a compact valley within the middle-range Himalayas, the Jammu region is mostly a mountainous terrain with a range from the low-lying Shivaliks to the high point of Pir Panchal range. Ladakh is high altitude dessert with sparse population. These three regions have had no shared history earlier than 1846 when these were brought together by the Dogra rulers. Prior to that, the trajectory of the three regions followed altogether different paths. While Jammu region comprised a number of semi-autonomous principalities with some kind of outside control, Ladakh was a part of the Silk Route and connected more with Tibet and Central Asia than with any other part of what has now become the state of J&K. Kashmir meanwhile was an insulated valley with varied outside influences. Since the fourteenth century, it came to be under the control of 'outsiders': first the Mughals and then the Pathans, Sikhs and Dogras.

Kashmir is largest in terms of its population, followed by Jammu which claims parity with Kashmir. As against the 54.92 per cent population of Kashmir, Jammu has 42.88 per cent population. Ladakh is geographically the largest but is sparsely populated region and it has a very small proportion of the population of the state (2.18%).

Of all the three regions, it is the region of Kashmir which is culturally more homogenous as compared to the regions of Jammu and Ladakh. Here, almost the whole population, with the exception of a minuscule minority of one kind or the other, share the same religious, linguistic, cultural and ethnic character. As already stated, around 95 per cent people here are the followers of Islam. Of these, a large part is composed of the Sunni Muslims. Most of them also share the language as almost all the people located in the Valley are Kashmiri-speaking. The exceptions are the Gujjars and Paharis who live in the outer fringes of the Valley.

The Jammu and Ladakh regions are, however, internally much more heterogeneous. Jammu region, in fact, has the greatest complexity. Despite some kind of cultural continuity, one finds a lot of internal differences—not only on the basis of religion but also on ethnic–cultural basis. Both the Hindus and Muslims of Jammu region are therefore internally differentiated. The Muslims are divided on the caste and tribal bases. Thus the Pahari Muslims, most of whom identify themselves as Rajputs, perceive themselves as a distinct social group having more in common with the Rajputs among Hindus as compared to non-Rajput Muslims. Like the Rajput Muslims, there are Gujjars who though are devout Muslims define their identity more on the basis of their ethnocultural and tribal background. They have affiliations with Gujjars (mostly Hindu) of northern India. Another distinct category of Muslims within Jammu region is that of the Kashmiri-speaking Muslims who are concentrated in the district of Doda but also have presence in the Poonch–Rajouri subregion. Besides these, there are the Dogra Muslims of the Jammu–Udhampur belt (Chowdhary 2010, 120–121).

Hindus are similarly differentiated on the basis of their linguistic–cultural patterns. Thus, besides the caste divisions which we will be discussing later, there are cultural–linguistic differences among the Dogras, Punjabis, Paharis, Poonchis, Bhaderwashis, Sirajis, etc. Although there are a lot of internal complexities, yet on the basis of cultural–linguistic differences one can find at least three different subregional patterns here—first, that of the dominant Dogra subregion; second, that of the Pir Panchal area; and the third of the Doda belt. The Dogra subregion comprising the districts of Jammu, Samba, Kathua and Reasi is a predominantly Dogri-speaking area with an overwhelming Hindu population. It has a small presence of Muslims. The Poonch–Rajouri subregion comprising the two districts of Poonch and Rahouri is predominantly constituted of Gujjar and Pahari people, with a large number of them being Muslims. This subregion, however, has a significant presence of Hindus. The Doda subregion, comprising the three districts of Doda, Kishtwar and Ramban, is a Muslim-majority area to the south of Kashmir. With many people having originally come here from Kashmir, it has a large number of Kashmiri-speaking people, mostly Muslims. It has also a very substantial population of non-Kashmiri speaking Hindus. This subregion in itself is a mini cultural microcosm of a number of languages and cultures including Baderwahi, Siraji, Paderi, Kashmiri and Bhalesi.

Having remained part of the Silk Route and having Central Asian linkage, the Ladakh region has its own historical and cultural trajectory. However, the region has its own complexity. Ladakhis are internally differentiated among the Tibetans, Argons and Balti tribes. Tibetans who follow Buddhism are the largest part of the Ladakhi region and are mostly located in Leh district. 'The Argons who are mostly confined to the Leh town and a few nearby villages are believed to be the descendants of the traders and merchants who mainly came from Kashmir or parts of Central Asia such as Kashgar, Yarkand, Khotan' (Shafi 2013, 3). With a tradition of intercommunity marriages between Kashmiri Muslim traders and Ladakhi women, a sort of mixed culture was introduced in Ladakh. The Argons were known as the offspring of such marriages.

A large population of Kargil comprises the Baltis who follow Shia Islam. In the border areas of Turtuk, there are also followers of Nurbakshi sect of Islam. Besides these, 'there is a small section of Shina-speaking Sunni Muslims in Drass, who are distinct from the Kashmiri-speaking Muslims and the Balti-speaking Shias in the rest of Kargil' (Puri 2001). Geographically, the area of Ladakh may be divided into seven parts: Sham (lower), Tod (upper), Zhung (centre), Nubra, Changthang, Purig and Zanskar (Dar, 2017).

Caste and Tribe

Caste continues to operate as a significant marker of identity and marks its presence in a variety of ways. Not only Hindus but many Muslims also define themselves in terms of caste categories. This is particularly true of Jammu region. Here Rajputs form a dominant caste—both in terms of their numbers as well as in terms of their influence. Being part of the ruling classes, part of the clan of Dogra rulers and closely associated with the court, the Rajputs have also been the privileged landowners who were most adversely impacted by the land reforms and had to surrender large portions of land to the state in the 1948–1950 period. However, even so they have continued to remain influential with many of them being part of the bureaucracy and armed forces. In the Pahari belt, Rajputs form a strong group among the Muslims. They are all converted Muslims (Malik 2009, 4–6). Before accession, the Muslim Rajputs outnumbered the Hindu Rajputs. With the division of the state, many of them got to be located across the LoC. Following the cultural rituals that they share with Hindu Rajputs, the Muslim Rajputs in Poonch and Rajouri observe endogamy and prefer to marry among the fellow Rajputs only. Like the Hindu Rajputs, the Muslim Rajputs have also had the tradition of joining the armed forces.

Apart from Rajputs, it is the Brahmins who form a dominant class of the Jammu region. They are numerically as large as the Rajputs and though traditionally linked with land and state jobs, they have been among the first to take to education and therefore dominated the bureaucracy in the post-accession period. They, along with Rajputs, also form the political class. It is between these two caste groupings, the Rajputs and the Brahmins, that much of the social privileges and positions within the society are distributed.

Along with these two dominant classes, there is a smaller number of Mahajans, the trading classes, who have been mostly urban-based and controlled the economy of the small towns. Khatris, mostly of Punjabi origin, are the other dominant groups in the Jammu region.

Among the Hindus of Jammu region, there are large numbers of Jats who are mostly migrated from the Pakistani side and have been settled in the border areas of the Jammu region. These are cultivating communities, though a large part of them have also joined the armed and police forces. Though there is no recognition of other backward castes in the state, the Jats have been demanding the status of OBC. There are a few backward castes such as Labana, Jogi and Saini who are mostly urban-based artisans.

Although caste does not operate in Kashmiri Muslim society in the manner that it operates within Hindu communities, however, there are some kinds of distinctions and hierarchies which have been maintained traditionally. Syeds, Pirs and Ulemmas have traditionally been given a superior space in society due to their lineage. They are seen to be the descendants of Prophet Muhammed. They are also respected for their foreign origin. Besides these, there are also the lower castes which include the Watals, Dums and Wagyas. The difference that exists between the highly placed castes such as those of Syeds, Mughals, Pathans, Qureshis are also to found among the Muslims of Pir Panchal. These are also called Ashrafi Muslims having their foreign origin.

The Kashmiri Pandits are a one-caste community—mostly Saraswat Brahmins—with the exception of a minuscule Vaishya group.[6] They

[6] T. N. Madan argues that historically there were all the four varnas in Kashmir, besides all the castes, subcastes and sects. It was after the arrival of Islam, and particularly during the reign of Sultan Sikander, that Pandits were forced to flee Kashmir.

> Not only did he destroy practically all the Hindu temples of Kashmir, he also compelled his Hindu subjects to choose between Islam, exile and death. Whereas some chose one of the latter, the majority of those who had resisted the missionaries now accepted defeat. It was thus that the Hindus of Kashmir, along with whatever Buddhists had remained, were

are internally differentiated on the basis of their occupational history. As Saraswat Brahmins, they have two subcastes: the public servants or Karakuns, and the priestly class or the Bhasha Bhatta or the Gors (with Karakuns asserting higher status to that of the Gors).[7] Each of these castes are further divided into exogamous *gotras*. 'Within each *gotta* there are families which are identified by surnames called *zat* or, relatively rarely, *karma*' (Madan 2008, 121).

A large population of the Hindu society, especially of Jammu region, is comprised of the Dalit population (see Table 2.5). As per the 2011 census, they form around 7.36 per cent of the total population of the state and 17.06 per cent of the total population of Jammu region.[8] Their number is much larger in districts such as Samba (26.80%), Udhampur (24.97%), Jammu (24.96%) and Kathua (22.91%).[9] As per the 2001 census data, there were as many as 500 villages which had more than 50 per cent SC population and 735 villages with more than 40 per cent population.

The districts of Doda (13.03%) and Reasi (12%), which are Muslim-majority districts, also have significant Dalit populations. The larger population of Dalits is rural. It was in 1956 that the state of J&K notified the Scheduled Castes (SCs).[10] Of these notified castes, Meighs (Bhagats), Chamars and Dooms are the largest castes. While Meighs comprise around 30–35 per cent of the Dalits, they are followed by

> nearly wiped out and Islam established in Kashmir in the fourteenth century. It seems that only a handful of Brahmins still survived in Kashmir at the time of Sikander's death in 1414; tradition puts the number at eleven. It is from them that the Pandits of today are said to be descended. (Madan 2008, 119)

Madan goes on to refer to Zain ul Abdin, or Budshah, who encouraged Pandits to return to Kashmir and accommodated them in the state administration. Taking decision to learn Persian, the new court language, they became *Karakun* comprising civil servants and revenue collectors.

[7] Madan mentions a minuscule number of a third urban subcaste: the Buher. 'The Buher (also called Bohra) are Khattris, probably of Punjabi origin' (Madan 2008, 121).

[8] There is a very small Dalit population in Kashmir region. Of the 13 SCs, only two castes, namely Watal and Ratal, are to be found there.

[9] The SC population of Jammu and Samba districts is mainly comprised of Meighs, Chamars and Batwals. Dooms form the largest numbers of SCs in Kathua district.

[10] The 13 notified castes included: Bharwala, Basit, Batwal, Chura, Chamar/Ramdasi, Dhyar, Doom/Mahasha, Gardi, Jolaha, Meigh/Kabirpanth, Ratal, Saryara, Watal.

Table 2.5 *Dalit Population in Jammu Region*

District	Total Population	Number of People belonging to SC	Percentage of SC
Jammu	1,529,958	377,991	24.71
Samba	318,898	91,835	26.80
Udhampur	554,985	138,569	24.97
Reasi	314,667	37,757	12.00
Kathua	616,435	141,224	22.91
Doda	409,936	53,406	13.03
Kishtwar	230,696	14,307	6.20
Ramban	283,713	13,920	4.91
Rajouri	642,415	48,157	7.50
Poonch	476,835	556	0.12
Jammu Region	5,378,538	917,722	17.06

Source: Census of India (2011).

Chamars[11] who are around 25–30 per cent of the SC population. Dooms also form a significant part of the Dalit population. The Chamars and Bhagats are the two better-off Dalit groups.

Dalits are internally differentiated and do not treat each other at par. As Sikand notes, 'The Dalits of Jammu, as elsewhere, are not a homogenous category, being divided into more than a dozen castes. Internalising the logic of the Brahminical system, some of these castes claim to be superior to those considered to be below them in the caste hierarchy' (Sikand 2010).

Like elsewhere, Dalits of the state follow various sects and identify themselves as Ravidasi, Kabirpanthi and Radhasoami. Meighs are basically followers of Kabir. Chamars are meanwhile, Ravidasis. Between Meighs and Chamars there is a lot of competition.

[11] Chamars are either Jatoi Chamars or Chandal Chamars. It is Jatoi Chamars who form part of the government services. A very small number deal with leather work.

Scheduled Tribes

As per the 2011 census, Scheduled Tribes (STs) form around 12 per cent (11.91%) of the total population of the state. The Gujjars, Bakkerwals, Gaddis and Ladakhis are recognized as the STs of the state. Despite the persistent demands, the ST status was not recognized for quite some time. It was in 1989 that eight communities of Ladakh, namely Chhangpa, Garra, Mon, Balti, Boto, Prigpa, Beda and Prokpa, were recognized as STs. In 1991, the demand for Gujjars and Bakkerwals was acceded and four communities including Gujjars, Bakkerwals, Gaddis and Sippis were granted the ST status. As per 2011 census, the ST population of the state stands at 14.9 lakhs. Of these various tribes, the Muslims are the largest (13.2 lakhs) and are followed by Buddhists (1.0 lakh) and Hindus (67,000) (Centre for Policy Studies 2016a).

Of the 12 ST communities, eight ST communities are from Ladakh and comprise of Buddhists and Muslims. However, it is the Gujjar–Bakkerwal community, concentrated in Poonch and Rajouri but spread in all parts of the state including Kashmir, who form the largest number of STs (Gujjars form 65.77% of the total ST population; with 7.1% Bakkerwals, their strength adds up to around 73%).[12]

Traditionally, both the Gujjars and Bakkerwals were nomadic communities. Some Gujjars became the owners of land after the land reforms, but many continued to remain nomadic. However, in last few decades, a large part of Gujjar community has come to be either totally settled or semi-settled. The Bakkerwals however have continued to remain nomadic and for that reason are more marginalized as compared to the Gujjars. Among the Gujjars, a small upper crust has been created following the formation of the

[12] As per the religious affiliation of the STs, Gujjars and Bakkerwals, who form almost three-fourths of the ST population, are all Muslims. The Bots and Changpas of Leh district are Buddhists. Bali and Purigpa located in Ladakh and Brokpa, Drokpa, Dard and Shin located in Ladakh and Kashmir are Muslims. Gaddis and Sippis located in Jammu region are Hindus.

Gujjar–Bakkerwal Board in 1976 and recognition of their ST status later. However, as compared to the SCs, the upward mobility of this community is quite slow. And with the exception of a very small class of elite, the general condition of these two communities remains quite poor. As per the data from the Statistical Profile of Scheduled Tribes in India 2013, though, the STs of the state are in much better condition when compared to the national figures; however, the data about the basic socio-economic indicators does not give a happy picture. Thus, as the poverty data shows, compared to the national average of ST rural and urban (47.4% and 30.4% respectively), the state's figures for STs who are below the poverty line are much lower (15% for both rural-urban combine). However, the state falls among those states that have lower literacy rate among STs (50.6% compared to the national literacy rate of 58.92%. The situation is worse in some of the districts, for instance, 39.4% in Reasi). The state is also not well placed in terms of number and area of landholdings by STs. As per the agricultural census 2010–2011, while there was an increase in the number and area of landholdings by STs in the rest of India, for this state there was a decline. In fact there was highest decline in J&K.

Despite being granted the ST status, the right to political reservation under Article 332 of the Indian constitution has not been granted. Hence, unlike the SCs for whom seats are reserved in the Legislative Assembly and Panchayats, the STs have been granted reservation only at the Panchayat level. There is no such reservation for them within the Assembly. With Article 370 being invoked, the state governments do not feel obliged to extend the provision of political reservation for the STs. Similar demands for extending certain social welfare laws for certain groups of STs are similarly rejected on the ground of the special constitutional status of the state. As an instance one can refer to the Forest Rights Act which does not apply to the state. The Act passed as Scheduled Tribes and Other Forest Dwellers (Recognition of Rights) Act, 2006, provides a number of rights to the forest dwellers including those related to access, ownership, and rehabilitation and management of forests (Nazeer 2015).

DIVERSITIES, MULTIPLE IDENTITIES AND POLITICAL ASSERTIONS

MULTIPLE LEVELS OF ARTICULATION OF MARGINALIZATION

For a thorough understanding of the politics of the state it is important to focus on the implication of the complex pattern of diversities on the identity politics of the state. Since diversities have an intricate nature, it leads to a complex social and political setting in which there is a multiple context of discontent and multiple identity assertions. Within each context of diversity—be it religion, region, subregion or tribe—there are multiple perceptions of marginalization. With reference to religion, for instance, there are different 'minority' perceptions. This is true of Muslims as well as the Hindus. Muslims of Kashmir, while asserting the 'Muslim-majority character' of the state, see themselves as 'minority' vis-à-vis the Hindu majority in India. The Muslims located in Jammu region perceive their marginalization vis-à-vis the Hindu majority in the region. Although the Muslims in Ladakh, particularly in Kargil, outnumber Buddhists, yet they define their marginalization with reference to the domination of the Buddhists in the politics of Ladakh. Hindus of Jammu meanwhile see themselves as a 'minority' in the context of the Muslim majority character of the state. The Kashmiri Pandits refer to their marginalization vis-à-vis the Kashmiri Muslims.

It is not, however, the demographic factor of religion that underlies the context of multiple perceptions of marginalization within the state. Ethnic–cultural, regional and subregional context of marginalization is more profound in this state. Thus Kashmiri sense of marginalization vis-à-vis the Indian State is reflected more at the ethnic rather than at the religious levels. Kashmiri identity politics, therefore, rather than asserting the Muslim identity, invokes the 'Kashmiri' identity. It is for this reason that the boundaries of Kashmiri identity politics whether defined by 'autonomy' or 'azadi' do not cross the Valley of the state, and Muslims of other parts of the state, whether in Jammu region or in Ladakh, see themselves external to this identity politics.

In Jammu and Ladakh regions, it is the 'regional' context of marginalization that gets to be articulated. For both the regions, the dominant politics has revolved around the power imbalance in favour of Kashmir region; its dominance and control over the political decision-making and power positions; and the 'neglect', 'deprivation' and 'discrimination' of the other two regions. This politics is defined by a persistent feeling that there is an inbuilt unevenness within the state with Kashmir region not only getting most of the political attention from the Centre but also controlling the political power and development resources within the state. In Jammu region, therefore, the political demands have ranged from regional autonomy to separate statehood for Jammu region. In Ladakh, there has been the demand for separation of Ladakh from the Kashmir dominance and the Union Territory (UT) status.

Regional identity politics, however, is not exhaustive but is supplemented and even countered by subregional identity politics. Such politics has been asserting both in Jammu and Ladakh and emanates from the backwardness of peripheral areas of these subregions. While sharing the regional sense of deprivation, these peripheral areas feel excluded not merely from the larger politics of the state but also from the dominant politics of the region.

At another layer, the context of marginalization is articulated at the level of 'community' and tribes. Hence the Gujjar and Pahari identity politics which though mutually exclusive and competing with each other is basically a reflection of the socio-economic marginalization of these two communities. Located at the periphery of society, with lower levels of literacy, education and other parameters of social and economic development, these communities in the process of vying for state patronage have competing identity politics—Gujjar versus Pahari politics. This politics is of more recent origin and has emanated from the recognition of the ST status to the Gujjars. Asserting that they are similarly situated as Gujjars and as backward, the Paharis demand similar benefits of reservation for educational and employment purposes.

Multiple Identity Politics: The Nature of Demands

Much of the identity politics of the state is related to the conflict situation with Kashmir Valley being the 'theatre' of conflict. As explained in the last chapter, though rooted in the pre-accession period, the Kashmiri identity politics took particular shape in the period after Accession and has been manifested in various forms ranging from 'autonomy' to 'demand for plebiscite' and 'azadi'. This politics has mainly been based on the question of the state's relationship with Indian state. This politics is neither homogenous nor linear. It has significant internal differences and has changed its forms depending on the situation and context. Thus in the initial post-Accession period this politics was manifested through the demands and negotiations around the special status of the state under Article 370 of Indian Constitution. This was the period when the dominant form of identity had taken ethnoregional form. There existed a parallel religious basis of Kashmiri identity politics, but it operated more on the fringes. From 'autonomy', the direction of this politics was changed to the demand for 'plebiscite' in post-1953 period. Although this politics took an antagonistic form vis-à-vis the Indian State, yet it continued to be ethnoregional in nature. In post 1975 period, it changed its form once more to 'autonomy'. It was the slogan of 'azadi' that came to define the core of this identity politics in the post-1989 period of militancy and separatism. Though the dominant streak of this politics continued to be ethnoregional in nature, the constituency of religion started expanding in this phase. 'Azadi' in itself remained an amorphous concept with multiple meanings, though the central point where all these different meanings converge continued 'renegotiating' and 'reorganizing' the state's relationship with the Indian State. The politics of 'autonomy' meanwhile, though pushed to the margins, was kept alive by the NC and other Kashmir-based mainstream political parties including the PDP that brought in the agenda of 'self-rule'.

This particular context of identity politics, has its specificity linked with Kashmir's history, logic and circumstances and does not exhaust the whole variety of identity politics within the state. Contours of politics change when we look beyond Kashmir valley. Here the logic of identity politics revolves around the power politics and the development issues. Hence rather than the larger issues of relationship between the state and the Centre, the identity politics operates at the level of interregional relationship. In the same way in which 'New

Delhi' remains the reference point for the identity politics in Kashmir, in Jammu and Ladakh regions, the reference point of the identity politics remains the 'dominance' of Kashmir vis-à-vis the two other regions of the state. The manifestation of this politics has taken varied shapes ranging from the demand for regional autonomy to reorganizations of the state, the demand for Jammu state and the demand for the UT status for Ladakh region.

Development issues assume greater importance at the subregional levels where the peripheral status gets reflected in the overall context of backwardness. The demands here get articulated in the form of 'reorganization' of administrative set-up of the state so that there is greater flow of resources and subregional autonomy for development purposes. In more articulated form the demand is raised for Hill Councils. Two parallel kinds of demand for Hill Councils are articulated in Jammu region: the demand for Chenab Valley Hill Council in the three districts of Doda, Kishtwar and Ramban comprising the Doda belt, and the demand for Peer Panchal Hill Council in the twin border districts of Rajouri and Poonch.

Political Divergence: The Three Regions and the Political Divide

One important fact that needs to be noted about the nature of identity politics, particularly at the regional levels, is not only its multiple forms and expressions, but also the context of political divergence.

The three regions of the state, namely Jammu, Kashmir and Ladakh, are distinct not only in terms of their terrain, geography and climatic conditions, but also in terms of their sociocultural and political patterns. Brought together as parts of the single entity of princely state of J&K only in the recent past (1846), regions have maintained their distinct regional identities. There has been no common sense of belonging vis-à-vis the state over and above that of the particular regions, and at no point of history, before or after accession, has any attempt been made to develop the sense of commonality among the three regions. With each region having its own historical trajectory of politics and therefore its own sense of political aspirations and goals, it continues to operate as a distinct political unit, albeit with internal complexities.

Before the period of Accession, the direction of politics of each of the three regions was quite distinct. It was in Kashmir region that there was a prolonged period of political mobilization right from the 1920s onwards. This process became much more intensive after the political movement attained mass character towards the end of the decade of the 1930s. However, such process of political mobilization remained mostly confined to the territorial limits of the valley. With the exception of a brief period (1931–1939) when Muslim Conference brought the Muslims of J&K together at one platform; the direction of politics of Jammu and Ladakh remained different from that of Kashmir. Unlike Kashmir, there was no mobilization of masses here, and it was the interest of the socio-economic and political elite that was reflected in the politics of these two regions. In Jammu particularly, the political developments were influenced by the larger politics of the subcontinent in general and neighbouring Punjab in particular, and by the time the partition took place, there was competitive Hindu and Muslim political mobilization on communal lines.

The three regions went through altogether different kinds of experiences during the time of Partition and the Accession. While Kashmir remained mostly insulated from the implications of partition, in Jammu and Ladakh, the implications were felt in greater depth. In both the regions, there was social and political turbulence as these got impacted by internal rebellion, tribal invasion and war. Ultimately when the ceasefire took place, a substantial part of these two regions came to be under the control of Pakistan. The division of the state had its own implications ranging from communal bloodshed to the displacement of a large number of people. By the time normalcy was restored, both the regions, but particularly Jammu region, had experienced a lot of upheaval and disruptions. Apart from the bitter memories of Partition bloodshed, there were the live issues of rehabilitation of mass of refugees.

After Accession, the political divide that existed between Kashmir region, on the one hand, and the regions of Jammu and Ladakh, on the other, was widened, for various reasons. For one, there was no sense of partnership in these regions vis-à-vis the fast-changing legal and political arrangements. The changes were structural in nature and adversely impacted the dominant classes located in Jammu region. While the land reform legislations had dispossessed a large number of rich landowners, the abolition of monarchy took away the privileges of many members of the aristocratic classes who were intrinsically linked with the royal patronages one way or the other. These classes being very influential in the society controlled the political discourse of the region and sought to define the developments as against the interest of the region as a whole. The changes therefore were projected in a context of binary of 'pro-Kashmir' and 'anti-Jammu'. The denial of compensation to the landowners whose surplus land was compulsorily acquired by the state, for instance, was seen not in the 'class' terms but in 'regional' terms.

However, it was not only the very privileged classes which were affected by the changing socio-economic policies, but the 'not-so-privileged' groups were also affected. The socio-economic structure of the region was quite different from that of Kashmir and therefore the policies of the NC whose logic emanated from its rootedness in Kashmir did not go well with a large number of people in Jammu region. Apart from the privileged big landowners, there were a large number of landowners belonging to the middle and lower levels. With much of the land in the region falling in the *kandi* (infertile) belt, their level of productivity was relatively much lower. The uniform ceiling legislation for the fertile land in Kashmir and infertile areas of Jammu region, therefore, had the implications of affecting these not-so-well-to-do landowning classes. Trade was another source of livelihood and the urban centres of the region had a large number of traders. With the exception of very few who could be characterized as rich business class, most of these were petty traders and could be defined at best as part of the lower middle class. These people came to be adversely impacted by the new government's policy of nationalization and permit system. Finally, following both the regional and family traditions, a large part of the earning population of the region was linked with the armed forces at different levels, mostly in the lower ranks.

These people were adversely affected by the decision to abandon the Dogra forces. Hence a large number of people were demobilized.

Due to its lack of connect with other regions, the policy framework of the newly formed NC government could not respond to the sensibilities and peculiarities of other regions. As a consequence, there was a sense of unease in these regions, particularly in Jammu. This was more so since the NC, the dominant political force within the state, had failed to take roots here and had no connect with the people in general. The entrenched classes of the region, therefore, succeeded in giving a direction to the prevailing sense of discontent and turning it into the 'anti-Kashmir' sentiments. The two regions came to be defined in a zero-sum relationship.[13]

Added to this remained the ideological divide among the three regions. The political arrangements that were extended to the state after the accession followed the logic of the NC's politics and its emphasis on the state's autonomy. The background to the autonomy politics was clearly located in the specificity of the identity politics of Kashmir, with no similar base in Jammu or Ladakh regions. The popular response to this politics in these regions, therefore, ranged from 'indifference' at best to 'hostility' at worst. However, with the passage of time, the identity politics of Kashmir shifted its goalpost from 'autonomy' to 'plebiscite' and in the period of militancy to 'azadi'. This generated further ideological distance of the other two regions vis-à-vis the Kashmir region.

In whichever form the Kashmiri identity politics has been manifested, it is the issue of the state's relationship with India that provides an emotional substance to this politics. In response, an equally emotive response is generated in Jammu region since neither the politics of 'autonomy' nor of 'azadi' has any resonance here. The incongruity of the political aspirations of the two regions gets manifested through a

[13] This is not to argue that there were no beneficiaries of the NC's policies in Jammu region. A large number of Dalits benefitted from the land reforms and like the Kashmiri peasantry became landowners overnight. However, these Dalits were not mobilized and did not have a political voice in the region. They, therefore, could not contribute to the political discourse of the region. They sought rather to fit in the regional discourse.

strong expression of antagonism towards these goalposts, on the one hand, and a strong counter-expression against 'Kashmiri nationalism' via the assertion of 'Indian nationalism', on the other.

The specificity of Kashmir's politics and its ideological stances since the 1950s became a major factor in the lack of cohesiveness in the politics of the state. The political developments that overtook Kashmir region barely touched the other two regions. Whether it was the politics of 'autonomy' in the pre-1953 phase (or later in the decades of the 1970s and 1980s), the 'plebiscite' politics in post-1953 stage or the later 'azadi' politics—it did not extend to Jammu or Ladakh. Because of its ethnolinguistic basis, it did not even involve the Muslims of these regions. While the Muslims of Ladakh totally remained unaffected by these streaks of politics, in Jammu region, one could see its limited effect among the Kashmiri-speaking Muslims of the Doda belt. However, even these Muslims of Kashmiri origin did not go whole hog with the Kashmiri politics as they were faced with their own distinct political issues related more to development rather than the identity politics. The other Muslims of the region, including the Paharis and Gujjars in Rajouri–Poonch belt, meanwhile were faced with altogether different issues linked with their border status, the continuous volatility of the border and the problems of divided families across the LoC.

When compared with the Kashmir's identity politics, the dominant politics of the Jammu and Ladakh regions has followed altogether different directions. While Kashmir region has been involved in the politics of contestation of the state's relationship with India, Jammu's politics has been scripted by the politics of regional deprivation and regional discrimination. Ladakh's dominant politics meanwhile has been characterized by the demand of UT status. Such politics in both the regions is located mainly in the context of power politics. There is a widely shared perception in both these regions that the Kashmir-based political elite dominates the power politics and their major concerns are also located in the development of this region only. Hence, the regional politics in Jammu and Ladakh is based on the issues of regional deprivation and neglect, and the political elite in these regions often uses the agitational methods to raise their political concerns.

INTERNAL DIVIDE: TRAJECTORY OF POLITICS OF JAMMU AND LADAKH

Jammu's Regional Politics

Due to various kinds of disruption in the region, Jammu faced a political vacuum in 1947. Of these, the most significant disruption was related to the division of the state because of which a large portion of the state came under the control of Pakistan. The period was also known for a lot of violence, communal rioting and displacement of people. There was an influx of refugees and a general sense of uncertainty among the people. Unlike Kashmir, the NC did not have any base here. Although there were some progressive leaders who were associated with the left politics or the NC, but there was no mass mobilization in the direction of progressive politics. The Indian National Congress could have found enough following in the region had it made an effort. However, due to its decision not to compete with the NC and leave the political space open for this party, it discouraged all such attempts to organize the local branch of the Congress Party. It was only in 1965 that the Congress formally entered the politics of the state.

This vacuum was filled in by locally organized Praja Parishad, which though had some identification with the Bharatiya Jana Sangh operated in an autonomous manner. It was this organization that took upon itself the task of giving a direction to the regional politics of the state in the ideological orientation of RSS and Bharatiya Jana Sangh—that of opposing the special constitutional status of the state and demanding the abolition of Article 370. In its effort to appeal to the popular sensibilities of the time, this organization linked these ideological issues with the generally perceived feelings of regional neglect and launched a major agitation in 1952, which was supported not only by the Bharatiya Jana Sangh but also by other Hindu Right organizations. It raised the slogan of one constitution, one flag and one symbol, and projected complete constitutional integration of the state with India as Jammu's aspiration. The support for the agitation went much beyond the ideological base of the Hindu Right organizations. It also came from multiple groups such as the refugees, traders and transporters, who were either being adversely affected by the changed policy matters or from those sections of society which felt that their concerns were completely neglected by the state government. There was a general sense of neglect and lack of partnership in whatever changes were taking place.

Over the period, the politics of regional neglect transcended its Hindu Right base and came to be defined as the 'legitimate' politics of the region. Parties other than the Bharatiya Jana Sangh seeking to establish base in the region also sought to raise the issue of regional neglect. From time to time, there have been prolonged agitations in Jammu around the issues related to establishment of educational institutions, share of seats in professional colleges, engagement of local people in state offices, location of secretariat, formation of districts and other administrative offices, etc. During every such agitation, the discourse of regional discrimination has been further articulated.[14]

Balraj Puri who has raised the issue of Jammu's regional discontent in much of his work, has argued that the issue even though expressed in material terms, is psychological in nature. In his understanding rather than the material imbalance between Kashmir and Jammu region, it is the political imbalance within the state that gets manifested through the politics of regional discontent. Referring to the centralized structure of power in which there was no political parity between Kashmir and Jammu regions, he attributed the regional discontent to the lack of political empowerment of regional and subregional units. He therefore suggested the reorganization of the internal structure of the state on federal principles—the five-tier federal structure in which the powers are decentralized from the Centre to the state, region, district and panchayats.

[14] In 1967, there was a major agitation in which the issues of regional discrimination, particularly in the areas related to education, employment and development resources, were raised. The constitution of the Gajendragadkar Commission followed this agitation. Another major regional agitation erupted in 1979 around the employment issues. Although it started in Poonch, it eventually spread to the whole region. This agitation was followed by the Sikri Commission. There have been other agitations around the issue of formation of districts, share of seats in professional colleges, employment share of these regions, etc.

The lack of political empowerment of the regions other than Kashmir was noted by the Gajendragadkar Commission that was appointed in the mid-1960s to look into the grievances of Jammu and Ladakh regions. The Commission clearly emphasized the lack of political parity between Kashmir region on the one hand and Jammu and Ladakh on the other as the basis of regional discontent. The Commission thus stated:

> Even if all the matters were equitably settled, we feel that there would still be a measure of discontent.... In fact, we consider that the main cause of irritation and tension is the feeling of political neglect and discrimination, real or imaginary, from which certain regions of the state suffer. (Report of the Jammu and Kashmir Commission of Enquiry, 1968, 83)

It therefore suggested political ways to deal with this feeling. Thus it recommended that 'a convention should be established that if the chief minster belongs to one region, there should be a deputy chief minister belonging to other region. By another convention, the number of the cabinet ministers belonging to the regions should be equal.'

The regional imbalance in the power structure which generated a sense of political marginalization in the region right since 1947 onwards was as much a consequence of the demographic factor as of the political factor. Of the two regions, Kashmir being larger in terms of population had a greater number of Assembly seats. But more important than the larger number of MLAs from Kashmir, it has been the disproportionate influence of Kashmiri political elite in the politics of the state. For the historical reasons, Kashmiri leadership has been dominating the politics of the state right from the beginning. Thus, for the first two and half decades of power politics, the state was dominated by the NC which drew its leadership mainly from Kashmir region. Although during this time, the NC held its sway in Jammu region as well, but the NC leaders from Jammu region were always at best placed at the middle level and therefore did not have the stature of top-level leaders and did not enjoy as much influence in the party as the Kashmir-based leaders did. Also since the party had its mass base in Kashmir, much of its cadre had been drawn from that region only. The situation did not change much after the NC was converted into the Congress in 1965.

Although Congress had larger base in Jammu region, even the Congress continued to be dominated by the Kashmir-based leaders.

The context of power politics changed in the more recent period when Jammu came to have a larger share in power politics. However, despite this change, the sense of political marginalization continues. Source of much of this lies in the disproportionate attention that the Kashmiri politics and the Kashmiri political elite draw because of the conflict situation. In any case, when it comes to the Centre–state relations, the bargaining power has been lying much more with the political elite of Kashmir region.

One of the grouses that underlies the sense of political marginalization in Jammu region is that all political arrangements that have been formally incorporated in the structure of the state politics have followed the logic of Kashmir's politics. Whether it is Article 370, the land reforms or other state policies, or the various accords like the 1952 Delhi Agreement or the Indira–Sheikh Accord of 1974—all these have emanated from the context of Kashmir's politics. In all this, Jammu has had no role to play. With no sense of partnership in these political arrangements, the sense of ownership or the involvement that one sees in Kashmir is missing in Jammu region.

Ladakh's Regional Politics

Like Jammu, Ladakh was also severely impacted by the events in 1947. With the tribal invasion a large part of Ladakh came under Pakistan's control and the region faced the problems of rehabilitation of Buddhist refugees. However, what defined the direction of Ladakh's politics in the post-1947 period was the relation of this region with Kashmir. Administratively, the region being a part of the Kashmir division and people here faced not only a sense of administrative but also political marginalization. With Kashmir being engulfed in conflict politics, such a sense of marginalization was further enhanced. Hence from the beginning it was the idea of separation of Ladakh from Kashmir that came to define the logic of Ladakh's politics. To quote Martijn van Beek, 'Kashmir and Ladakh both claim the right to self-determination, although Ladakhi leaders have said that they have opted for accession to India; and while Kashmiri movements seek to free the region from India, Ladakhi movements have for decades sought to 'Free Ladakh from Kashmir' (van Beek 2004, 196).

The politics of Ladakh from the beginning has been mostly defined by the Buddhist elite situated in Leh district. It is only recently that the Kargil leadership has started making its presence felt. The demand for separation of Ladakh is basically the demand emanating from Leh district. This demand was formally raised as early as 1949 when Chewing Rigzin, President of Buddhist Association of Ladakh, submitted a memorandum to the Prime Minister of India and asserted that Ladakhis 'are a separate nation by all tests—race, language, religion, culture—determining nationality' (Puri 1982, 273).

In Puri's analysis, much of Ladakh's grouses emanated from the failure of the state to recognize the Ladakhi identity, leading the Ladakhi leaders to look towards Tibet for the recognition of its identity. However, with Tibet itself losing its status due to its conflict with China, and with the growing strategic importance of Ladakh due to the Sino-Indian War, the Ladakhi identity has been manifested in the identification with India and Indian patriotism. This explains the demand for the greater integration with the Centre via the route of UT status (Puri 1982, 273).[15]

Apart from other things, it was the consequence of structural changes initiated by the NC in the immediate post-Accession period that led to anti-Kashmir response in Ladakh.

The Ladakhi politics right from the early 1950s has highlighted the issue of regional neglect. That the state government dominated by Kashmiri leaders did not pay attention to the requirements of Ladakh and that Ladakh remained invisible in the policies and budget allocation remained the major complaint of Ladakhi leaders in the initial

[15] The initial leadership was provided by Young Men Buddhist Association, which opposed the idea of Ladakh being linked with Kashmir. The reason for this lay in the political stance being taken by Kashmir, especially the conflict angle and the possibility of a plebiscite. This group did not want Ladakh to be part of such a situation in which the future of Ladakh is uncertain. The demand from the beginning was to exclude Ladakh from any such process where the linkage of Ladakh with India is disturbed.

decades following the Accession. One of the major problems of Ladakh relates to its economy. There are not many sources of livelihood. Land is a scarce resource. In the absence of much agricultural activities beyond subsistence level, much of Ladakh's economy has been dependent on the presence of army (due to an extensive border with China and Pakistan). Of late, tourism has picked up. But other than that, there is lot of economic handicap of the region which feeds into the discontent of the people. It was as late as 1974 that Ladakh was opened for tourism. However, the state did not take much initiative in that process. Foreign tourists and private initiatives have resulted in boost in tourism in Leh. Kargil is still to catch up in this field. Such discontent is more acutely felt as the educated class is increasing and there are not many avenues of employment. Until 1990 there were no institutions of higher education and Ladakhis had to move out of Ladakh to get even college education. (The first college was established in Leh in 1990 and soon another college in Kargil.) In the situation of the backwardness of the region, much of the demands that have been raised have related to 'more resources, faster development, and greater control over decision making' (van Beek 2001, 373).[16]

One major agitation in which the issues of Ladakh's discrimination were raised took place in 1989. Though initiated against the Kashmiri traders to begin with, this agitation not only took an anti-Kashmir stance but also an anti-Muslim stance. It was during this agitation that demand for UT status for Ladakh became more sharpened and soon after the agitation the idea of Hill Council was fructified. Two Hill Councils (one each for Leh and Kargil) were offered to the region.

Subregional Politics

Beyond the regional identity politics, there lies another layer of identity politics that operates at the subregional level. This identity politics has been asserted both in Jammu and Ladakh regions. In Jammu, it

[16] There has also been the demand for special consideration of the area. In 1962 during the Sino-Indian war, the region had been centrally administered under the North-East Frontier Agency (NEFA) arrangement. When this status was withdrawn, there was demand for continuation of this arrangement (van Beek 2004, 202).

has been reflected in the twin districts of Poonch–Rajouri, on the one hand, and the Doda belt, now comprising the three districts of Doda, Kishtwar and Ramban, on the other.

The subregional identity politics emanates from three reasons: first neither the Jammu nor Ladakh region is homogenous and the pulls and pressures that are manifested because of the internal differentiations take shape of the subregional political demands and politics. The second reason for the subregional identity politics lies in the very nature of the regional politics both of Ladakh and Jammu regions. This politics though makes claim of representing the whole region, however, does not take into cognizance the plurality of the region and does not sufficiently represent the issues of the peripheral parts of the region. Thus even while 'discrimination' remains central to the discourse both of Jammu and Ladakh regions, this discourse does not focus on real pockets of backwardness—Doda belt and Poonch-Rajouri districts in the Jammu region and Kargil in the Ladakh region. Much of this discourse merely echoes the elitist concerns of the core constituency of these regions—the Hindu-dominated urban areas of Jammu region and the Buddhist dominated Leh in Ladakh region. Third, the reflection of the regional politics as it is articulated in the Jammu and Ladakh regions is based on regional-cum-religious binary of Muslim Kashmir, Hindu Jammu and Buddhist Ladakh; this tends to exclude the Muslim populations, both of Jammu and Ladakh.

What gets reflected in the subregional politics therefore is a sense of double marginalization since the peripheral parts of both Jammu and Ladakh region feel neglected both as part of their respective regions vis-à-vis the politics of Kashmir and also vis-à-vis the dominant politics of the region of which these subregions are parts.

MARGINALIZED SECTIONS AND IDENTITY POLITICS

The overarching context of identity politics that operates in the state is either related to conflict situation or is oriented towards elite demands and therefore leaves no space for the articulation of the issues related to the marginal sections of society. Despite the fact that the state has multiple layers of discontent and has gone through various phases of protest politics, however not many progressive movements around the socio-economic issues have been organized in the post-1947 period. This is despite the fact that the NC had represented a tradition of a politics aimed at socio-economic transformation, the impact of which could be seen till the early years of the 1950s in the form of land reform legislations, progressive economic policies, educational reforms and the broad-based socio-economic content of the Directive Principles of State Policy as enshrined in the Constitution of J&K.

The socio-economic content that was to be seen in the movement politics went missing in the post-1950 period as the Kashmiri identity politics entered a new phase. With political identity being privileged over socio-economic identities, this politics lost its progressive face. Social movements that emerged elsewhere in India completely bypassed this state and neither the Dalit politics, nor the women's politics, nor the OBC politics, nor any other kind of social movement politics could be witnessed here. In fact, other than the purely political issues of discrimination, neglect of the region, subregion or the like—there has not been space for any other kinds of politics. Even within the ongoing political identity politics, the issues related to marginal, weaker or downtrodden classes have not been raised. For instance, the Dalit politics which has been asserted in neighbouring state of Punjab has not touched the state of J&K. This is despite the fact that Dalits form quite a large part of the population in largely Hindu parts of the state (every fourth person in Jammu, Samba and Kathua, and every fifth person in Udhampur and Reasi is a Dalit). One of the reasons that has been attributed to absence of Dalit assertion in the state is the relatively better position of Dalits compared to their counterparts in other northern states.

One peculiarity about the Dalits of J&K has been that a significant number became the beneficiaries of the land reforms. In the kind of caste structure that existed in the region, the Rajputs were the biggest absentee landowners followed by the Brahmins. The backward classes including the Lohars, Tarkhans, Masons and Dhobis followed occupations with fixed income. Dalits formed the most marginalized class that was engaged in actual cultivation process and therefore became the beneficiaries of the policy of the redistribution of the land (Verma

1994, 368–369). They also benefitted from the educational policy of the state. Though the state had laid down a policy of compulsory schooling even before the Accession (the *Jabri* schools or the forced schools at the time of Maharaja Hari Singh) it was only after the land reforms that some Dalit children could afford to take advantage of the universal and free education that was made available by the NC government.[17] Reservation policy that was later extended to them also benefited the Dalits.[18]

All this helped Dalits in this state achieve an upward mobility. In comparative terms, the SCs of J&K reflect a better socio-economic profile in relation to their counterparts in many north Indian states including Punjab, Haryana, Rajasthan and Uttar Pradesh. One can get a comparative picture from the census data and the Socio Economic and Caste Census (SECC) of 2011. As per the 2011 census data, the literacy rate of SCs in J&K is 70.2 per cent which is higher than the average Indian literacy rate of 66.1 per cent and many other north Indian states (Punjab 64.8%, Haryana, 66.9%, Rajasthan 59.7%). The SECC data meanwhile gives further details that reflects a comparatively better position of Dalits in this state. It shows, for instance, that only 4.46 per cent SC households in this state are involved in manual casual labour as against the national average of 12.40 per cent, and 14.73 per cent in Bihar, 17.45 per cent in Haryana, 28.88 per cent in Punjab, 11.31 per cent in Rajasthan and 14.44 per cent in Uttar Pradesh.[19] Households with salaried jobs in government is 18.49 per cent for J&K as against the national average of 3.96 per cent. Figures for other

[17] The compulsory education was started by Maharaja Hari Singh during the 1930s itself. Later on this policy of compulsory education was vigorously followed by Sheikh Abdullah's government. The benefits of education did trickle down to Dalits, especially after the land reforms, when some Dalits were able to send their children to schools.

[18] Although due to Article 370 the provision of reservation was not automatically extended to the SCs, it was following an agitation by the Dalits and a fast unto death which ultimately led to the death of Bhagat Amarnath that the provisions of reservation were extended to the state.

[19] The percentage of the landless SC households delivering major part of their income from manual casual labour is 21.88 per cent for this state against the national average of 54.67 per cent. In Punjab it is 77.20 per cent, 76.21 per cent in Bihar and 74.30 per cent in Haryana.

states are: 2.42 per cent for Bihar, 4.67 per cent for Gujarat, 6.52 per cent for Haryana, 6.09 per cent for Punjab, 3.93 per cent for Rajasthan and 2.94 per cent for UP. The data for monthly per capita consumer expenditure (rural) for SCs for this state is ₹1,753 as compared to the national average of ₹1,252 (₹996 for Bihar, 1,710 for Haryana, 1,660 for Himachal Pradesh, 1,785 for Punjab, 1,389 for Punjab, 1,004 for Uttar Pradesh).[20]

On the whole, one can agree with Verma that '...there has been considerable improvement in the condition of Dalits in the state'. He notes that 'a sizeable group of elitist class consisting of bureaucrats, military–police officials, professionals and politicians has emerged over the years' (Verma 2010, 370). The land reforms followed by the reservation policy have helped create a small layer of middle class among Dalits. Bhatia notes:

> though very few members of this community could reach the higher echelons of bureaucracy, there were many who were able to benefit from lower cadre government jobs. This has helped create a lower middleclass layer of SCs, and over the generations, a small urban middle class. (Bhatia 2014, 948)

However, there are a large number of Dalits who continued to remain marginalized. The benefits of the land reforms were not evenly spread among all the subcastes of SCs. While the Meighs got the maximum benefit, there were other subcastes such as Mahashas, Batawals and Chamars who did not get any benefit, mainly for the reason that these were urban-based castes and were not occupationally associated with the land.

However, there is another reason for lack of Dalit assertion in Jammu region. This relates to the larger politics of the region defined by the issues of regional discrimination. This politics in many ways obfuscates the contradiction between the upper and lower castes in the region and rather diverts the direction of all politics in Jammu

[20] For urban, it is ₹1,955 for the state, as against the national average of ₹2,028, ₹1305 for Bihar, ₹2,164 for Haryana, ₹2,817 for Himachal Pradesh, ₹2,024 for Punjab, ₹1,974 for Rajasthan and ₹1,523 for Uttar Pradesh.

versus Kashmir politics. While issues related to regional discrimination and regional deprivation are raised, Dalits are incorporated into this politics. If there is any kind of Dalit politics, it is related to issues related to reservation. The associations such as All India Confederation of SC/ST Organizations (AICSCSTO), J&K, play important role in this process. However, the issues of intercaste relationship do not take the shape of organized Dalit politics.[21]

Like Dalits, women have also not been able to organize themselves into a movement politics. In fact, there is no women's constituency in the state despite the fact that women's issues lie at the centre of the conflict discourse. There are not many credible organizations which articulate women's issues or voice concern from gender perspective. In fact, one can see that women are divided around the larger battle lines drawn by the competitive identity politics within the state. Hence, rather than pursuing issues from the gender perspective, these are pursued from larger context of identity. That way, the women's identity politics is subsumed by the larger context of competitive identity politics.

One example that can be put forth for explaining as to how the women's issues are subordinated to the larger identity issues, relates to the controversy linked with women's right to retain the permanent resident certificate (PRC) after marrying outside the state. By an administrative practice, till 2004, women who married outside the state lost the privileges entitled to the permanent residents as their PRC was marked 'valid till marriage'. However, when this practice was declared invalid by a High Court decision in 2004, there were strong protests in Kashmir on the ground that the decision went against the basic tenets of the Kashmiri identity politics. So much was the pressure on the then ruling PDP that it introduced a Bill in the state legislature

[21] That is also the reason that except for a brief period, the BSP has not been very successful in this state. In 1996, the party won four seats and polled 6.43 per cent votes at the state level. In Jammu region, its share of votes was 11.19 per cent. In 2002, it could win only one seat with a vote share of 4.5 per cent at the state level and 6.83 per cent in Jammu region. In 2008 and 2014, it could not win any seat and its share of votes was also drastically reduced.

that proposed to disqualify women from holding the PRC after marrying outside the state.[22]

One major concern related to women emanates from the negative sex ratio in most of the districts of the state. The state, as per the 2011 census, is among the very few states of India where the sex ratio is going inverse direction. From 892 females per thousand males in 2001, the number has gone down to 883 in 2011. The inverse direction of sex ratio has brought national attention to the state of J&K. This is mainly for the reason that in the last one decade, there has been a relative improvement in the sex ratio for most of the other states. There are only three states including J&K which have experienced inverse sex ratio. With a deficit of 117 women for every thousand men, the state seems to have travelled backwards. In 1901, the sex ratio of the state was recorded at 882 per 1,000 men. Even after 110 years, the sex ratio, as per 2011 Census data is 883 per 1000 men. This is really a worrisome situation since it is an indicator that despite a constitution with lofty principles of equality, women continue to face a high level of prejudice.

However, what is actually alarming is the data related to child sex ratio (CSR) which is still lower than the overall sex ratio. For every one thousand male children there are only 859 female children. This means that between the female and male children, there is a gap of 141 female children. Although these are the only two districts in the state which have a CSR at less than 800, there are 13 other districts of the state which are placed much below the national average of 914: Anantnag and Badgam (832 each), Rajouri (837), Pulwama and Kathua (836 each), Kupwara (854), Ganderbal (863), Baramulla (866), Srinagar (869), Kulgam (882). Shopian (883), Udhampur (887) and Bandipora (893). It is only Reasi (921), Kishtwar (922), Ramban (931), Doda (932) Leh (944) and Kargil (978) which are placed above the national average.

[22] The way the issue of rape and murder of an eight-year-old Gujjar girl in early 2018 evoked regional and communal identity politics also reflects how the serious concerns related to women are subordinated to competitive identity politics of the state. Rather than being seen as a 'gender issue', it was seen both in Kashmir and Jammu as a 'community issue'.

Another critical issue related to women's empowerment is about the state of literacy and education. It is a matter of great concern that in a state which had committed itself to universal education and had provided for free education up to the university level, there is around 42 per cent female illiteracy. However, when we go into details, we find that there are districts which have still worse rates of female literacy. More than half the female population in districts such as Badgam, Bandipora, Ganderbal, Kulgam, Ramban, Kishtwar and Reasi are illiterate. The worst rate of female literacy is in Ramban where 60 per cent of women are still illiterate. The situation is worse in rural areas. In the rural areas of Ramban, for instance, only 38.52 per cent females are literate.

To Conclude

This chapter focusing on the social diversities and political divergence within the state has emphasized the plural character of the state. It has sought to extend the imagination of the state beyond the Kashmir Valley and brought focus on the multiple identity politics. It has specifically sought to draw attention on the intra-state political differences that operate at the regional level.

The underlying argument, while focusing on the social diversity and political divergence within the state, relates to the context of complexity that characterizes the nature of both internal politics and the conflict situation. It is this complexity that gets to be reflected when we shift our focus beyond the identity politics of Kashmir. It is then that we get to see the interplay of multiple identity politics at the level of the state.

Complexity of internal politics also draws our attention to the additional intricacy to the context of conflict. It is through the internal politics that we can understand how besides the two recognized dimensions of conflict (the external and internal dimensions), a third dimension is added because of the lack of internal political consensus on the fundamental issues confronting the state.

References

Bhatia, Mohita. 2014. '"Dalits" in Jammu and Kashmir'. *Asian Survey* 54 (5): 941–965.

Bhat, Fayaz Ahmad, and P. K. Mathur. 2011, July–December. 'Ethnic Plurality in Jammu and Kashmir: A Sociological Analysis'. *Man in India* 91 (3–4): 577–596.

Centre for Policy Studies. 2016, 29 February. 'Jammu and Kashmir: Hindus No More Have a Place in the Valley'. Religion Data of 2011: XV Jammu and Kashmir. http://blog.cpsindia.org/2016/02/religion-data-of-census-2011-xv-jammu.html (accessed on 27 August 2018).

———. 2016a, 24 December. 'Scheduled Tribes of Northwest India: Jammu & Kashmir and Himachal Pradesh'. Religion Data of Census 2011: XXXIII JK-HP-ST. http://blog.cpsindia.org/2016/12/religion-data-of-census-2011-xxxiii-jk.html (accessed on 27 August 2018).

Chadha Behera, Navnita. 2000. *State, Identity and Violence: Jammu, Kashmir and Ladakh*. New Delhi: Manohar Publishers.

Chowdhary, Rekha. 2010. 'Identity Politics of Jammu Region'. In *Identity Politics in Jammu and Kashmir*, edited by Rekha Chowdhary. New Delhi: Vitasta.

———. 2015. *Jammu and Kashmir: Politics of Identity and Separatism*. New Delhi: Routledge.

Dar, Mohd. Ashraf. 2017. 'Political History of Ladakh (Pre 9th to 12th CE)', *Historical Research Letter*, Vol. 41. https://www.iiste.org/Journals/index.php/HRL/article/viewFile/37838/38920, (accessed on 9 November 2018).

Lawrence, Walter R. 1895. *The Valley of Kashmir*. London: Oxford University Press.

Madan, T. N. 2008. 'Religious Ideology in a Plural Society: The Muslims and Hindus of Kashmir'. In *Muslim Communities of South Asia: Culture, Society and Power*, edited by T. N. Madan. New Delhi: Manohar Publishers.

Malik, Mohd Latif. 2016, 6 October. 'OBC Reservation Row in J&K'. *Daily Excelsior*. http://www.dailyexcelsior.com/obc-reservation-row-jk/ (accessed on 27 August 2018).

Malik, M. Mazammail Hussain. 2009, 1 November. 'A Case Study of Rajouri District in J&K'. *Epilogue* 3 (11): 44–43.

Nazeer, Zubair. 2015, 13 August. 'Tribals in Jammu and Kashmir: A Need for Forest Rights Act'. Countercurrents.org. http://www.countercurrents.org/nazeer130815.htm (accessed on 27 August 2018).

Puri, Balraj. 1982, 20 February. 'Route of Ladakh's Integration'. *Economic & Political Weekly* 17 (8): 273–275.

———. 2001, 28 April–11 May. 'The Mosaic of Jammu and Kashmir'. *Frontline* 18 (09). http://www.frontline.in/static/html/fl1809/18091110.htm (accessed on 27 August 2018).

Puri, Luv. 2005, 1–14 January. 'A Struggle for Survival'. *Frontline* 22 (01). http://www.frontline.in/static/html/fl2201/stories/20050114003303600.htm (accessed on 27 August 2018).

Rao, Aparna. 1999. 'A Tortuous Search for Justice: Notes on Kashmir Conflict' (Article 7). *Himalaya: The Journal of the Association for Nepal and Himalayan Studies* 19 (1): 12.

Report of the Jammu and Kashmir Commission of Inquiry (Gajendergadkar Commission). 1968. Ranbir Government Press.

Shafi, Sumera. 2013, August. 'Identifying the "Other" in Buddhist–Muslim Transformative Relations'. Issue Brief #234. New Delhi: Institute of Peace and Conflict Studies (IPCS).

Sikand, Yoginder. 2001, 20–26 January. 'The Changing Course of the Kashmiri Struggle: From Nationalist Liberation to Islamist Jihad?' *Economic & Political Weekly* 36 (3): 165–204.

———. 2010, May 20. 'Dalit Perspectives on Religion and Inter-Community Relations'. TwoCircles.net. http://twocircles.net/2010may20/muslim_hindu_relations_jammu_province_part_8.html (accessed on 27 August 2018).

Verma, P. S. 1994. *Jammu and Kashmir at the Political Crossroads*. New Delhi: Vikas Publishing House.

———. 2010. 'Dalits in Jammu and Kashmir'. In *Identity Politics in Jammu and Kashmir*, edited by Rekha Chowdhary. New Delhi: Vitasta.

Van Beek, Martijn. 1998, May. 'Ladakh Balti'. *Himal*. http://old.himalmag.com/component/content/article/2461-Ladakhi-balti.htm (accessed on 1 November 2017).

———. 2001. 'Public Secrets, Conscious Amnesia, and the Celebration of Autonomy for Ladakh'. In *States of Imagination: Ethnographic Explorations of the Postcolonial State*, edited by Thomas Blom Hansen and Finn Stepputat, 365–390. Durham, NC: Duke University Press.

———. 2004. 'Dangerous Liaisons: Hindu Nationalism and Buddhist Radicalism in Ladakh'. In *Religious Radicalism and Security in South Asia*, edited by Satu Limaye, Mohan Malik, and Robert G. Wirsing, 193–218. Honolulu, HI: Asia-Pacific Centre for Security Studies.

Politics of Separatism
1989–2010

3

The politics of separatism that overtook the Kashmir Valley in the post-1989 period has gone through various shifts. On the basis of these shifts, one can identify three major phases of separatism—the phase of militancy, the post-militancy phase of separatism and the recent phase of separatism. While the discussion on the recent phase of separatism will be taken up at the later stage, this chapter focuses on the first two phases of separatism.

It was in the post-1987 period that separatist politics overtook Kashmir in a big way. Although the stage for the militancy was set by the indigenous factors, however, it had its external basis with Pakistan supporting and even controlling various militant groups. However, militancy was not unlinked to the popular separatist sentiment. In fact, it was the popular separatist sentiments in Kashmir that actually provided legitimacy to the militancy. Ultimately, it was the gradual withdrawal of the popular support and therefore the legitimacy to the armed militancy that caused its decline. Separatism, therefore, though intricately linked with militancy, has its own trajectory that preceded and has followed the phase of militancy.

With the decline of militancy, separatism entered a new phase and came to be manifested through mass response. Massive anti-state demonstrations, street protests and stone pelting marked the separatist politics of this phase. Prolonged agitations that lasted for months together (as in 2008 and 2010) were the high points of this phase of separatism. This phase brought about a generational change as the youth born and brought up in the situation of violence and militarization took the centre stage. It also saw a shift towards the more extreme positions, rejection of moderate leadership and moderate political positions, and also an extended space for religious radicalism.

THE FIRST PHASE OF SEPARATISM

Armed Militancy and Popular Separatism

Although this phase of separatism started in the post-1987 period, while reflecting immediate sense of disillusionment with the democratic sphere of politics, particularly its lack of autonomy, its long-term roots lay in the earlier phase of separatism that had taken shape during the 1953–1975 period. It was during this earlier phase that the psyche of separatism had taken shape. Although the expansion of democratic space in the 1975–1983 period had pushed back the separatist politics, however, the developments that took place in the later period brought this politics back to the centre stage. In a way, therefore, the separatist politics that emerged in the post-1987 period was a continuation of the 1953–1975 period. It was the similar contestation of the finality of accession and similar demand for 'self-determination'.

However, despite this continuity, the separatism that emerged in this phase was quite distinct as compared to the earlier phase. Militancy was its dominant feature and its major manifestation. However, the phenomenon of militancy was intermeshed with the popular separatism. As almost the whole Kashmiri society was swept away by the separatist sentiment, at least in the initial phase, the kind of intensity that was reflected on the streets of Kashmir was certainly exceptional. With a new aggression vis-à-vis the Indian State, there were massive demonstrations reverberating with 'azadi' slogans almost on daily basis. Situation was so volatile in 1989–1990 period that it not only led to the collapse of the law and order but to the total erosion of all democratic spaces. While the writ of the state was challenged, the role of the political actors, especially in the mainstream politics, was completely rejected. The defiance and resistance of people to the commands of the state and authority of government was displayed in a variety of ways.

The two phenomena—that of militancy and the popular separatist sentiments—were interconnected and it is the linkage between the two that made this phase quite distinct.

Another peculiarity of this phase was that it reflected an intermeshing between the external and internal factors. The external factor came into operation when young Kashmiris frustrated with the local developments, particularly the choking of the democratic space, took the decision to take up arms and cross the border. Pakistan fully exploited the situation not only by giving material and moral support to militancy but also seeking control over it. Thus, while the outbreak of militancy and mass separatist upsurge in post-1987 period was purely because of the internal factors, its sustenance was due to the external factors. During the period, there evolved a complex intertwining between the internal and external factors—with one reinforcing the other.

Finally, what clearly distinguished this phase of separatism from the earlier one was its break from the traditional politics revolving around the persona of Sheikh Abdullah. As a matter of fact, there was a reassessment of the history of the Kashmiri identity politics and the role played by Sheikh Abdullah in it. What was clearly rejected was his decision to disband the Plebiscite Front and take to power politics following an accord with New Delhi. Rather than being seen as the 'hero' of Kashmiri politics, he was now projected as the failed leader who 'betrayed' the Kashmiri cause.

Outbreak of Militancy: Linkage between Militancy and Popular Separatist Response

Following the debacle of 1987 Assembly election, the political situation of Kashmir was quite unsettling and there were different manifestations of public discontent. Joining militancy by local Kashmiri youth was one such manifestation. It was the imprisonment of Mohammed Yousuf Shah, the MUF candidate from Amirakadal (who later on came to be known as Sayeed Salahuddin, the chief of Hizbul Mujahideen), which provided a trigger for the youth to take up armed militancy.

His close aids and election agents joined the Jammu and Kashmir Liberation Front (JKLF) and took the decision to cross the border for militant training. By the middle of 1988, these trained militants had started coming back and registering their presence in Kashmir (Bose 2003; Puri 1993; Schofield 2000; Widmalm 2002). Two explosions in the centre of the Srinagar city, in the telegraph office, were among the first militant incidents. The responsibility for these explosions were taken by the JKLF (Sahni 1999). Militancy at this stage was of symbolic nature and was aimed more at recording the presence of militants and attracting international attention rather than harming people. It was around the year 1989 that militancy took a full-blown form. By this time, thousands of Kashmiri youth had been recruited as armed militants.

Among some of the high-profile militant attacks in 1989 that established beyond doubt the space that the militants had carved for themselves included that on Yusuf Halwai, the NC activist who was seen to be associated with the electoral rigging during the Assembly elections; killing of Justice Neelkanth Ganjoo, the judge who had pronounced death sentence on Maqbool Bhat, the founder of JKLF; and on BJP leader Tika Lal Taploo. In December, with the kidnapping of Rubaiya Sayeed, the power of the militants came to be displayed publicly[1] (Pachauri 1989). By 1990, there were more high profile cases of militant killing which included those of Lassa Koul, the Director of Srinagar Doordarshan; Dr Mushirul Haq, the Vice Chancellor of Kashmir University; and H. L. Khera, the General Manager of HMT (Sahni 1999, 129).

Militancy, as it overtook the Valley, did not exist in vacuum and was closely linked with the popular separatist sentiments. Following the 1987 Assembly election, there was an outburst of anger which was expressed in various kinds of protests. Throughout the years of 1987 and 1988, Kashmir remained disturbed. The agitational mood, however, was intensified in 1988. Protests that year were organized

[1] Rubaiya Sayeed, the daughter of Mufti Mohammed Sayeed, the then Home Minister of India, was kidnapped in December 1989 by militants of JKLF group. After a negotiation mediated by a few prominent Kashmiris, she was released in exchange of five top-level detained militants.

around disparate issues such as Darbar Move, hike in power tariff and even following the news of General Zia's death. However, by 1989, the protests were clearly focused on the 'azadi' politics. Frequency of protest demonstrations increased and people in large numbers started participating in these, chanting the 'azadi' slogans. To express the anti-India sentiment, complete bandhs were observed on days of national importance such as the Republic Day and the Independence Day; anniversary of Maqbool Bhat's hanging on 11 February; and Sheikh Abdullah's death anniversary (declared as a *Youm-i-Nijad* [Deliverance Day]) (Bose 2003; Sahni 1999; Schofield 2000).

The 'azadi' politics had fully taken a shape by this time. What was peculiar was that the sentiment was spread across the board. Not only the young people but people of all generations were emotionally involved in this politics and were convinced that 'azadi' was around the corner. The sentiment was equally shared by the students, petty shopkeepers, the business class, the housewives and even the government officials. Further, the response was not limited to the city of Srinagar but spread throughout the Valley of Kashmir.

By the year 1990, militancy had taken deep roots in Kashmir Valley and there was an intensified popular separatist response. What contributed to such a response was the stringent state retaliation. Seeking to control the situation in the streets, the violence that was resorted to by the security forces led to an intensified protest demonstration. By February and March, some of the processions were reported to be so large as to have comprised lakhs of people. Massive gatherings were also witnessed during the funerals. One such funeral which saw huge participation of lakhs of people was that of Ashfaq Wani, a prominent JKLF militant (Bose 2003, 103).

It was from this widespread sentiment of separatism that militancy drew its legitimacy. People generally approved of the militant activities and celebrated the youth involved in it. Seen as the youth icons and the new heroes, they were owned by the common Kashmiris as their 'own boys'. The death of a militant became an occasion of celebration and his funeral attended by thousands of people became an important space for mobilization for 'azadi' politics. Special affection was shown for them by the women who sang wedding songs during their funerals (Sobhrajani 2008). The status of 'martyr' was granted by the society to the dead militants.

On the whole, one can argue that militancy and separatism though were two different phenomena, yet these were quite intrinsically linked with each other in the initial stage. The strategies of popular politics of 'azadi' were different from those of the militants, and unlike the protest marches of unarmed civilians, the militants were armed with sophisticated and modern arms and directly targeted the security forces and other symbols of the state. However, notwithstanding this difference, there was a close linkage between the two. Militants at this stage were very much linked with the society. They were often showing their presence in the public spaces, and during processions or funerals, they were openly mingling with people. Their acts of violence were glorified by the people. In sum, the militancy was seen as a legitimate political activity and violence against the state was seen as the most appropriate mechanism for separatist politics (Chowdhary 2016, 105–108).

One of the reasons for such linkage between militancy and popular separatist politics was that militancy at this stage had its indigenous base. It was the internal political conditions which had led to the birth of militancy and all the militants were local youth and hence were owned by the people. This was to change in the latter period when militancy came to be controlled by Pakistan and the militant cadre came to be comprised of the outsiders.

Ascendancy of Separatism: Collapse of State Authority and Shrinking of Space for Democratic Politics

The situation, as it evolved in the early period of militancy, led to a complete breakdown of state authority. In the face of massive demonstrations on everyday basis, the state found it difficult to enforce its writ. There was a mood of open rebellion and apart from the antistate processions, there were various other signs of popular defiance including the hurling of Pakistani flags, following the Pakistani rather than the Indian time and changing the names of places. People even stopped paying taxes (Verma 1994, 263).[2] Curfews, which were the only instrument available with the state to enforce its authority, were openly defied. 'Civil curfews', which were actually calls of complete shutdown by militant groups, were fully observed. On the days of such civil curfews, all shops would be closed, no transport would ply, no educational institution would work and even the public offices would not be functional.

Significantly, the popular response was more or less spontaneous. Apart from the militants, there was no specific overarching organization to direct and organize the popular response. It was in 1993 that the All Party Hurriyat Conference came into existence. Till that time, it was either the writ of various militant organizations which was being followed on the ground or people on their own were manifesting their separatist inclinations.

It was, on the whole, a stage of 'euphoria' with people believing that 'azadi' was imminent.[3] Almost the whole of the valley seems to have been swept away by this sentiment. Although militancy was seen as an important instrument of achieving the azadi, people were convinced that their participation in the street demonstrations would also contribute to the process.

In such a mood of overwhelming separatist sentiment, the mainstream politics was the major casualty. Since much of the popular separatist response was linked with the reaction to the 1987 Assembly election, there was a strong resentment not only against the NC and

[2] Jagmohan, who served as the governor of the state, thus notes about the tax collection as he found it in January 1990: 'The State machinery was incapable, and even unwilling, to collect even routine taxes like entertainment tax and excise duty. By the end of the year, the arrears on this account alone amounted to ₹24 crores' (Jagmohan 2006, 374).

[3] The sentiment that 'azadi' was imminent was shared by Kashmiris. The political developments at the international level, particularly the changing situation in East Europe, contributed to the expectation of Kashmiris. As Bose notes:

> International events played a significant role in steeling insurrectionist resolve in the late 1989 and early 1990. The first Palestinian *intifada* against Israeli occupation was an important reference point, as was the collapse of repressive one-party regimes in central and eastern Europe after mass demonstrations in the autumn of 1989.... The young Kashmiri guerrillas, for their part, were inspired by the 1989 Soviet withdrawal from Afghanistan in the face of Afghan *mujahideen* resistance.... (Bose 2003, 111)

Congress party but against the political class per se. Daunted by the separatist sentiment, the political class, in itself, had withdrawn from the political scene (Chowdhary and Rao, 2003, 15–16). Even though the government held on to power till January 1990, its effectiveness was very much in question. Unable to deal with the situation, it ultimately resigned making way for the Governor's rule that was followed by President's rule for a prolonged period.

That the competitive politics had become irrelevant and that there was no space for this politics in Kashmir was clear in 1989 itself when the Parliamentary election was organized. Such was the reluctance of the political parties to come forward to contest election that the NC could win all the three seats without any competition. While a few independent candidates competed with NC in Baramulla and Anantnag, it won the Srinagar seat without a contest. The electoral exercise was almost farcical with people choosing to stay away from the whole process. As a consequence, in the two constituencies where polling was held, the voter turnout did not exceed 5 per cent (Chowdhary and Rao 2003a, 196).

Besides the de-legitimization of the mainstream politics, it was also the threat of militant violence that had serious implications for the mainstream politics. Right from the middle of 1989, the political workers and leaders across the party lines had become the targets of the militant violence. Not only the high profile leaders but the cadre as well as the ordinary ground workers of the political parties were vulnerable targets of the militants. With militancy gaining the supremacy and the violence becoming the major tool of separatism, the vulnerability of the political class was increased and most of the political party leaders and cadre went in complete hibernation. Only those who had shifted sides and joined the separatist politics could remain active.

Nature of Militancy: Initial Period

As already stated, militancy as it emerged in Kashmir in the 1988–1989 period was indigenous. The first generation of militants were those who were deeply involved in the 1987 Assembly election and were associated in some way with the MUF. It was the HAJY group comprised of four young Kashmiris (mostly having the urban lower class background), namely Hamid Sheikh, Ashfaq Wani, Javed Mir and Yasin Malik, which took the lead in initiating militancy in Kashmir.[4] This group had earlier formed the Islamic Students League and during the 1987 Assembly election, its members had worked as associates and election agents of Mohammed Yousuf Shah. Shah who contested election from Amirakadal constituency in Srinagar was defeated and the HAJY group took the decision to join JKLF formed by Maqbool Bhat in 1964 in Pakistan-administered Kashmir. Under the leadership of this group, JKLF was able to mobilize and recruit a number of young Kashmiris into militancy. For the next three years, the JKLF was the most popular militant organization of Kashmir (Sahni 1999).

Pakistan initially supported JKLF despite ideological difference with this organization. As against the official position of Pakistan that J&K be merged with it, the JKLF stood for the goal of complete independence for the whole of undivided state including the part in Pakistan's control. The spontaneity and suddenness of the decision of young Kashmiris to opt for militancy had taken Pakistan by surprise and it did not want to leave the opportunity being provided to it on a platter. Hence, it readily extended all the support that the JKLF required. However, the Pakistani establishment was never comfortable with its political stance. Therefore, while supporting the JKLF, its intelligence agency ISI created its own militant organization, the Hizbul Mujahideen. Apart from the Hizb, ISI launched a number of other militant organizations to be active in Kashmir. These included Al-Umar Mujahideen and Ikhwan-ul-Muslimeen. Many of these organizations were actually the breakaway groups of the JKLF. These organizations along with Hizb were created to outmanoeuvre the JKLF. Among the first actions of Hizb and these organizations was the elimination of the cadre of JKLF—either by killing them or by providing information about them to the Indian security forces. By 1993 much of the cadre of JKLF had already

[4] The term 'HAJY' represented the first letters of the names of the four militants: Hamid, Ashfaq, Javed and Yasin.

been eliminated and the militant space was dominated by the Hizb (Noorani 2000). Yasin Malik was forced to withdraw from militancy and declare support for Gandhian strategy of non-violence. Control of the militancy thereafter was in the hands of Pakistan and its intelligence agency, the ISI.

With the withdrawal of the JKLF from the scene, the ISI-controlled Hizbul Mujahideen became the dominant militant organization in Kashmir. Despite the fact that this organization was not as popular as the JKLF, it used the local influence of Jamaat-e-Islami to generate its local support base. By 'creating war-fighting institutions through the Jamaat's party cadres and their kin and local sympathisers', it could operate as an indigenous organization (Staniland 2014, 76–77). With JKLF out of the scene, local Kashmiris have been identifying with the Hizb, not because of its ideology but because of its local nature.

Political Face of Separatism: All Party Hurriyat Conference

While the popular separatist sentiment and militancy were the two manifestations of separatist politics, initially there was a vacuum so far as the political representation of separatism was concerned. It was in 1993 that the All Party Hurriyat Conference (APHC) was organized. This thereafter became the political face of separatism.

The Hurriyat Conference was an overarching organization that brought to its fold varied kinds of socio-religious, political and militant organizations active at that point of time. While there were a few organizations with political background, such as the Awami Action Committee, Jamaat-e-Islami, Jammu and Kashmir People's Conference, Muslim Conference, People's League, there were also socio-religious organizations such as Auquaf Jama Masjid, Islamic Study Circle, Jamiate Ulam-e-Islam, Jamiat-e-Hadania, Jamiat-a-Ahle-Hadit and Anjuman-e-Tablig-ul-Islam. The militant organizations like JKLF were also its components. Among other components included various associations such as Kashmir Bar Council, Employees and Workers

Confederation, All Jammu & Kashmir Employees' Federation, Islamic Student League and Muslim Khwateen Markaz.[5]

Besides being amorphous in terms of its composition, the Hurriyat Conference was also internally differentiated in terms of the ideological goals pursued by its components. The range of difference was so large that it almost reflected contradictory positions. Typical in this way was the ideological difference between the two leading organizations, namely the Jamaat-e-Islami and the JKLF. Thus while complete independence of the undivided state of J&K from both India and Pakistan was the goal of JKLF, merger with Pakistan was the goal of Jamaat. While the Jamaat saw the Kashmir question from the perspective of religion, the JKLF saw it from the political perspective. The Jamaat's goal of establishment of an Islamic State was not acceptable to JKLF. It emphasized on the ethnic identity of Kashmir and referred to *Kashmiriyat* as the basis of its political ideology.

However, despite all these internal differences, the Hurriyat Conference represented a common platform for the purpose of giving a political direction to the militancy as well as popular separatist sentiment. Since it had come into existence at a time when there were inner conflicts among the militant groups and there were increasing cases of confrontation between the JKLF and the Hizbul Mujahideen, its major role was not merely to mediate between different militant groups but also to act as a bridge between the people and the militant groups. Representing the separatist sphere of politics, this organization was to play a major role in internationalizing the conflict politics and sustaining it at the ground level.

However, its role kept on changing in different phases of separatist politics. During the peak of militancy, when separatism was basically driven by the violence at the ground level, it sought to present itself as a political body that attempted to bring about a cohesiveness in

[5] The APHC worked through its executive council which was comprised of seven members: Syed Ali Shah Geelani of Jamaat-e-Islami, Umar Farooq of Awami Action Committee, Sheikh Abdul Aziz of People's League, Moulvi Abbas Ansari of Ittihad-ul-Muslimeen, Professor Abdul Gani Bhat of Muslim Conference, Yasin Malik of JKLF and Abdul Gani Lone of People's Conference.

the resistance politics, despite the differences at the ground level. The significance of its role at that time can be gauged from the fact that it came into existence when there was absolutely no space for any kind of politics and there was a lot of internal disorder. Not only the mainstream political organizations had gone under, but even within the separatist sphere there was no 'political' initiative. There was already a mushrooming growth of militant organizations which were not only operating in an autonomous manner but in certain ways also at cross purposes. Meanwhile, there was a fratricidal war going on among the militant organizations. Such chaos was further compounded by the entry of foreign jehadis on the one hand and a number of fundamentalist organizations on the other. While the former sought to redefine the goals of the Kashmiri separatist politics by giving it global Islamic tinge, the latter sought to intervene in the societal processes by issuing dictates for enforcing cultural, religious and moral codes.

In this situation, Hurriyat operated, at least initially, as an umbrella organization that not only brought different kinds of autonomously operating organizations under one fold but also channelled the separatist politics in one direction. It also had the internal function of mediating between different militant organizations, and between the militant and the political organizations. Gradually, it came to be recognized as the only political organization that represented the separatist voice in Kashmir.

Changing Nature of Militancy and Its Delegitimization

The initial phase of militancy that was locally rooted and purely an indigenous response was to undergo gradual changes as the number of militant organizations started proliferating and as non-local elements started entering the scene. This was specifically so after the end of the Afghan war. With the Mujahideen exiting Afghanistan, they started entering Kashmir and dominating the scene of militancy. By 1995 a number of organizations such as Harkat-ul-Mujahideen (HUM), al-Barq, al-Omar, Harkat-ul-Ansar and Lashkar-e-Toiba (LeT) were operating in Kashmir. What was particular about these organizations was that these were non-local organizations and were not familiar with the local sensibilities. As Ganguly notes:

> Unlike the various Kashmiri insurgent groups, these organizations and their members proved to be especially vicious in their tactics and strategies. Lacking any blood-soil relationship with Kashmir, they were far more prone to engage in rapine and violence. Their lack of regard for the local population as well as their differences with other insurgent groups increasingly contributed to sanguinary and internecine battles. (Ganguly 1997, 125)

Much of the agenda of these non-local organizations was linked with the concept of global jehad. In a situation where militancy and separatism were having indigenous roots to begin with, the idea of jehad was alien. More particularly so because conflict was mostly articulated in its ethnic context. However, in the euphoria of challenging the authority of the Indian State, the role of jehadi organizations was accepted and initially the presence of foreign militants was also welcomed. That's why these foreign militants were termed with approval as 'guest militants'. There was certainly a constituency in Kashmir which justified the presence of the foreign militants on religious grounds. It was the same constituency which saw the Kashmir question as part of the unfinished agenda of Partition. However, for the larger number of people, the conflict was purely of political nature and was not in any way linked with global agenda of jehad.

With the change in the nature of militancy, there was also a subtle change in the nature of the relationship between militancy and popular separatist politics. This change however, could not be reflected on the surface for a long time for the simple reason that after the middle of 1990, there was not much space for the expression of popular response. With the overall dominance of the militant organisations and the counter-violence and militarization by the State, there was no space for articulation of popular voices. Kashmiri society, however, was under a siege not only because of the pressure from the state but also from the militant organizations. Violence being the only instrument of expression; there was no space for debate or dissent. The society had gradually become muted. Though the popular separatist sentiment remained strong, however, it did not have the similar linkage with militancy that existed in the initial period (Khan 2012, 27–34).

By the middle of the 1990s, there was certainly an internal rethinking in Kashmir about the situation, particularly the ongoing violence. There was still an identification with the local militants, but on the whole, the kind of support that was available for militancy earlier was missing. The militants killed, especially the local ones, were still regarded as 'martyrs', but the militancy in general was not a celebrated phenomenon. By this time the impact of violence on Kashmiri society was quite intense and there was a sense of exhaustion as well. The proliferation of militant groups had introduced all kinds of elements into militancy, including those in search of quick power and money. This class of militants did not get the kind of respect the first generation of ideologically committed militants received. The element of 'criminalization', in any case, gave an altogether different image to the militancy. Aparna Rao has referred to the changed nature of militancy and the implications that it had for Kashmiri society. To quote her:

> While ISI trained and armed them, these young men proclaimed that the duty of every Kashmiri was to fight a jehad for social and political justice. This justified extortion, kidnappings, forcible entry into Muslim homes, and even torture; for if one was not ready to take up arms, or give one's son or younger brother to the armed movement, one should at least pay. Road blocks to collect 'donations' for a variety of militia (many gave receipts) or for a local mosque were the order of the day. All this led to resentment among wealthy Muslims, many of whom began to leave the Valley and stay in India or in the West. It also ultimately led to numerous factions and even gun battles within and between the militia. The overall result was an atmosphere of intense fear and a collapse of the productive part of the economy. (Rao 1999, 16)

More than the local militants, it was the foreign militants against whom there was a strong sense of antipathy. As already stated, these militants were not familiar with the local culture and often their acts hurt the Kashmiri sensitivities. For instance, the threat of banning the Amarnath Yatra by Harkat-ul-Ansar in 1994 and abduction of foreign tourists by Al-Faran in 1995 were some situations that didn't go very well with local Kashmiris. The Yatra particularly was seen as a part of Kashmiri culture. However, more emotional was the response to the burning of the Chrar-e-Sharief, the revered Sufi shrine which was occupied by Mast Gul, a Pakistani mercenary trained in Afghanistan (Rao 2008, 645).

By the middle of the 1990s, the Kashmiri society felt sufficiently pressurized by the 'gun culture'. The ascendancy of violence over everything else had taken a toll not only in terms of the number of people killed but also in other ways. With the overwhelming fear of gun, the society had become totally muted. Along with this there was the psychological trauma linked to prolonged violence. Further, as time passed there was a growing sense of disillusionment with militancy. As Puri notes, 'the militants lost their original élan due to a number of reasons: a continuous proliferation of groups, confusion and division in their ranks, regarding their ultimate objective, and Pakistan's changing policy towards different groups of militants' (Puri 1993, 78). However, most importantly, it was the criminalization of the militants—their acts of extortion, abduction and looting—that generated a negative response towards militancy. There was also a silent response against the fundamentalist agenda imposed on the society. Right in the beginning of the period of militancy, there was mushrooming of such organizations which took upon themselves the role of enforcing social, religious and moral codes and issuing diktats with the threat of violence. In the process of striving towards radical Islamization, attempts were made to ban all those practices which were seen to be 'anti-Islamic' and reflecting the 'Western' influence. Thus a ban was imposed on cinema halls, video parlours and beauty salons. Attempts were made to restrict the mobility of women and to restrain their visibility in the public spaces.[6] Veiling remained a major issue throughout the 1990s with several militant organizations issuing diktats from time to time asking women to veil themselves.

[6] Among the organizations that imposed the dress and moral codes on women was the all-women organization Dukhtaran-e-Millat, headed by Asiya Andrabi, which not only campaigned for Islamic dress code for women but got involved in street campaigns against the use of jeans and cosmetics by women. Itself a group of all veiled women, it insisted on use of veil by Kashmiri women.

Delegitimization of Militancy: Role of Moderates

As we can see, much before the global delegitimization of armed militancy (post 9/11), militancy in Kashmir had already been delegitimized. The unquestioning support that was available to the militants in the initial period was withdrawn by the middle of the 1990s. However, due to the overwhelming presence and influence of the militants, the public response could not be articulated within the Kashmiri discourse for a long time. And when it was articulated by a topmost separatist leader, he had to pay a heavy price for it. Abdul Gani Lone was assassinated in 2001 months after he had publicly initiated a debate around the role and relevance of militancy in Kashmir.

Lone was quite vocal about his critique of the militants, specifically the foreign militants or jehadis and had been suggesting a change of strategy—shunning militancy and giving a political turn to resistance politics. He was actually the most prominent separatist leader who had been consistently favouring the shift away from militancy and towards a political resolution. There were others also including Abdul Ghani Bhat and Mohammad Abbas Ansari who had the similar perspective. 'Shortly after his release from jail in 1997, G.M. Bhat set the ball rolling, with an interview that distanced the Jamaat-e-Islami from the Hizbul Mujahideen, and called for an end to the "gun culture"' (Swami 2003). And when he took the office of Chairman of APHC in 1999, he talked about the need of an internal dialogue between separatists and mainstream parties. Ansari had also been suggesting replacement of violence by the dialogue process. In 2003, he expressed the desire of the separatists to travel to Pakistan to persuade the militants to lay down the gun so that a dialogue process could be initiated (Swami 2003).

The changing moderate stance was, however, not acceptable to all the separatist leaders. There were many within the Hurriyat Conference who were in favour of continuity of armed militancy and who saw any compromise on the issue of dialogue as a sell-out on the part of separatists. Syed Ali Shah Geelani was the most prominent spokesman of this section of the separatists. He and Lone actually entered into a long debate on this issue.

The debate took place around three inter-related questions. The first question was regarding the nature of the Kashmiri movement—whether it was a political or religious movement. The second question was in relation to the role and relevance of militancy. And the third question related to the role of jehadi militants in the movement. The position of Geelani was that the movement was a part of global jehad and therefore it was religious in nature. And this not only legitimized the role of militancy but also justified the role of jehadis (Chowdhary 2002, 2398–2399). In his opinion, Kashmir conflict arose from the unfinished agenda of Partition. Being a Muslim-majority state, it was an inevitable part of Pakistan. Religion, therefore, had an important place in the context of conflict and also explained the role of foreign jehadis in it. While questioning Geelani, however, A. G. Lone took the position that religion had no role whatsoever in the Kashmir conflict. It was an indigenous and political conflict with no connection with global jehad. There was a specific context of Kashmir's political history which was linked with Kashmiri identity politics. To see it as a religious movement was to distort its nature and not only to add an external dimension to it but to be insensitive towards the local sensibilities. Lone further emphasized the distinct nature of the state which despite being a Muslim-majority also had a multi-religious character. Taking a position that the conflict had a religious character or restricting it to the Muslims alone, in his opinion, didn't do justice to the religious, cultural and regional diversities of the state. To quote him:

> We believe in the undivided state of J and K, which is disputed and yet to be settled. Its formal settlement is to be done by the people of the state by a fair plebiscite, without going into the question whether it is a Muslim issue or another issue. It is a complicated issue because this disputed territory is not inhabited by the Muslims alone. There are other faiths as well. Then there are regions, Jammu, Kashmir, Ladakh, Azad Kashmir, Northern Areas, Gilgit.... (Cited in Chowdhary 2002, 2399)

On the question of militancy and jehadi militants, Lone took the position that the militancy had played its role in internationalizing the movement, but had now exhausted its relevance. He stated:

> [Militants] have played their part in bringing the Kashmir issue out of the cold storage. Now is the time for diplomatic and political approaches. We must take stock of the situation. Now it [militancy] is becoming a disadvantage for the movement. Now violence has no place. We expect the militants to take note of this fact. (Chowdhary 2002, 2399)

Though Lone was assassinated soon after, his ideas ultimately came to dominate in the separatist politics. By the time peace process was launched in 2002–2003, the idea of militancy becoming irrelevant was being openly pursued. How dominant this idea had become was reflected during the visit of leaders of moderate Hurriyat faction to Pakistan where they openly stated the negative consequences of violence in Kashmir. Mirwaiz Umar Farooq was reported to have stated that 'We have already seen the results of our fight on the political, diplomatic and military fronts which have not achieved anything other than creating more graveyards.' And further that 'as far as the APHC is concerned, we are not prepared to sacrifice any more of our loved ones' (Swami 2007).

The position taken by the moderates was a reflection of the mood of the people at the ground level. They not merely wanted an end to the violence but also some movement forward in the process of resolution of conflict. The moderates were, therefore, in a position to take flexible position despite the threat they faced from the hardcore elements, particularly the militants. Off and on, they were threatened by the militants and were also intimidated by the separatist hardliners like Geelani. However, the situation at the ground level was so dynamic that moderates felt emboldened to suggest change in strategy as well as to make the conflict resolution process more negotiable (Swami 2007).[7]

Much of this dynamism was also a reflection of the changing response of the Indian State under the leadership of Atal Bihari Vajpayee. As Prime Minister of India he had started taking initiatives for establishing peace between India and Pakistan right from the time

[7] Geelani would continue reminding the moderates that the militants could not become irrelevant in Kashmir because they had created the space for separatist politics. During one of his meeting with journalists, he stated that 'leaders who are today talking of ending militancy owe their popularity to these militants only'. He further stated that 'Jehadist cadre took to the armed struggle after the complete failure of democratic institutions in the State' (Swami 2007).

he came to the helm of affairs. After his unsuccessful Lahore visit in 1999 that was followed by the Kargil War and later the militant attack on the Indian Parliament, he took fresh initiatives for the peace process in 2002. What particularly appealed to the Kashmiris was his comprehensive approach to the peace process in which for the first time in the history of conflict an attempt was made to tackle both the external and internal dimensions of the conflict through the dialogue process. While offering dialogue with Pakistan, Vajpayee had offered the dialogue to Kashmiri separatists as well. Meanwhile, acknowledging the lack of democratic space in Kashmir, he had also committed himself to a 'free and fair election' which took place in 2002 under the gaze of media.

With the Government of India for the first time acknowledging the 'political' question of Kashmir and seeking to engage Kashmiris in resolving it, the political environment in Kashmir was invigorated and people not only responded to the democratic processes but also became hopeful for the 'honourable exit' from the conflict situation. This certainly had its implications for the moderates, who were sufficiently empowered and occupied the centre stage of separatist politics.

This period of 'hope' and 'optimism' in Kashmir lasted even after the Vajpayee government was replaced by the Manmohan Singh government. The fact that there was some movement forward and that the status quo was changing in certain crucial areas helped sustain the hope. The most important development of the Manmohan Singh phase was the opening of the routes on the LoC and the plying of buses (and later trade) on the Srinagar–Muzzafarabad and Poonch–Rawalakot routes. Although dialogue with the separatists was suspended after an initial meeting with a few separatists, the Round Table Conference dialogues and reports of the five Working Groups of the Prime Minister were the important developments. However, as trouble started erupting in Pakistan, the peace process and dialogue came to a total halt after 2007.

Assessment of Separatism in Its First Phase

An assessment of separatism in its first phase shows that the separatism was not only driven by militancy, but also reflected a strong linkage between militancy and popular separatist sentiment. It was the indigenous basis of militancy and its local roots that generated strong societal approval of this phenomenon. However, as the militancy came to acquire an external character, it was delegitimized. Notwithstanding its delegitimization, militancy continued to remain at the centre of Kashmir's separatist politics for many more years.

Notwithstanding the delegitimization of militancy and its later decline, the popular separatist sentiment remained intact. Even while the democratic space was extended and the mainstream politics gained credibility, this sentiment remained unscathed. In popular sensibilities, the mainstream politics—'the politics of governance' as it came to be clearly defined—operated at a different level and didn't have much implications for the separatist politics which was linked with the situation of conflict. Hence even while the Assembly elections, like the ones held in 2002 and 2008, were participatory and sufficiently legitimized, these were not seen as having challenged the separatist sphere of politics.

The popular separatist sentiment continued to manifest and assert itself even when the separatist leadership and organization started facing the challenges. As we shall see below, the Hurriyat, the only separatist organization, was faced with multiple challenges arising not only because of the multiple splits that it faced in 2003 but also because of the expansion of the democratic politics. Much of the expansion of the democratic politics was due to the shifting of the agenda of the Hurriyat Conference to the mainstream space. This had definitely put a dent on the efficacy of the Hurriyat Conference; however, despite such challenges, the popular separatist sentiment continued to thrive.

Hurriyat Conference: Strength and Fragility

Hurriyat as the face of the separatist politics had made its presence felt towards the later half of the 1990s. It would issue regular statements, organize public protests, and give calls for bandhs and hartals. However, with the restoration of the mainstream political processes, its major role was manifested in enforcing 'poll boycott'. The Hurriyat leaders would indulge in extensive campaigns to enforce the boycott. They organized meetings and rallies in different parts of the Valley. Until the 2002 Assembly election, the Hurriyat's role in the boycott politics was very effective. Although it was partially due to the threat of militants that the legitimacy of electoral process generally remained contested, but mobilization by the Hurriyat Conference leaders also contributed to it. Even in the 2002 Assembly election, there were a number of constituencies in Central Kashmir where the voter turnout was so low that electoral process was almost rendered to be farcical in nature. However, with every election since 2002 assuming a competitive and participatory nature, its call for boycott started becoming ineffective.

Hurriyat came into prominence during the post-2002 peace process since its claim to represent the Kashmiri separatist sentiment was acknowledged not only by Pakistan but also by the Indian government. It was officially engaged by the Vajpayee government in the dialogue on behalf of Kashmiris. While the extremist elements within the Hurriyat, prominently Syed Ali Shah Geelani, rejected any such engagement which did not formalize the process of tripartite talk between India, Pakistan and Kashmiris, the moderates led by Mirwaiz Umar Farooq were quite happy that the Indian government was ready to talk to Pakistan and Kashmiris, even though not on the same table. It was in this process that the Government of India had two rounds of talks with the moderate faction of the Hurriyat Conference. The process might have continued had the Vajpayee government not been defeated in the 2004 Parliamentary elections. The Manmohan Singh government initially tried to continue with this process of engaging the separatists but later abandoned the process in favour of Round Table Conferences initiated by Prime Minister Manmohan Singh (Chowdhary 2016, 220–224).

The internal divisions within the Hurriyat had however started weakening this organization by the beginning of the millennium. By the time the 2002 Assembly election took place, the approach towards the electoral politics had become a major issue among the different factions of the Hurriyat Conference. Among all the separatists, Lone was soft on the idea of electoral politics. It is not clear however whether he toyed with the idea of elections for the larger question of settlement of conflict or for power politics. By all indications it was the former idea rather than the latter that appealed him. However, his assassination much before the 2002 Assembly election made it difficult to presume as to what would have been his approach towards election. However, his party (the People's Conference) under the leadership of Sajad Lone fielded proxy candidates in this election. This became a sore issue between Geelani and the moderates. Geelani's demand that the Hurriyat membership of the People's Conference be suspended was resisted by the moderates.

It was not only the question of fielding the proxy candidates by the People's Conference but also the response of the moderates in general towards the 2002 Assembly election that became the issues of contention within the Hurriyat Conference. Responding to the changing situation in which the Vajpayee government was seeking to engage the separatists, the moderates led by Mirwaiz Umar Farooq did not aggressively campaign for the poll boycott. This generated a feeling within the extremist camp led by Geelani that the moderate camp was too flexible and deviating from the set position of the Hurriyat Conference. As a result of the differences that were widened, the Hurriyat Conference was formally split in September 2003. Rather than a two-way split, it was multi-level split since apart from Geelani who formed his own Hurriyat Conference named Tehreek-e-Hurriyat, Yasin Malik of JKLF and Shabir Shah also opted out of the organization.

The multi-level split of the Hurriyat Conference resulted in fragmenting this organization in general and weakening of the moderate forces within the separatist politics in particular. The failure of the moderates to achieve any tangible progress in the conflict resolution led to a general sense of disillusionment in Kashmir. The separatist space, as we shall see in our assessment of the next phase of separatism, came to be dominated by the hardcore extremist elements.

POST-MILITANCY PHASE OF SEPARATISM

With the decline of militancy in the period after 2003, the separatist politics of Kashmir entered a different phase with a focus on popular protests. Although there was a strong linkage between the popular response and militancy in the first phase, militancy was the central point around which separatist politics manifested. By 2003, the situation had started changing and by 2007–2008, there was a substantial decline of militancy. As per the data provided by the home ministry, militancy had peaked during the period of 1990–1996 but had started declining significantly by 2003 (see Table 3.1). As compared to 1995 when there were 5,938 incidents of militancy, these had declined to 3,401 in 2003, 2,565 in 2004, 1,990 in 2005, 1,667 in 2006, 1,092 in 2007 and 708 in 2008. As against 1,341 civilians killed in 1996, 795 civilians were killed in 2003, 707 in 2004, 557 in 2005, 389 in 2006, 158 in 2007 and 91 in 2008. While 2,020 terrorists were killed in 2001, the number of terrorists killed was 976 in 2004, 917 in 2005, 591 in 2006, 472 in 2007 and 339 in 2008. By 2011, this number had come around to 100 (see Table 3.2).

Decline of militancy changed the very nature of separatism. It became more intense in its manifestation. Also with the role of militancy being significantly minimized, the external factor was minimized and separatism became much more locally rooted. Rather than being sustained by Pakistan's material and moral support, separatism was now bolstered through the support of local Kashmiris.

Both with the decline of militancy and the extension of democratic politics, public space was activated in which people could come out and take part in the protests. This space had gone under in 1990. The mass demonstrations that had come to characterize the popular Kashmiri response in 1988–1990 period were no more available as the violence and militarization had taken complete control of the situation in early 1990. However, it was after the 2002 Assembly election that the situation started changing, not only due to the decline of militancy but also because of the conscious efforts made by the newly installed Mufti government to ease the militarized situation.

While political voices could be more freely voiced in the public space, political actors could freely use this space for political mobilization. It was reflection of this phenomenon that more than a year before the next Assembly election was due, the political parties had started organizing political rallies on competitive basis in 2007. For any other place, holding of political rallies would not make any news, but in Kashmir where political parties and leaders had withdrawn from the

Table 3.1 *Militancy-related Data: 1990–2003*

	1990	*1991*	*1992*	*1993*	*1994*	*1995*	*1996*	*1997*	*1998*	*1999*	*2000*	*2001*	*2002*	*2003*
No. of incidents	4,158	3,765	4,817	5,247	5,829	5,938	5,014	3,420	2,932	3,071	3,074	4,522	4,038	3,401
Civilians killed	461	385	634	747	820	1,031	1,341	971	889	873	847	996	1008	795
Security Forces killed	155	143	189	198	200	237	184	193	236	355	397	536	453	314
Terrorists killed	550	844	819	1,310	1,596	1,332	1,209	1,075	999	1,082	1,520	2,020	1,707	1,494
Foreign terrorists killed	14	12	14	90	122	85	139	197	319	305	436	625	508	470

Source: Ministry of Home Affairs, Annual Report (2003–2004).

Table 3.2 *Militancy-related Data: 2004–2015*

	2004	2005	2006	2007	2008	2009	2010	2011	2012	2013	2014	2015
No. of incidents	2,565	1,990	1,667	1,092	708	499	488	340	220	170	222	208
Civilians killed	707	557	389	158	91	71	47	31	11	15	28	17
Security Forces killed	281	199	151	110	75	79	69	33	38	53	47	39
Terrorists killed	976	917	591	472	339	239	232	100	50	67	110	108
Foreign terrorists killed												

Source: Ministry of Home Affairs, Annual Reports (2012–2013 and 2015–2016).

scene in the wake of militant violence, it was a big thing. For around a decade or so, no political activity could be organized in the Valley and no political actor from the mainstream arena (including those holding political power) could move around freely in the Valley.

As the democratic space started becoming available and political activities started being organized, popular protests also became the norm. Although there were incidents of protests and demonstrations even in earlier years, the frequency and intensity of protests started increasing by 2007. That year, apart from the protests against the administrative policies of the state (for instance, those related to the establishment of a new college or reorganization of tehsils), there were protests around the issue of human rights violations. One of the major issues that led to a number of protest demonstrations was linked to the killing of five people in alleged 'fake encounters' by local police and CRPF. Following an investigation which led to exhumation of bodies, there was huge resentment in the Valley leading to protests throughout the year 2007 (Chowdhary 2011).

While the protests against the alleged 'fake encounter' killings lasted throughout the year, there were many other protests in the year 2007. In April, there were protests against the killing of a civilian in Tral; in July there were massive protests in Handwara against the rape and killing of a minor girl in Langate. In September there were protests in Kupwara over the killing of a student, and in October there were protests in Kupwara against the killing of a teacher by security forces.[8]

What was peculiar about these protests was that these were spontaneous and were held in different parts of the valley including the remote areas. Many a times, the response by the security forces, particularly the killings of civilians became the basis of civilian resentment and started a cycle of protests and violence. However, it was in the period between 2008 and 2010 that Kashmir witnessed the most intensive phase of separatist upsurge.

[8] There were protests on other issues as well. There were protests including those demanding the remains of Maqbool Bhat on the anniversary of his hanging on 11 February, on the death anniversaries of Mirwaiz Mohammad Farooq and A. G. Lone in May and against conferring knighthood on controversial writer Salman Rushdie.

In 2008, there was eruption over the Amarnath land row which lasted almost the whole of the summer and gave a new turn to separatist politics. This agitation took place at a time when democratic politics seemed to have been sufficiently entrenched with political parties involved in the electoral campaigning. Since the Assembly election was due sometime in October–November 2008, the election mood had overtaken the Valley with political parties holding massive rallies all over the place. The intense separatist eruption that took place in July 2008 was, however, to change the political mood of the Valley. For the next few months, rather than the electoral spirit, it was the separatist assertion that was reflected on the streets of Kashmir.

What triggered the agitation in Kashmir was the state government order related to diversion of 40 hectares of forest land to the Shri Amarnath Shrine Board (SASB) for the purposes of erecting prefabricated structures during the period of pilgrimage. Mass eruption took place as there emerged a contention that such diversion of land was a part of the 'state conspiracy' to facilitate the settlement of outsiders and to bring about a 'demographic change' with the ultimate purpose of altering the 'Muslim-majority' character of the state. So intense was the Kashmiri response that the government was forced to take back the order. However, as the withdrawal of the order led to an agitation in Jammu region, the commitment by the government to make alternate arrangements for the pilgrims led to another, longer phase of agitation in Kashmir (Chowdhary 2008).

The agitation took a separatist turn from the very beginning. It was like a replay of the 1989–1990 period of mass response, with similar kind of massive demonstrations resounding with the slogans against the state. However along with the usual 'azadi' slogans, new slogans like 'India Go Back' were raised. Again, as a reminder of the earlier period of separatism, the same kind of defiance against the state was shown—the curfew and other restrains imposed by the state were observed by non-compliance and shutdown calls by the separatist leadership were faithfully followed. The normal life in the Valley was totally derailed with all business activities stopped, all educational institutions closed, transport services suspended and even government offices made non-functional. This agitation made it evident that despite the success of the competitive politics and extension of democratic space since 2002, the separatist sentiment had not gone under but on the contrary was alive and could overtake the Valley to the extent that it could push the democratic politics to the margins.

While the separatist leadership that was facing crisis due to the internal divisions of the Hurriyat Conference, on the one hand, and the 'hijacking' of their agenda by the mainstream political parties, on the other—contributed in the process of separatist mobilization—the agitation reflected spontaneous popular response. Protests were not organized by the separatists under a planned separatist programme but these erupted spontaneously, at least in the beginning. It was in response to the emerging situation that the separatist leaders were compelled to respond to the popular mood and provide leadership. Of course, the separatist leadership did play a role of making a calendar of events for sustaining the agitation, for giving calls for marches, and for giving coherence to whatever was happening on the ground, but one could see that the leadership, rather than being autonomous, was rather being driven by the mass response.

An analysis of the mass separatist sentiment of that time clearly shows that it was marked by the prevailing sense of cynicism that had gradually overtaken the Valley following the stalling of the peace process. The optimism that had been generated during the early years of the Vajpayee government's initiatives had given way to a sense of disillusionment. Such a sense of disillusionment was further aggravated by the cases of killing of non-combatant Kashmiris in the alleged 'fake encounters'. It was the overall sense of frustration with the ground situation and the stalled political engagement in which a space was created for renewed assertion of separatism.

With a growing critique of the moderate politics and the 'flexibility' that had been shown in 2000–2007 period, there was a significant change not only in the nature of the separatist politics but also in the leadership. The separatism that manifested now was very aggressive, extremist and radicalized with the leadership shifted to the hardcore elements. Syed Ali Shah Geelani known for his inflexibility and non-negotiability of his views on 'self-determination' emerged as the key leader of the resistance politics.

What could be seen as the most significant outcome of the agitation was that it started the process of separatist indoctrination of the mass of Kashmiri youth. By the time the agitation ended, the youth had become central to the politics of separatist assertion. They were visible in the streets confronting the security forces. The stone-pelting youth, thereafter, became an integral part of the separatist politics.

Agitational mood continued throughout the year 2009. Very early into the Omar Abdullah-led NC–Congress coalition, the protests resurfaced around the allegation of rape and murder of two women in Shopian. The protests, to begin with, were local but later on spread to various parts of the Valley including Srinagar, Baramulla, Sopore, Bandipora and Pulwama districts. Although this issue kept flaring up throughout the year 2009, there were many other issues around which protests took place in that year; for instance, killing of a 12-year-old boy by tear smoke shells and that of a 25-year-old person when he did not respond to a warning near the security picket in north Kashmir.

The agitational mood in Kashmir continued during the beginning of 2010. Three different cases of killing of uninvolved youth by the CRPF and BSF had instigated protests in the initial couple of months that year. These protests were intensified with the reported killings of three civilians in a 'fake encounter' in Machail sector of the Kupwara district. This started a new intensified phase of protest. It was during the protests against these killings that 17-year-old Tuffail Mattoo was killed. His killing triggered a cycle of protests, violence and killings which ultimately led to the 2010 summer upsurge. On the whole, 120 young people were killed during this upsurge which lasted for six months.

Like the 2008 agitation, the 2010 agitation led to collapse of the authority of the state.[9] For around five months, there was a complete

[9] The law and order situation as it existed, few months into the agitation, has been described by Shujaat Bukhari in the following words:

> According to official figures, as many as 872 incidents of stone-throwing took place in June and July, in which 1,456 police and CRPF personnel were injured. In just six days, from July 30 to August 4, the situation took a turn for the worse as a large number of public and private property was destroyed. In the wave of anger that consumed the Valley, nine police stations, police posts and SOG (special operations group) camps, eight government

shutdown—the educational institutions, business establishments, shops remained closed and all other activities were halted. The government's business also could not take place as the public offices could not be operationalized and all the energies of the state were diverted towards quelling the protests. There was an intense display of pro-'azadi' sentiments on the streets as massive anti-state demonstrations and stone pelting incidents became the order of the day (Parthasarathy 2010).

Mainstream politics became the major casualty of the situation. Political leaders were not only marginalized but were also under tremendous pressure due to the overwhelming separatist mood all around.

The 2010 agitation was mostly a youth agitation and reflected the completion of the process of generational shift that had started in 2008. This was a generation of youth who were born and brought up during the period of militancy and had imbibed an altogether different political culture as compared to the generation that led the separatist politics till now. Impacted by violence and militarization they were much more cynical and aggressive. Crossing the class barriers, the youth romanticized the idea of 'azadi'. Apart from the stone pelters belonging to the lower classes, there were the youth of the middle and upper middle classes who were active on the social media and aggressively pursued the ideals of 'self-determination' and 'liberation'. While many among the former were the rootless youth having no promise of economic future before them, the latter were educated, many of them pursuing professional and technical degrees. Their involvement in the agitation, irrespective of their class background and their social location, was quite intense (Chowdhary 2010).

The overwhelming presence of youth in the agitation not only invigorated the separatist politics and gave it a new lease of life but also redefined its character. It came to be characterized by the logic of singularities, losing in the process the shades of different ideological streaks and shades that were till now reflected in the separatist politics. Syed Ali Shah Geelani, who till now represented as one of the major political voices in the separatist politics along with scores

vehicles and a coach of a train, one railway station, two houses of political activists and 13 government offices were destroyed. (Bukhari 2010) of other separatist leaders including Mirwaiz Umar Farooq and Yasin Malik, became the only political voice of separatism. So raised was Geelani's stature that even those opposing his ideology of Kashmir merging with Pakistan accepted his leadership mainly for the reason of his 'consistency' and his 'inflexibility'. The other two leaders who were the driving force of the agitational politics at this time, namely Masarat Alam and Asiya Andrabi, represented the same shade of politics as that of Geelani. Chairman of the pro-Pakistan Muslim League and general secretary of Geelani's faction of the Hurriyat, Alam, had the reputation of being extremely hardline and was seen to be the mastermind of the agitation (Bukhari 2010a). Asiya Andrabi also reflected her conservative Islamist and pro-Pakistan ideology.

The pro-Pakistan Islamist politics that till now was at the fringes of separatism now occupied the central space. And as the agitation moved forward, it started coming under the pressure of popular expectations. The overall aggression so increased that even the well-known hardliners found it difficult to fit in with the popular expectations. For instance, Syed Salahuddin, the Hizb Commander and the Chairman of the United Jehad Council, during the agitation had to face the flak when he advised the protestors to go slow. He was warned that 'those who will try to sabotage the ongoing agitation won't be spared. This is tantamount to making a sell-out of the martyrs' (*Daily Excelsior*, 2010). Even Syed Ali Shah Geelani's appeal for non-violent protests, after he was released from prison, was seen by many as a 'compromise'.

To Conclude

Despite the similarities between the two phases of separatism, the post-militancy phase had its own peculiarities. Driven by the scepticism on the ground, it didn't have much space for flexible or negotiable positions. Being manifested mainly through the action of the youth in the streets, it became much more aggressive and radicalized. That is the reason that the moderate leadership that had dominated the separatist politics in the earlier years was not only marginalized but also became discredited. The leaders like Mirwaiz Umar Farooq and the team that he led were condemned for the 'moderation' and 'flexibility' shown by them in the earlier phase of separatism. More particularly, their role in participation in the peace process was critiqued as having 'compromised' the goals of the movement.

With the generational shift being the major manifestation of the separatist politics, the post-militancy separatism was to undergo further changes in the times to come. The 2008–2010 period of separatism, as we will see later, was to lay the foundation of another phase of separatism as was reflected in the post-2014 phase. This third phase of separatism driven by the youth was to reflect not only extreme hardline positions but also a bent towards religious radicalism.

References

Bose, Sumantra. 2003. *Kashmir: Roots of Conflict: Paths to Peace*. Cambridge, MA: Harvard University Press.

Bukhari, Shujaat. 2010, 14 August. 'Valley on the Fire'. *Frontline* 27 (17). http://www.frontline.in/static/html/fl2717/stories/20100827271712900.htm (accessed on 30 August 2018).

———. 2010a, 11–24 September. 'Key Players'. *Frontline* 27 (19). http://www.frontline.in/static/html/fl2719/stories/20100924271904100.htm (accessed on 30 August 2018).

Chowdhary, Rekha. 2002, 22–28 June. 'Kashmir: Lone's Liberal Legacy'. *Economic & Political Weekly* 37 (25): 2398–2400.

———. 2008, November. 'J&K: Once Again on the Brink'. *Seminar* #591. http://www.india-seminar.com/2008/591/591_rekha_chowdhary.htm (accessed on 10 September 2018).

———. 2010, September. 'The Second Uprising'. *Economic & Political Weekly* 45 (39): 10–13.

———. 2011, November. 'Kashmir: The Summer of Unrest'. *Seminar* #620. http://www.india-seminar.com/2011/620/620_rekha_chowdhary.htm (accessed on 10 April 2018).

———. 2016. *Jammu and Kashmir: Politics of Identity and Separatism*. New Delhi: Routledge.

Chowdhary, Rekha and Nagendra Rao. 2003, 4 January. 'Elections 2002: Implications for Politics of Separatism'. *Economic & Political Weekly* 38 (1): 15–21.

———. 2003a, January–June. 'Jammu and Kashmir: Political Alienation, Regional Divergence and Communal Polarisation'. *Journal of Indian School of Political Economy* 15 (1–2): 189–219.

Daily Excelsior. 2010, 25 July. 'Protestors Burn Salahuddin's Effigy'. http://www.dailyexcelsior.com/web1/10july25/news1.htm#4

Ganguly, Sumit. 1997. *The Crisis in Kashmir: Portents of War, Hopes of Peace*. New York and Washington, DC: Cambridge University Press, co-published with Woodrow Wilson Center.

Jagmohan, 2006. *My Frozen Turbulence in Kashmir*, 7th edition. New Delhi: Allied Publishers.

Khan, Mohammad Ishaq. 2012. 'Evolution of My Identity vis-à-vis Islam and Kashmir'. In *The Parchment of Kashmir*, edited by Nyla Ali Khan. New York: Palgrave Macmillan.

Noorani, A. G. 2000, 30 September. 'Jammu and Kashmir: Contours of Militancy'. *Frontline* 17 (20).

http://www.kashmirlibrary.org/kashmir_timeline/kashmir_files/militancy_noorani.htm (accessed on 1 November 2017).

Pachauri, Pankaj. 1989, December. 'Rubaiya Sayeed: Abduction Anguish, India Today'. http://indiatoday.intoday.in/story/kashmiri-militants-releases-rubaiya-daughter-of-union-home-minister-mufti-mohammed-sayeed/1/324242.html (accessed on 1 November 2017).

Parthasarathy, Malini. 2010, 4 August. 'Understanding Kashmir's Stone Pelters'. *The Hindu*. http://www.thehindu.com/opinion/lead/Understanding-Kashmirs-stone-pelters/article16120870.ece (accessed on 30 August 2018).

Puri, Balraj. 1993. *Kashmir: Towards Insurgency*. New Delhi: Orient Longman.

Rao, Aparna. 1999. 'A Tortuous Search for Justice: Notes on the Kashmir Conflict'. Article 7. *Himalaya: The Journal of the Association for Nepal and Himalayan Studies* 19 (1): 9–20.

———. 2008. *The Valley of Kashmir: The Making and Unmaking of a Composite Culture?* New Delhi: Manohar Publishers.

Sahni, Sati. 1999. *Kashmir Underground*. New Delhi: Har-Anand Publications.

Schofield, Victoria. 2000. *Kashmir in Conflict: India, Pakistan and the Unending War*. London: I.B. Tauris.

Sobhrajani, Manisha. 2008, April. 'Jammu and Kashmir: Women's Role in the Post-1989 Insurgency'. *Faultlines* 19.

http://www.satp.org/satporgtp/publication/faultlines/volume19/Article3.htm#7 (accessed on 8 March 2009).

Staniland, Paul. 2014. *Networks of Rebellion: Explaining Insurgent Cohesion and Collapse*. Ithaca, NY: Cornell University Press.

Swami, Praveen. 2003, 16–29 August. 'Growing Schism'. *Frontline* 20 (17). http://www.frontline.in/static/html/fl2017/stories/20030829005701900.htm (accessed on 30 August 2018).

———. 2007, 27 January–9 February. 'Martyrs Sans Cause'. *Frontline* 24 (02). http://www.frontline.in/static/html/fl2402/stories/20070209003003200.htm (accessed on 30 August 2018).

Verma, P. S. 1994. *Jammu and Kashmir at the Political Crossroads*. New Delhi: Vikas Publishing House.

Widmalm, Sten. 2002. *Kashmir in Comparative Perspective: Democracy and Violent Separatism in India*. London: Routledge Curzon.

The Exodus of Kashmiri Pandits

4

One of the major implications of militancy and separatism in the post-1989 period has been the mass migration of Kashmiri Pandits from Kashmir Valley. Despite being small in number, the Pandits had a very significant presence in Kashmir. Not only they were located throughout the Valley but also they were holding public positions which linked them with the whole society. Apart from being teachers and doctors, they had strong presence in the upper and lower ranks of bureaucracy. Their presence was also very crucial for upholding the concept of Kashmiriyat or defining Kashmir as a composite culture. In an overwhelming Muslim-majority society, they were the only ones who while sharing the common cultural ethos of Kashmir were defined as the 'other' of the overwhelming Muslim population of Kashmir.

KASHMIRI PANDIT–MUSLIM RELATIONSHIP BEFORE MILITANCY

Common Cultural Ethos

The common cultural ethos did not mean that there existed no difference whatsoever between the Kashmiri Muslims and the Pandits. T. N. Madan has noted as to how the distinctions between the two communities were maintained, especially in the rural areas. Apart from the difference of dress, he notes the differences of speech. He also notes the context of purity–impurity practised by the Pandits. Muslims, in his understanding,

> are regarded in principle as being ritually impure. They are referred to as mlechchha (of lowly birth, outsider); theirs is the world of tamas (darkness,

> ignorance). Muslims are outside the pale of values by which a Pandit is expected as a Hindu to order his life. In practice, however, Pandits consider some Muslims as less polluting than others. (Madan 1972, 108)

While keeping these distinctions intact, the Kashmiri society still had sufficient space for the plural and even shared cultural ethos. As Trisal notes:

> It is between the verses of Lal Ded and teachings of Sheikh Noor-ud-Din that the ethos of Kashmiri plural society lies. Their precepts, verses and sayings formed the core of Kashmiri culture.... This gave rise to that peculiar social relationship, among Kashmiris belonging to different faiths, which can be termed as the basis of Kashmiri identity. (Trisal 1995, 735–740)

Lal Ded, or Lalleshwari, is a fourteenth-century mystic poetess of Kashmir who continues to influence the day-to-day life of common Kashmiris through the use of *Vakhs* (verse saying). Born in a Hindu Brahmin family, she renounced her family in her twenties and during her spiritual journey came in contact with Sufi Saint Sheikh Noor-ud-Din. In her fight against the ritualistic and rigid religious and Brahminic practices, she became a very popular figure of Kashmir who 'probably laid the groundwork for the propagation of Islam among the Kashmiri populace by the Rishis. Furthermore, her verses illustrate the union of the streams of Shaivite philosophy and Sufism in fourteenth-century Kashmir' (Zutshi 2004, 22).

Apart from Lal Ded, it is the influence of Sheikh Noor-ud-Din on the life of people which is seen as the reflection of the syncretism between the Hindu past and the Islamic present of Kashmir. He is known to have continued the mystic legacy of Lal Ded. To quote Prem Nath Bazaz:

> ... [Noor-ud-Din] founded the order of the 'Rishis' or 'Babas' who carried the torch of Humanism, religious tolerance and Hindu–Muslim unity from generation to generation for over four centuries. ... The 'Rishis' wielded tremendous influence over the educated and the illiterate. Many of them had both Hindu and Muslim names; in fact it was difficult to call them either Hindu or Muslim. (Bazaz 1995, 492)

Much of syncretism in Kashmir, many argue, flows from the very evolution of Islam. Most of the people adopted the religion through the influence of Sufi saints. The Sufi saints, rather than imposing the religion, adapted it to the existing cultural practices. English observers of the late nineteenth and early twentieth century in Kashmir seem to have been struck by the lack of difference between Hindu and Muslim places of worship and worshippers. They found shared popular religious tradition especially in the countryside. Thus Walter Lawrence noted a strong confluence between Islam and Hinduism and lack of rigidities among the Muslims as well as the Hindus. It is because of this reason that many scholars noted that both the Muslims and Hindus were quite different from their religious counterparts in the rest of the subcontinent. They did not reflect the kind of rigidities that were to be found among the Muslims and Hindus elsewhere. Meanwhile, it was the shared language and culture that worked as the greatest bond between the two communities.

Modernity certainly placed a lot of pressures on both Muslims and Pandits to shed their non-conformist ways and it was the result of these pressures that one could see some partial attempts made to introduce orthodoxy in these religious communities. However, such efforts did not go very far in changing the existing practices and both the communities continued to remain, more or less, unorthodox in the expression of their religious practices. Wakhloo refers to the language, living style, culture and genetic origin of Kashmiri Hindus and Muslims. 'The cultural heritage is common to all, giving rise to many common customs and rituals at the time of birth, marriage and death. Many Hindu children had Muslim foster-mothers and vice versa' (Wakhloo 1992, 379). Gul Mohd. Wani similarly emphasizes the cultural commonalities between the two communities. He notes:

> Needless to say, a Kashmiri Muslim shares many intellectual and cultural commonalities with a Kashmiri Pandit which are unique to Kashmiri setting. I would like to underline that Muslims in Kashmir have retained their pre-Islamic last names such as Koul, Bhat, Razdan, Dar, etc. Moreover, there exists many similarities in the rites of death, birth and marriage between the two communities. (Wani 2012, 136)

What made the relationship between the Kashmiri Pandits and Muslims unique was the fact that the Kashmiri Pandit society was all Brahmin with no lower castes, leading to what Rai calls a forced 'relationship of ritual and economic interdependence' between the two communities. To quote her, 'In the absence of the full panoply of jatis that characterised Hindu society elsewhere, the Pandits, whose caste status excluded them from either manual labour or work deemed polluting, relied heavily on Muslim specialist groups for the provision of essential services and liturgical goods' (Rai, 2004, 40).

Economic and Political Differences: Class Question and the Gap between the Two Communities

Despite the cultural continuity between the Kashmiri Pandits and Muslims, there was huge economic gap that existed between them.[1] The Pandits were mostly associated with the state and were not only controlling a large portion of state jobs but also formed one of the largest classes of landowners. As compared to other communities, they were more flexible in their approach to modern ways of life. With the change in political regimes, they could adapt themselves to the requirements of the new rulers. During the Afghan rule they learnt the Persian language and became proficient in it and later were the first ones to master the English language. Because of their association with the state, they were able to improve their economic status. With their hold on the state jobs, particularly the revenue-related jobs, Pandits 'had converted these privileges into acquisition of substantial land wealth' (Rai, 2004, 50).

The economic gap between the two communities therefore led to the political gap as well. The Pandits did not identify with the political movement that evolved in Kashmir during the post-1931 period. With the exception of a few leading examples like Prem Nath Bazaz who joined Sheikh Abdullah in secularizing the Kashmiri identity politics in the mid-1930s, the Kashmiri Pandits kept themselves away from the politics of Muslim Conference. Even when the Muslim Conference

[1] In the opinion of Rai, it was the Hindu nature of the state that was significantly responsible for creating the economic gap between the two communities. 'The Dogra Maharaja needed to substantiate their claim to legitimacy in Kashmir as Hindu rulers by associating with them its powerful Hindu minority, while the Kashmiri Pandit community was concerned to hold on to its privileged access to government employment' (Rai 2004, 123).

got converted to the National Conference, they did not identify with it. The very nature of political demands of the Kashmiri movement, especially those related to increasing their share in state employment, generated a negative response from the Pandits. Already they were facing challenge from Punjabi Hindus. As per the state policy of Maharaja Pratap Singh, many Punjabis had been incorporated into the state administration. This was resented by the Pandits and they had already started 'Kashmiri for Kashmiri movement' demanding the reservation of state jobs only for the residents of the state.[2] Now, the possibility of Muslims also joining the state services in large numbers directly hurt their interests.

It was not only the Pandits who saw Muslims in terms of their antagonistic interests, but Muslims also saw Pandits in the same manner. Leaders like Sheikh Abdullah, who later rose above their religious identity politics, also attributed the backwardness of Kashmiri Muslims to their religious identity and the prejudice against the Muslims by the Hindu rulers. It was only in the later years that Sheikh formally invited the Pandits and the non-Muslims to join the anti-feudal and anti-monarchical struggle. It is a different matter though that with the exception of a few like Prem Nath Bazaz, the Pandits neither joined the movement nor owned it in any way.

It was the conflict of interest of the two communities that gradually led to a silent tension between them which came into open during and after the 1931 riots.

1931 Riots: Impact on Kashmiri Muslim–Pandit Relations

While the Muslims trace the origin of the political awareness in Kashmir to the mass upsurge on 13 July 1931, the Pandits remember it as a day when they were faced with communal violence. The background to the incident lay in the police action against Kashmiris who

[2] It was following this movement that the State Subject Law of the state that distinguished and privileged the 'mulkis' (residents of the state) from the 'non-mulkis' (outsiders) was passed.

were protesting the arrest of one Abdul Qadir, a non-Kashmiri butler serving with the British Resident, for making an inflammatory speech against the Dogra ruler. In the police action 26 Kashmiri Muslims died and many suffered injuries. It was following this that there was mass upsurge which bordered on a communal response. Bazaz has described the situation:

> The jail firing which killed several Muslims created great resentment in the mob mind against the Hindus. So when the procession reached Maharaja Gunj, a busy trade centre of the city, Hindu shops which had been closed ... were broken open and looted. A serious rioting followed not only at Maharaja Gunj but also at several parts of the city, notably Vicharnag and Nowshehra. Hundreds of Hindu houses and shops were denuded of their contents and the inmates badly handled. Three Hindus were murdered and 163 wounded. The rioters held the northern part of the city for three hours until the military came and occupied it.... (Bazaz 2011, 130)

This incident of rioting had a major impact on the social and political relationship between the two communities. The cultural bondings of the two communities were clearly impacted, at least to some extent. Taking note of the impact of the riots, Mridu Rai notes:

> Take for instance the practice common to both Hindus and Muslims, which Lawrence and others delighted in describing, of worshipping nagas (serpent deities) at the many springs of Kashmir. This tradition of collective worship broke down rather dramatically in 1931, in the aftermath of riots in which the Kashmiri Pandits and Muslims confronted each other in a competition for the political and economic resources of the Dogra state. (Rai 2004, 42)

Zutshi, however, makes a distinction between the cultural and economic issues underlying the Pandit–Muslim relationship. She argues that whatever happened in 1931 was not as much due to the religious animosity between the two communities as because of economic and political reasons. To quote her:

> ... tussle between Kashmiri Muslims and Kashmiri Pandits in and after 1931 was more about political and economic representation than religious antagonism. Kashmiri Muslims, tired of being excluded from education, the government, and the lower rungs of the administration, rallied around the cry of 'Islam in Danger' raised by youth recently returned from British

> India with professional degrees. Significantly, the looting following the Central Jail incident was concentrated in the Vecharnag locality of Srinagar, home to Kashmiri Pandit petty administrators and moneylenders.... The rioting on July 13, 1931 was not that of a frenzied mob looking to kill in the name of religion, but one intended to redress the immediate economic grievances of Kashmiri Muslims. (Zutshi 2004, 224)

EXODUS AND AFTER

Situation Before the Exodus

Despite the strong political differences between Kashmiri Muslims and Pandits, the two communities were culturally bonded and lived a mixed life in the post-1947 period. There was mutual trust and there was no major incident of communal tension. Describing the situation before militancy, Sanjay Tickoo, a Kashmiri Pandit activist representing the Kashmiri Pandits who did not migrate in 1990 and associated with Kashmiri Pandit Sangharsh Samiti, notes that even when one could not say 'that (Kashmiri Pandits and Muslims) were brothers in arms, living in each other's homes or something before 1989. Yes, there was an unmistakable tolerance and respect for each other ... violence was unheard of' (Essa 2011). There was some tension between the two communities in the late 1960s around the issue of marriage of a Kashmiri Pandit girl with a Muslim. In 1986 communal violence broke out in South Kashmir with Hindu temples and Pandit houses being targeted. In the words of Praveen Swami, these were Kashmir's 'first post-independence communal riots, in the form of attacks on the Pandit-owned homes and on Hindu temples in south Kashmir' (Swami 2007, 158). The situation however started deteriorating during the time of militancy. The relationship between the two communities was clearly affected. The violence that overtook the Valley had created an environment of uncertainty. However, what affected the Kashmiri Pandits the most was the high-profile killings of Kashmiri Pandits. Among these high profile killings included that of Justice Neelkanth Ganjoo (a judge of the High Court of J&K, who was targeted by the militants for having awarded the death sentence to Maqbool Bhat), Tika Lal Taploo (a lawyer by profession and also a member of the BJP's national executive body), Lassa Koul (Director, Srinagar Doordarshan), Sarvanand Premi (a noted poet) and Prem Nath Bhat (an advocate by profession and also an RSS activist). Apart from these killings, there were other kinds of targeted killings of Kashmiri Pandits.[3] Many were killed because they were seen as 'informers' and 'agents of Indian intelligence agencies' (Bose 2003, 120–121).

The overall situation of violence in general, and the news of high profile killings of the Pandits in particular, certainly affected the Kashmiri Pandit community and they felt increasingly insecure in the Valley. It was this insecurity that ultimately led them to take the decision of leaving the Valley. While a few families left because they were personally caught in the situation of violence, many more left because of the general sense of fear and the feeling that the Pandits were being targeted and killed in large numbers. Verma notes, 'They felt very much threatened in an atmosphere of unabated violence' (Verma 1994, 254).

However, it was the overall environment which seems to have affected the Kashmiri Pandits. The time they left the Valley was the one in which there was complete chaos, not only because of the presence of militants but also because of the everyday phenomenon of massive protest marches. The state authority had almost gone missing and the 'azadi' processions seemed to have overtaken the Valley. What was the added factor was the mix of religion with politics and religious slogans being chanted along with the political slogans. To quote Bose, 'The sight of huge pro-Azadi demonstrations chanting Islamic religious slogans across the valley in January–February 1990 may have further intimidated local Pandits and contributed to their exodus' (Bose, 2003, 120–121).

The use of the religious places for issuing threats and intimidating the minorities was a reality of that time. To quote Wajahat Habibullah who was posted as Special Commissioner in Anantnag in 1990:

[3] Among the most gruesome murders included that of a nurse of Soura Medical College Hospital who was also gangraped and another woman who was not only raped and killed but her body was also sliced in small pieces at a sawmill. Many of these killings were attributed to JKLF.

> That the Pandits were apprehensive was hardly surprising.... Places of worship, like the one in Anantnag, where the majority went, were being used to issue threats to them over loudspeakers. I learnt later that these inflammatory sermons, and their reverberating public applause, were audio recordings circulated to mosques to be played over loudspeakers at prayer time. (Habibullah 2015)

Mention can also be made of the threats issued through the newspapers[4] and through the posters and notices being pasted on the Pandit houses.

On the whole, there was an intimidating environment in Kashmir at the time when the Pandits left. There was a strong presence of those militant organizations which insisted on imposing the dress and other cultural codes. This was also the time when the cinema halls were closed, video parlours and beauty parlours were banned and people were asked to abide by religious norms.

Sumantra Bose notes that by 15 March 1990, 'the Pandit exodus was substantially complete' (Bose 2003, 120–121). There are different versions on the exact number of the Pandits who migrated. However, as per Wajahat Habibullah, 'Nearly 70,000 families fled in the turmoil of 1990–92, and even though the violence was brought under control, most of the remaining families left thereafter' (Habibullah 2015).[5]

Discourse of Ethnic Cleansing vs Engineered Migration

The whole issue of exodus of Kashmiri Pandits has been mired in controversy. Among the multiple discourses that have evolved in the post-exodus period, one relates to the discourse of 'ethnic cleansing',

[4] One can refer to the narration of Col. Tej Kumar Tikoo who notes, 'On Jan, 04, 1990, a local Urdu newspaper, Aftab, published a press release issued by Hizb-ul-Mujahideen, asking all Pandits to leave the Valley immediately. Al Safa, another local daily, repeated the warning' (Tikoo 2015).

[5] According to official records, '62,000 migrant families, comprising Pandits, Sikhs and some Muslims, are registered with the government in Jammu, Delhi and in other parts of India' (Wani 2015a).

and the other relates to that of 'engineered migration'. As per the first discourse, terror was used in a systematic manner to 'cleanse' Kashmiri Pandits from the Valley. This argument negates the tradition of coexistence of the two communities and focuses on the continued 'persecution' of Pandits. Inevitably, in this argument, the persecution of Kashmiri Pandits precedes 1989. While the pro-Muslim attitude of the state is held responsible for 'a silent migration' of Pandits from Kashmir even before the rise of militancy, the 1990 exodus is attributed to the religious nature of the Kashmiri movement.

The idea of 'Islamism', fundamentalism and religious mission as the reason for Kashmiri Pandits being pushed out of Kashmir has been officially pronounced by Panun Kashmir, the most vocal organization of Kashmiri Pandits. In its Margdarshan Convention held in Jammu on 26 December 1991, this organization passed the Panun Kashmir Resolution which attributed the migration of Kashmiri Pandits to 'a Muslim religious crusade aimed at the secession of the state'. The major tenets of this crusade, according to the Resolution, are 'Kashmir having a Muslim majority and aiming to become a part of Pakistan on the basis of religion and destruction of all institutions that stand for democracy and secularism'. The Resolution explicitly blames 'communalism and fundamentalism' as the reason for the exodus of Kashmiri Pandits. It states:

> ...Kashmiri Hindus faced a deliberate, steady and relentless squeeze of their constitutional, political and legal rights and were forced into a slow exodus. In the process, nearly three lakh Hindus have already left the valley during the last four decades.

Further, it states:

> As a part of 'the grand strategy' for the attainment of the Islamic and fundamentalistic State of Kashmir, communal elements and terrorists are bent upon 'annihilating the Kashmiri Hindus' as a result of which their exodus has been made inevitable. (Panun Kashmir Resolution, 1991)

As opposed to this, there lies the discourse of 'engineered migration'. As per this discourse, the exodus of Kashmiri Pandits resulted with a conscious and active role played by the state, particularly by the then governor, Jagmohan. Many in Kashmir give the argument that the exodus of Kashmiri Pandits was a conspiracy of the Indian State to deal sternly with the local population of Kashmir. The Pandits, as per this discourse, were scattered all over the Valley and they were allowed to leave the Valley so that security forces could deal with the local population through militaristic means. This view is held by the separatists as well by many others in Kashmir. For instance, Nayeem Ahmad Khan, a member of Hurriyat Conference, made a statement that 'A few migrant Pandits are hell bent to malign the Muslim population of the valley. The fact remains that the Muslims had nothing to with the migration of Kashmiri pandits. It was the then Governor of J&K, Jagmohan, who forced them to leave the valley' (Greater Kashmir 2015).

However, the reality was much more complex than as portrayed by simplistic understandings of the reason of the mass exodus of Kashmiri Pandits. Neither it was the case of the Kashmiri Muslims operating in a planned manner to throw Kashmiri Pandits out, so that Kashmir could become an Islamic society, nor the Pandits left because their migration was 'engineered'. The reality is much more layered and different. To quote Trisal:

> In the late 1989, when militancy surfaced in the valley, the Muslims in general, whether as a neighbour, friend or colleague, asked their Pandit brothers not to leave their homes and provided security to them. Many Muslims accommodated Pandit families in their houses to save them from militant attacks. There are instances when Muslim ladies, at the risk of their lives, stood at the doors of Pandit houses, to stop militants from entering their houses. Not only this, but when militancy gained the upper hand and the common Muslim himself came under the threat of the gun, timely information was provided to the Pandits so that they could flee to safety. (Trisal 1995, 735–740)

H. N. Jattu, President of All India Kashmiri Pandits Conference, also notes the helplessness of the Kashmiri Muslims: 'Our Muslim neighbours were also rendered helpless. No Muslim family was in a position to protect the Pandits. Had they done so, they too would have been eliminated' (cited in Razdan 1999, 242–243). Jattu refers to the killing of Mirwaiz Mohamad Farooq, who had assured the protection of Kashmiri Pandits.[6]

A reflection of the complexity of the situation is provided by M. M. Khajooria, the retired director general of police of the state. Referring to the impact of the threats issued by the militants to Pandits asking them to leave the Valley, he notes:

> The recipients of the threatening letters at first reacted quite non-seriously. They felt reassured on account of the lack of support for such antics, which were considered abhorrent to the basic value system traditionally dear to the Kashmiris. The impact of such warning was thus slow to take effect. Nevertheless, the campaign persisted. The confusion was further confounded by indications of lack of unanimity amongst the militant outfits on the 'solution'. The threats to 'get out of Kashmir' were matched by gestures of goodwill and touches of 'compassion' through the delivery of much needed fresh vegetables during curfew hours on the very doorsteps of some Hindu families in Srinagar—by courtesy of 'extremist brothers'. While sceptics interpreted these moves as an integral part of the 'cat and mouse' game, others saw in these a ray of hope. These strong cross-currents only created a somewhat muddled picture of the inter-communal relations in the valley. But in the very nature of things, the twilight period was bound to fade out—sooner than the optimists hoped for. (Khajooria 1998, 227)

So how does one understand the role of the community—neighbours and friends—in the issue of exodus? To quote Badri Raina:

> Two broad readings of that moment offer themselves: one, that the exodus of January 1990 had the full endorsement of the Kashmiri Muslim population; and, two, that the ordinary lot of Kashmiri Muslims were as much at the receiving end of an organised militant putsch as the Pandits, and,

[6] To quote Jattu, Mirwaiz had:

> warned his followers not to cast even verbal aspersions at Kashmiri Pandits, when the sacred relic of the Prophet was misplaced from Hazratbal shrine in 1964. During the 1986 communal disturbances in south Kashmir, he again stood like a rock to ensure the safety of Pandits. Even in 1989 and early 1990, when militancy was its peak, he came upto Ganpatyar, the citadel of Pandits in the city. He assured me that the Pandits would not be harmed. That is what Islam, as known to Kashmiri Muslims, preached and the martyred Maulvi Farooq followed. No wonder, he was slain in his own house in broad daylight in the valley of Kashmir. (cited in Razdan 1999, 242–243)

> although many Muslims across the Valley willed the Pandits not to leave, they were too helpless and afraid to do much more than to so will in view of both nasty admonitions from hostile ideologues and guns on the street. (Raina 2015)

It was on the whole a situation of confusion and chaos when the gap of communication between the communities had increased. That is why when the Pandits left, the Muslims thought they had abandoned them and left to safer places.

Kashmiri Pandits, however, rue the fact there was no organized voice from anyone representing the majority community to give them a sense of assurance and stop their exodus. Neither the separatists nor any other kind of political leaders, nor the community leaders, took any initiative to stop them from fleeing Kashmir. Of course, when the peace was relatively established, there were voices of regret, but as Moti Lal Bhat notes, 'it was too late, and people had already left ... they should have come forward to the minority. It is the moral duty of the majority to look after the minority and include them ... if you are in a minority you face a psychological threat' (Essa 2011). Jattu, similarly notes:

> The Pandits had become the prime soft targets for the wielders of the gun. Open and humiliating threats were served on them through the print media. We had to flee leaving everything behind. Secondly, no one stopped us either. No Muslim leader came to tell us that regardless of the movement they were leading, Pandits would be safe and should not flee from their homes. (Razdan 1999, 243)

Implications of Exodus

One of the major implications of the exodus of Kashmiri Pandits from Kashmir has been that the very essence of the political movement came under questioning. As Schofield noted, 'Their departure meant that the militant groups, like the JKLF, who maintained that their objective for the state included all the occupants of the former princely state, could no longer claim to represent Hindus...' (Schofield 2003, 152). Rather than being defined a movement that represented all the Kashmiris, it was now seen as a movement of 'Kashmiri Muslims'. Most importantly, as Bose notes, the going away of Pandits 'exposed a critical flaw embedded in the "independent Kashmir" concept—its complete inability to accommodate the multiple political allegiances regarding sovereignty and citizenship that exist even in the Kashmir Valley' (Bose 2003, 124). A major fault line between the political orientations of the Kashmiri Muslims and Pandits came to the surface, and the exit of the Pandits could be seen as a statement that despite their cultural bonds the political differences were quite significant.

Added to this has been the implication of increasing gap in the inter-community relations. Militancy has played an important role in shattering the faith which existed earlier between Kashmiri Muslims and the Kashmiri Pandits. Referring to different perspectives that developed between the Muslims and Pandits, Hangloo notes that 'at the popular level ... both the communities failed to view the crisis in an appropriate perspective.... The contacts between the communities that had been broad based shrank because of the suspicion and mistrust, heightened by the instigation of mainstream communal politics, which was consistently on the ascendance from 1986 up to 2005' (Hangloo 2012, 50–51). Hangloo states that 'there has been misrepresentation of facts on both sides, which has created a wedge between the two communities' (Hangloo 2012, 56).

Radicalization both of the Kashmiri Muslims and the Pandits has been another consequence of the exodus. The religious dimension of identity became prominent in both the communities. With Kashmiri Pandits gone, the Kashmiri society lost the factor of 'diversity' and in the process its pluralist culture was deeply impacted. On the other hand, the Kashmiri Pandits were also radicalized and in many cases reinvented the past which did not refer to the shared culture ethos but which highlighted the oppression of the minority Pandits at the hands of the majority Muslims. Rather than remembering the peaceful times that they had in the pre-militancy period, their narrative has been centring on the past when the community was persecuted by the Muslim rulers. However, the project of reinvention of the memories is not limited to the Kashmiri Pandits only. There is a similar process among the Kashmiri Muslims who have been selectively emphasizing on the negative side of the relationship between the communities and projecting the Pandits as the historical oppressors of the Muslims.

That much of the problem is linked with the generations that have grown in the period of militancy has been acknowledged by many. To quote Hangloo:

> ... the generations born in the late 1980s and after, among both Muslims and Hindus, have no idea of Kashmir's harmonious cultural fabric, because these generations were born and raised in a period of turmoil, and after migration they have not lived Kashmiriyat. The Kashmiri Muslim youth born post 1990 in Kashmir are surprised when they are told about Pandits and their present plight, and the Hindu youth born post-1986 and 1990 display no concern for Kashmiri Muslims because they were born outside Kashmir, but more so because they have been brought up in an atmosphere charged with communalism and instilled with anti-Muslim sentiment. The spaces of socialisation and interaction that were available to both the communities in government offices, educational institutions, commercial establishments, religious places like Astans and Asthapans (shrines), and on social occasions in the neighbourhoods were all lost. (Hangloo 2012, 51)

Neerja Mattoo also notes that 'Young Kashmiris today have no idea of the inclusive voice our poets used in the past, or even if they do have a vague idea they are rather embarrassed by it and tend to dismiss it as a rare aberration' (Mattoo 2012, 89).

QUESTION OF RETURN

Most of the Pandits who left the Valley did not visit Kashmir in the initial decade. However, few of them have been now visiting Kashmir for brief periods, especially to go to the famous temple of Kheer Bhawani in village Tulamulla. In the process they also go back to their villages or localities and meet with their neighbours. In most of the instances, such meetings are reported to be very emotional. A lot number of people have been visiting the Valley for other reasons, including those related to their property.

However, the question of their return and resettlement in Kashmir is not very simple. To quote Shyam Kaul:

> As far as the general attitude of Pandits about their return to Kashmir is concerned, they certainly do not want to go back to live in the same conditions that forced them to flee their homes. They do not appear to be interested in stopgap proposals that have been emanating from the government from time to time. They will go back only when they are able to live with honour and in peace and security in their homes, as equal citizens of Kashmir. (Kaul 1998, 93)

Apart from the issue of security, the Pandit leadership raises the question of the political environment of the Valley and the political rights of the minority community. The question is raised in view of the majoritarian stance taken by Kashmiri leaders like Syed Ali Shah Geelani. Geelani for instance states:

> ... Should the right of self-determination be granted to us finally, Pandits, Dogras and Buddhists and even Muslims will be at liberty to vote as they like. The majority decision will have to be accepted by all. That is democracy. We will not allow anyone to adopt coercion during voting. Islam does not allow us use of force.... According to the basic tenets of Islam, politics and religion go hand in hand. Muslims cannot separate politics from religious life. They have to be Muslims in politics as they are Muslims in a mosque. (Cited in Razdan 1999, 209)

The Kashmiri Pandit leaders, however, reject the majoritarian approach and rather demand their own right of self-determination.

Successive governments have been working on the issue of return of the Pandits. The PDP government, when it came into power in alliance with the Congress in 2002, had spoken of its resolve to rehabilitate Pandits in their homeland with full security. In collaboration with the Central government, the party had prepared a detailed proposal to rehabilitate the Pandits. However, the proposal could not be implemented as there was a major incident of massacre of Kashmiri Pandits in Nadimarg village. These were the Pandits who had chosen to stay back in the Valley. Twenty-four of them were killed in the month of March in 2003 (Bedi 2003).

In the year 2015, the PDP–BJP alliance government announced a decision to rehabilitate Kashmiri Pandits. There was a proposal to set up cluster colonies to rehabilitate them. In order to give a concrete shape to the proposal, the Centre government had asked the state government to identify area in three different districts to make townships where the Pandits choosing to return to the Valley could be accommodated. However, this proposal triggered a huge debate. The idea of settling them in separate colonies has been objected to by the separatist and other leaders in Kashmir on the ground that it is a communal plan. It is argued that Kashmiri Pandits can be safe only in the mixed colonies. Since earlier also they had been living in mixed areas, they should be rehabilitated in their own places, where they were living before the exodus. The opposition to their return in cluster colonies has been coming from the political class across the ideological divide—from Geelani and Yasin Malik on the one hand to NC leaders on the other.

The general refrain is that 'Pandits are welcome' but not in separate areas and separate colonies. Even when the government stated that these will be composite colonies, the plan was equated with the Israel kind of cluster colonies in Palestine. The argument that is developed is that the smooth rehabilitation is possible only by reintegrating them back to their original places of living. But any idea of securitized areas for them is bound to be counter-productive since it would increase the gap of communication and would lead to further polarizing the society. For many, the idea of separate identified areas is a part of the hidden agenda of rightist elements in India. It has been argued that already existing arrangements of keeping Pandits (who have chosen to come back under the Central government's plan) in separate securitized zones has not been serving the interest of the Pandits. The isolation of these areas itself is symbolized by the very physical structures such as concrete walls and concertina wires as well as the security guards. This symbolizes the continued separation of the Pandits from the Kashmiri society.

The concern of the Pandits meanwhile is that they would not feel secure if they are not settled in secured areas. Moreover, there is the practical issue that the places where Pandits were living are no more available. Most of the displaced Pandits have sold off their property and need to live in the townships which are newly created by the state.

While the issue of return of Pandits remains controversial at the political level, the Centre for the Study of Developing Societies (CSDS) survey reflected that at the level of people, a larger number of people were interested in their return. Thus on being asked to express their opinion whether the government should bring back Kashmiri Pandits in Kashmir region, 82 per cent respondents in Kashmir region agreed during the 2002 post-poll survey (44.2% strongly agreed and 37.8% agreed); 73 per cent agreed during the 2008 post-poll survey (51.8% fully agreed and 21.3% somewhat agreed); and 66.8 per cent agreed during the 2014 post-poll survey (52% fully agreed and 14.8% somewhat agreed).

To Conclude

The controversy around the issue of return of Kashmiri Pandits clearly reflects the trust deficit that has evolved over the decades between the two communities. Since the time of the exodus in 1990, a great gulf has developed which cannot be bridged without any conscious and collective effort of both these communities.

Of all the fallouts of militancy and separatism, the exodus of the Kashmiri Pandits from Kashmir has been the most grave one and has had the implications not only for the Kashmiri Pandits but for the Kashmiri society per se. Kashmiri Pandits, of course, have gone through the pain of displacement as well as the crisis of identity. With its roots in Kashmir, its sense of being 'Kashmiri' without a connection with the Valley is the greatest issue for this community. However, there is a greater loss for the Kashmiri society, which in the absence of the most influential minority has become a one-religion society. In the absence of Kashmiri Pandits in Kashmir, the concept of 'Kashmiriyat' which is often invoked to impress the plural, syncretic and tolerant nature of the society gets to be questioned.

In political terms, however, the exodus of the Kashmiri Pandits raises intricate questions about the very nature of the separatist movement and points to its limits in the context of the social diversity and political divergence that the state represents.

References

Bazaz, Prem Nath. 1995. 'Secular Concepts in Kashmir Traditions'. In *The Story of Kashmir: Yesterday and Today*, Vol. 2, edited by Virender Grover, 735–740. New Delhi: Deep & Deep Publications.

Bedi, Rahul. 2003, 25 March. '24 Hindus Shot Dead in Kashmir'. *The Telegraph*. https://www.telegraph.co.uk/news/worldnews/asia/india/1425614/24-Hindus-shot-dead-in-Kashmir.html (accessed on 3 November 2018).

Bose, Sumantra. 2003. *Kashmir: Roots of Conflict, Paths to Peace*. Cambridge, MA: Harvard University Press.

Essa, Azad. 2011, 2 August. 'Kashmiri Pandits: Why We Never Fled Kashmir'. *Aljazeera*. http://www.aljazeera.com/indepth/spotlight/kashmirtheforgotten-conflict/2011/07/201176134818984961.html (accessed on 31 August 2018)

Greater Kashmir. 2015, 21 January. 'Jagmohan Engineered Pandit Migration: Nayeem Khan'. https://www.greaterkashmir.com/news/kashmir/jagmohan-engineered-pandit-migration-nayeem-khan/184313.html (accessed on 3 November 2018).

Habibullah, Wajahat. 2015, 16 April. 'Return to a Lost Paradise'. *The Hindu*.

Hangloo, Rattan Lal. 2012. 'Kashmiriyat: The Voice of the Past Misconstrued'. In *The Parchment of Kashmir: History, Society, and Polity*, edited by Nyla Ali Khan, 37–70. London: Palgrave Macmillan.

Kaul, Shyam. 1998. 'Migration of a Coffee House'. In *Jammu, Kashmir and Ladakh: Ringside Views*, edited by Shyam Kaul and Onkar Kachru, 242. New Delhi: Atlantic Publishers.

Khajooria, M. M. 1998. 'The Making of a Catastrophe'. In *Jammu, Kashmir and Ladakh: Ringside Views*, edited by Shyam Kaul and Onkar Kachru. New Delhi: Atlantic Publishers.

Madan, T. N. 1972. 'Religious Ideology in a Plural Society: The Muslims and Hindus of Kashmir'. *Contributions to Indian Sociology* 6 (1): 108.

Mattoo, Neerja. 2012. 'Syncretic Tradition and the Creative Life: Some Kashmiri Mystic Poets'. In *Islam, Women and Violence in Kashmir: Between India and Pakistan*, edited by Nyla Ali Khan. New York: Palgrave Macmillan.

Panun Kashmir. 1991. Resolution during Margdarshan Convention.

Raina, Badri. 2015, 25 April. 'Jammu and Kashmir: Return of the Natives'. *Mainstream* 53 (18). https://mainstreamweekly.net/article5626.html (accessed on 4 November 2018).

Razdan, Onkar. 1999. *The Trauma of Kashmir: The Untold Reality*. New Delhi: Vikas Publishing House.

Rai, Mridu. 2004. *Hindu Rulers, Muslim Subjects: Islam, Rights and the History of Kashmir*. London: Hurst & Company.

Schofield, Victoria. 2003. *Kashmir in Conflict: India, Pakistan and the Unending War*. I.B.Tauris.

Swami, Praveen. 2007. *India, Pakistan and the Secret Jihad: The Covert War in Kashmir 1947–2004*. New York: Routledge.

Tikoo, Tej Kumar, Col. 2015, 12 October. 'Kashmiri Pandits Offered Three Choices by Radical Islamists'. *Indian Defence Review*. http://www.indiandefencereview.com/news/kashmiri-pandits-offered-three-choices-by-radical-islamists/ (accessed on 4 November 2018).

Trisal, O. N. 1995. 'Kashmiri Pandit: At the Crossroads of History'. In *The Story of Kashmir: Yesterday and Today*, Vol. 2, edited by Virender Grover, 735–740. New Delhi: Deep & Deep Publications.

Verma, P. S. 1994. *Jammu and Kashmir at the Political Crossroads*. New Delhi: Vikas Publishing House.

Wani, Gull Mohd. 2012. 'Political Assertion of Kashmiri Identity'. In *The Parchment of Kashmir: History, Society, and Polity*, edited by Nyla Ali Khan, 125–153. New York: Palgrave Macmillan.

Wakhloo, Khemlata. 1992. *Kashmir: Behind the White Curtain 1972–1991*. New Delhi: Konark Publishers.

Zutshi, Chitralekha. 2004. *Languages of Belonging: Islam, Regional Identity and the Making of Kashmir*. London: Hurst & Company.

5 Restoration of Democracy in Separatist Context of Kashmir

Kashmir started witnessing erosion of the democratic space following the 1987 Assembly election. The NC–Congress government that was installed after this election worked under extremely difficult conditions. By the beginning of 1988, the popular resentment against this government had started taking the form of massive protest demonstrations. By the beginning of the year 1989, these protests had taken a clear-cut separatist direction. By this time, militancy had also taken a full-blown form and as a consequence the democratic processes were totally receded to the background.

How the democratic political space had crumbled in Kashmir was clearly reflected during the 1989 Parliamentary election. Though all the three Parliamentary seats of Kashmir were won by the NC, the election was a totally farcical exercise. In the situation in which call for boycotting the election was given by JKLF and other militant organizations, neither the parties were willing to contest election nor were the voters ready to vote. The incapacity of administration to meet the threat of the militants was reflected in Baramulla where a coffin that was placed outside the polling booth had this message that it was meant for the first person who would come forward to participate in polling (Behera 2006, 147). In the end, election was almost rejected with 95% of the voters staying away from the electoral process[1] (Chowdhary and Rao 2003, 196).

[1] While the MUF boycotted the election, other political parties did not participate. In the end, no electioneering took place, and the victory of NC candidates was registered

By the end of 1989 and beginning of the year 1990, the situation had turned to be so volatile that the normal functioning of the government had become difficult. Apart from the anti-state mass processions, almost on daily basis, there were militant attacks against the state functionaries and political leaders. As Bose notes, as a result of 'the JKLF's campaign of selective assassinations of alleged Indian spies and political "collaborators" in Valley' more than a hundred killings of political workers and other functionaries took place in a period of six months (Bose 2003, 108). It was in this situation that the state government was dismissed and the Assembly was dissolved. The political parties and leaders went into hibernation.

REVIVAL OF DEMOCRATIC POLITICS: 1996–2002

The situation continued to remain impacted by violence over the next few years. There was therefore no space for any kind of political activity, even in the separatist sphere. It was in 1993 that the APHC was organized to give a political face to separatism but in the intensity of militant violence and the counter-insurgency operations, there was almost a total political vacuum.

It was by 1994, when the counter-insurgency operations had succeeded in restoring the authority of the state, that attempts were made to install a political government and hold elections. By this time, the state was able to control militancy to a manageable level. But more significantly, there was the changed response of people towards the militancy because of which the Central Government could think of political initiatives in the state. On the ground there was a growing exhaustion with violence and an urge for some kind of normalcy.

However, there were certain issues in restoring the political processes. First, in context of the ascendancy of militancy and violence, there was not much available political space in which political initiatives could be taken. Moreover, since all mainstream political

uncontested in Srinagar constituency and contested against independent candidates in Baramulla and Anantnag with 5 per cent voter turnout.

leaders had retreated from the political scene, there was neither an appropriate political environment nor willing political actors to test the political waters. The situation was further compounded as the militancy was still at its peak and the separatist sentiments were still quite strong. With the delegitimization of the very mainstream politics, there was the apprehension that the election would become a farcical exercise.

In the situation in which there was complete reluctance of the political class to come forward to participate in any mainstream political activity, the NC was persuaded to start opening its channels in Kashmir. Assuming that the idea of 'autonomy' could work as an alternative to 'azadi' the Central Government started indicating that it could offer 'maximum autonomy' to the state. It was in this context that later Narasimha Rao, the then Prime Minister of India, used the famous phrase 'only the sky is the limit' (Ahmed 2000).

It is in this background that the NC sought its re-entry in the political arena of the state. Holding its first working committee meeting in five years, it attributed the deteriorating situation in Kashmir to the erosion of autonomy. It passed a resolution affirming that 'the time has come when this state of affairs should be reviewed in order to restore autonomy to its pristine and original form' (Chowdhary 2000, 2599). It was around the autonomy plank that the NC contested the Assembly election which was held in 1996.

To overcome the problem of holding elections in the presence of militants, the government took the help of 'renegades' or the surrendered militants. These militants had surrendered because many of them got disillusioned with the direction that militancy had taken over the period and many others had been forced to do so due to the pressure of the security forces (Syed 2000). However, by the mid-1990s they had played a significant role in helping the Indian security forces fight the armed militancy and weaken its hold in Kashmir. As a strategic policy, many of the surrendered militants were incorporated into the state police force. Many others were encouraged to become active in politics, float their own political organizations and contest the elections. Thus, Kukka Parrey's Awami League and

Hilal Haider's Awami Conference became active in Kashmir.[2] These ex-militants and their political organizations with the active support of the security forces succeeded in breaking the hold of militants in many areas of northern Kashmir and creating a space in which elections could take place.

However, the 1996 electoral process was not very 'normal' because militancy continued to dominate and violence severely disrupted the electoral process. Though the NC won the election with a massive majority and formed the government, its role in expanding the democratic space was quite limited for a number of reasons. For one, the electoral exercise in itself was under a cloud of controversy because of the role of security forces, on the one hand, and that of the counter-insurgents, on the other. Difficulties for the NC also lay in the ground situation which was dominated by separatist sentiments. Just by having an 'elected' government in place, it was not possible to shift the orientation of people from separatist to mainstream politics. The memories of 1987 Assembly election were still alive and the scepticism towards the mainstream political processes that had developed during that time continued to inform the Kashmiri common sense. The NC particularly carried the baggage of its role in pre-1989 period and was considered responsible for the loss of dignity of Kashmiris through its compromised position. Despite its slogan of Autonomy, it failed to turn the tide of 'azadi', not only because of the lack of its credibility but also because of its inability to get any positive response from the Centre. The party was actually snubbed by the Central Government over the issue of implementation of Report of the State Autonomy Committee which had recommended the restoration of pre-1953 position of the Centre–state relations. Without any discussion on the issue, the Central Government dismissed the demand of the NC. This response of the Centre 'had serious implications both for the political responses in Kashmir as well as for the political fortunes of the NC. While reinforcing the feeling of distrust towards the centre it had also the effect of further diminishing the political image of the NC…' (Chowdhary and Rao 2004, 1523).

[2] Kukka Parrey of Ikhawan-ul-Muslimeen, in fact, was one of the most powerful surrendered militants who participated in and won the 1996 Assembly election (Swami 2003),

However, notwithstanding all its limitations, six years of a 'political government in power' had its implications for the democratic politics. The cadre of the NC which was dormant throughout the early 1990s was activated and even at the village level, some minimum political activities started taking place. This itself was not a smooth process since the ground level workers were quite vulnerable and were the easy targets of the militants. The party, in fact, lost a large number of ground level workers in militant attacks (Chowdhary and Rao 2004).

Notwithstanding the legitimacy crisis, there was some opening for political processes by the time the NC ended its tenure of six years. For the redressal of their day-to-day problems, common people had started looking towards the government and the political class, and some linkage was established between the people and the political representatives. Despite all the risks that the NC cadre faced, it was successful in reviving politics at the grassroots levels. What helped the party was the network that it has had since pre-1947 period. This network somehow survived all the odds and could be used to restore the mainstream sphere of politics.

Some opening was also provided by the presence of legislators of the opposition parties. The legislators such as Mohd Yusuf Tarigami of CPM and Mehbooba Mufti of Congress along with her father, Mufti Mohammed Sayeed, started providing an alternative discourse in the context of militarized situation of Kashmir. Rather than pursuing a statist line, they started seeing the situation from the perspective of people and demanding end to the excesses by the security forces. They also were among the first within the mainstream politics to ask for dialogue with the separatists.

Mehbooba, who later took the initiative to form the PDP along with her father, gave a different direction to Kashmir's mainstream politics. Rather than maintaining a distance from the ground situation, she started connecting with people and empathizing with their sufferings. Through her politics, she particularly acknowledged the impact that militarization had made on the lives of people and started talking of 'peace' and 'dialogue'.

PARADIGM SHIFT IN ELECTORAL POLITICS: LEGITIMACY AND EXPANSION OF DEMOCRATIC SPACE

The 2002 Assembly election provided a very significant moment for restoring the mainstream political space in Kashmir Valley. For a situation in which the electoral politics had lost its legitimacy and the space for mainstream politics had been completely eroded, the 2002 Assembly election went a long way both in providing legitimacy to the electoral process and opening up a space for mainstream politics.

To understand the importance of the 2002 Assembly election, it needs to be emphasized that the legitimacy crisis of the electoral process has been a serious issue in Kashmir and with the exception of the 1977 and 1983 Assembly elections, all other elections were perceived as manipulated. This legitimacy crisis, however, did not remain confined to the electoral process but was extended to other areas of mainstream politics. It was generally believed that the successive state governments didn't enjoy political autonomy and even for the process of sustaining themselves in power were dependent on the Central Government. These were the commonly shared grievances—that democracy was a sham since Kashmiris did not ever get a fair chance to represent themselves; that there was no relationship between the voters' response and the electoral outcome; that governments were imposed from above and many a time changed without reference to the mandate of the people.

As a part of the peace initiative undertaken by the then Prime Minister Atal Bihari Vajpayee, special attention was paid to assuage the widely held belief that elections are generally manipulated and managed from above. Vajpayee made a public announcement committing a 'free and fair election' in J&K (*The Times of India* 2002). His commitment was followed with special arrangements for a transparent electoral process. The election took place under the national and international glare with civil society organizations and media taking keen interest in it. The assessment, on the whole, was that the election was quite free from governmental interference.[3] Unlike the 1996 elections, there were no allegations of coercion by the security forces or of the rigging by the government forces.

That people felt less threatened and intimidated during this election has been reflected by the CSDS data of the 2002 post-poll survey. On being asked to compare the level of fear during the 2002 Assembly election to earlier elections, 43.6 per cent respondents said that there was less fear in this election (17.8% said there was same level of fear as earlier election and 19.3% said that there was more fear in this election). To a question 'was there fear of strong intimidation' during the election, only 24.3 per cent respondents said that there was strong intimidation. While 33.8 per cent said that there was 'some intimidation' 35.9 per cent said that there was no intimidation. On the question of rigging, while a large number of respondents did not respond (43.2% saying DK/NR), 36.6 per cent said there was less rigging as compared to earlier elections. Only 7.3 per cent respondents said that there was more rigging than previous elections and 12.9 per cent said that level of rigging was same as earlier elections.

On the whole, the voter turnout was lower than the 1996 elections (29.60 per cent as against 46.17 per cent in 1996), but it had greater credibility because of the voluntary participation of people. This was an uneven election—there was great enthusiasm about the electoral process in certain areas like Northern Kashmir, in certain other areas, there was quite moderate voting and there were still other areas where the separatists' call for election boycott was followed. The rural Kashmir severely impacted by the violence was more receptive to the idea of elections as compared to the Central Kashmir which is mostly urban. In the northern districts of Kupwara and Handwara which had been affected the most by the violence unleashed by militancy, the election scenario was reminiscent of the pre-militancy era. Here,

[3] That the Assembly election was generally free from governmental interference was a conclusion reached by many independent observers. *The Hindu*, for instance, mentioned two such reports: the report *Jammu and Kashmir Elections 2002: How Free, How Fair* by a 22 member multinational team from the Rural Litigation and Entitlement Kendra, Dehradun, and the report by the Institute of Social Sciences, New Delhi, *Fair Elections under the Shadow of Fear* (Mody 2002).

election campaign was quite vibrant and huge rallies were organized by the political parties. Such process of electioneering had not taken place in Kashmir Valley since 1987 as there was delegitimization of everything linked with the electoral process and was seen as violating the spirit of separatism. Even in Anantnag and Pulwama which witnessed a very high level of violence during the electoral process, people were not completely intimidated and a moderate level of voting was recorded here.

For a situation in which the electoral process had been completely delegitimized, the moderate turnout was quite meaningful. Since there were no reports about coercion, whatever minimal was the level of participation, it was quite voluntary. However, there was an unevenness in the electoral trends. While compared to other two regions of the state, the voter turnout was quite lower in Kashmir Valley. However, within the region there were areas which had registered relatively higher voter turnout. Kupwara district, for instance, recorded a voter turnout of 53.22 per cent and it was followed by Budgam district which recorded 45.92 per cent voter turnout. Baramulla had a moderate voter turnout of 39.64 per cent. There were certain constituencies where the voter turnout was more than the state average of 44.02 per cent.[4] Many of these constituencies had been severely affected by militancy and the higher voter turnout here reflected an exhaustion with violence.

However, there were certain constituencies which had rejected the electoral process and voter turnout here was very low. The Srinagar district, for instance, recorded only 11.18 per cent voter turnout. There were constituencies in this district which generally boycotted the electoral process. The voter turnout, for instance, was as low as 3.06 per cent in Amirakadal constituency, 3.21 per cent in Habbakadal, 4 per cent in Batmaloo, 4.22 per cent in Khanyar, 4.75 per cent in Idgah, 4.78 per cent in Zadibal, 7.12 per cent in Hazratbal and 9.96 per cent in Sonawar.

[4] These included Gurez (76.60%), Chrar-e-Sharief (71.99%), Chadoora (69.82%), Uri (66.56%), Kupwara (55.29%), Langate (53.98%), Rafiabad (52.55%), Kangan (52.03%), Handwara (51.48%), Gulmarg (50.44%), Khansahib (49.43%), Lolab (47%) and Sonawari (55.48%).

Despite the moderate voter turnout in Kashmir region, what contributed to the credibility of the electoral process was the outcome of the election—the failure of the ruling NC to attain majority in the Assembly. The election therefore did not carry the image of being manipulated. For a state, where there were frequent instances of governments being formed or leaders changed from above without any reference to popular mandate (Sheikh Abdullah in 1953, Bakshi Ghulam Mohammed in 1962, Shamsuddin in 1965, Mir Qasim in 1975, Farooq Abdullah in 1984), the 2002 election provided an altogether new political setting in which the popular mandate gained centrality. This had the implications not only of making the electoral space vibrant but also adding to the credibility of electoral process. This was to go a long way in helping the expansion of democratic space (Chowdhary and Rao 2003a).

ALTERNATIVE POLITICAL DISCOURSE AND STRATEGIES OF MAINSTREAM PARTIES: PDP AND NC

In giving a boost to the democratic space, the emergence of PDP contributed a lot. The party was formed in July 1999 by splitting the Congress party. Eight MLAs of the party led by Mehbooba Mufti (who was at that time the leader of the Congress Legislative Party) came out of the party to establish the PDP.

Apart from breaking the hegemony of the NC in Kashmir, the PDP also changed the very discourse of the mainstream politics in Kashmir. The party from the very beginning provided an alternative discourse to the one available within the mainstream politics. What was peculiar about this discourse was that it was grounded in the prevailing conflict situation that sought to respond to some of the problems that the people were confronted with due to the violence and militarization. It reflected the mood of the people exhausted by a decade-old situation of conflict and sought to demand peace and dialogue. One of the objectives to form the party was 'to persuade the government of India to initiate an unconditional dialogue for resolution of Kashmir problem' (cited in Gilani 2016). Mufti Mohammed Sayeed after forming the party underlined the major objective of the party 'to convince the Government of India that bullets are no answer to the Kashmiri problems' and serious negotiations are needed to solve them. Hence mobilizing 'public opinion in the state and country in favour of persuading the Government of India to adopt a policy of understanding and reconciliation and initiate a comprehensive and unconditional dialogue' with Kashmiris was stated by him as the reason for floating the party. He also referred to the objective of mitigation of the problems of people and therefore laid it as the goal of the party to 'find ways and means to ensure that innocent people languishing in jails are released, migrants are brought back and rehabilitated, and the healing touch is administered to the victims of the violent turmoil in the state'. Referring to the mechanism of resolving the internal problems he cleared that the objective of the party was to 'fight for the restoration of complete autonomy to the state'.[5] The party not only asked for dialogue with the separatists but also with the militants. The unconditional dialogue with the militants remained one of the major thrusts of the party from the beginning (*Daily Excelsior* 2000).

What really helped the PDP find acceptance among the people within the larger context of separatism was its strategy to enter the mainstream space via the separatist agenda. The party faced a two-way competition—from the entrenched NC, on the one hand, and from the separatists, on the other. This party was no match to the NC whether in terms of its ideological foundation, its historical legacy, its cadre or mass base. However, more formidable than the competition from the NC was the challenge coming from the separatist politics. As the mainstream politics was totally delegitimized, the separatist politics captured the whole political space of Kashmir since 1989–1990. In

[5] Meanwhile, he also referred to the interregional relations and stated that it would be the goal of the party to 'advocate the formulation and implementation of proper policies for devolution of powers and distribution of resources among the three regions of the state, equitable economic growth, and advancement of understanding and co-operation among the various communities and regions' (Ahmad 1999).

this situation, it was really difficult for a newly established mainstream political party to find its feet within Kashmir.

The strategy that the PDP used to counter both the NC and the challenge of separatism was to adopt the separatist agenda. When the party contested the 2002 Assembly election, its manifesto included all those issues that were raised by the separatists at that point of time. Many of these issues related to the implications that militarization had for the people of conflict-ridden areas and included the demand for reduction of the strength of armed forces, repeal of Armed Forces (Special Powers) Act (AFSPA) and Disturbed Area Act (DAA), disbanding of Special Operation Groups (SOGs), probing all cases of missing youth and a commission to investigate custodial deaths. It also called for an honourable resolution of conflict (Manifesto of PDP, 2002 Assembly election). For this purpose, dialogue was seen as the major instrument of establishing long-term peace and was incorporated in the Common Minimum Programme (CMP) of the coalition government of which PDP was a major partner along with the Congress Party. The CMP referred to 'the power of "unconditional" dialogue over bullets to solve the state's problems'. It called for 'unconditional dialogue' with the MLAs and other segments of public opinion (SATP 2002).

Once in power, the PDP used the political discourse of 'healing touch' to legitimize its power and to expand the democratic base in Kashmir in the process. The party popularized the slogans like '*Goli se nahin, baat banegi boli se*' (problems won't be resolved by gun but by dialogue), peace with 'honour and dignity and not the peace of graveyard'. Soon after forming the government, Mufti Mohammed Sayeed gave a call for unilateral ceasefire during the holy month of Ramzan. He also called for unconditional talks with separatists arguing that such talks were a must in order to bring about a positive change in the situation (*The Asian Age* 2002). Later when the NDA government initiated talks with the separatists, he made a case for talks with the militant organizations like Hizbul Mujahideen. 'They are locals and thus are an important party' (*The Indian Express* 2003).

Taking the clue from the separatists, PDP focused its politics around the implications of militarization in Kashmir. It was the result of such a focus that soon after the formation of the PDP-led coalition government, there were certain visible changes in the ground situation. Most significantly, since there was a transformation in the role of police and security forces, harassment which people used to feel on everyday basis because of the roadside frisking was no more felt. Special care was taken by the government to see that not much inconvenience is caused to general public.[6] With the largest number of complaints of human rights violations being registered against the SOG, the PDP as per its commitment in its manifesto took the decision of disbanding this organization and merging it with the local police. It was decided that for handling militancy, there would be no special force. For cognizance of complaints, including those related to disappearances, police helplines were set up in Srinagar, Jammu and New Delhi (Bukhari 2003). Prevention of human rights violations was emphasized as the major priority of the government.

One of the ways by which the discourse of healing touch was popularized by the party was through the personal contacts that the party leaders, particularly Mehbooba Mufti, had with the victims of militarized actions by the state forces.[7] Rather than joining the government, Mehbooba Mufti, designated as vice-president of the party, actively maintained contact with the people. It was quite a successful strategy since it helped ground the party within the Valley.[8]

Among the first few actions taken by Mufti Sayeed as the CM of the state was to give attention to the release of the political prisoners. This was one of the major decisions which reflected the shift in policy

[6] As CM, Mufti succeeded in getting the approval of the security forces in mitigating some of the problems faced by the civilians in the context of militarization of civilian areas. On his insistence, the Government of India often intervened and instructed the security forces to 'tread carefully' in conducting operations in Jammu and Kashmir (Gilani 2004).

[7] In a situation of death of a person while in police custody, barely few months after the PDP–Congress government was formed, Mehbooba Mufti visited the family and promised strict government action (*The Hindustan Times* 2002).

[8] One can refer to the case of Zahoor's family, who was among five people killed in alleged fake encounter against those involved in Chattisinghpora killings. *The Indian Express* noted how his mother expressed her trust in Mehbooba and another member of his family stated that Mehbooba felt their plight (Islah 2002).

framework. Earlier soon after their release, some of the political prisoners were immediately re-arrested. Even while apprehensions were expressed by parties like BJP, Mufti defended the policy stating that 'Democracy is a battle of ideas. Let them (political prisoners) come out and put forth their point of view and we will put ours' (*The Indian Express* 2002).[9] In the first hundred days of the government, a number of high-profile political prisoners were released. These included a few top militants imprisoned for 12–13 years such as JKLF commander Nazir Ahmad Sheikh; Hizbul Mujahideen top militant Mohammad Ayub Dar; JKLF commander Showkat Ahmad Bakshi, accused in the abduction of CM's daughter Rubaiya Sayeed; JKLF Chairman Mohammad Yasin Malik; and senior leader of the APHC Syed Ali Shah Geelani (albeit on health grounds).[10]

The narrative of the PDP during this time was quite similar to that of the separatists. Keenly following the peace process and incorporating the political idioms that were being used at that time in their political discourse, the Muftis aggressively pursued the peace politics. Picking up the four-point programme of Musharraf (which comprised the ideas of self-rule, demilitarization, irrelevance of borders and joint control/management), they made it as the ideological plank of the PDP. Self-rule for instance, became one of the major ideological programmes of this party. Although defined a bit differently from Musharraf's

[9] He also stated that 'I sincerely believe in democracy. If we go out and talk to people, let Geelani or any other separatist leader do the same.... Let Yasin Malik carry on with his signature campaign. If he wants Kashmiris to play a role in resolving the dispute, we also favour that.' Arguing that there was a need for a momentum in the political process, he said, 'Once people are allowed to vent their anger when they are allowed to talk and protest, it helps to lower the significance of gun.... I want people to come out on the streets to air their grievances. It's part of the political process' (*The Indian Express* 2003).

[10] Another matter which the Mufti government emphasized as a part of its healing touch policy related to the rehabilitation of militants. Apart from the monetary assistance to be made available to surrendered militants, commitment was made for vocational training and self-employment schemes. Under the scheme, a surrendered militant could be entitled to a rehabilitation incentive of ₹1.50 lakh after spending three years of normal life. Further, a monthly stipend of ₹2,000 was approved to be paid to the surrendered militant. The policy also envisaged vocational training for self-employment at specified centres. However, those involved in heinous crimes were not to be covered under the scheme (*The Times of India* 2004).

plan, it had the potential of being catchy and reflecting PDP's central position in the ongoing engagement between India and Pakistan. PDP's concept of self-rule had two parts: internal and external. At the internal (Centre–state relations) level, the idea was similar to the NC's demand for autonomy. However, in application, its scope was much more limited and comprised only three demands: non-application of Article 356 of the Indian Constitution to J&K, elected governor of the state and separate civil service structure for the state.[11] At the external level, the concept of 'self-rule' involved the idea of regional councils and the fiscal autonomy of the state. With one regional council on each side of LoC, the party proposed joint/common management of certain affairs. As per the position taken by the Muftis, it was the collaborative and consultative mechanism between the two parts of the state which would ultimately lead to the conflict resolution.[12]

Among other ideas floated by the party included those related to 'free trade',[13] 'common currency'[14] and 'demilitarization'. The party also picked up the idea of irrelevance of borders as evolved from the peace process. When the cross-LoC (Uri–Muzaffarabad) bus service was started, the PDP projected this as the achievement of the party.

[11] Making a case for non-application of Article 356 to the state, Mufti stated, 'Article 356 should not apply to Kashmir. The Centre should not dismiss our government, which is elected by the people.' At the same time, he argued in favour of elected governor of the state and made a case for a local governor, alternatively to be elected from Kashmir and Jammu regions. Referring to the need of the local services, Mufti stated that 'We can have our own Kashmir Administrative and Police Service so that the real power is vested with the people of State.' As per Mufti, regional federation was also the part of the 'self-rule'. 'A consultative mechanism can then be evolved between the three units, Kashmir, Ladakh and Jammu, so that important issues are debated over' (Bukhari 2006).

[12] To quote Mufti Sayeed, 'The creation of such an institutional mechanism is imperative to address the issues of common concern in the state.' Further, till the time the political resolution would be achieved, the common economic concerns would lead towards the mutual cooperation between two sides (Indo-Asian News Service 2006).

[13] For obtaining fiscal autonomy, the party demanded the undivided state becoming a free trade zone. It also demanded compensation for pledging water of rivers flowing through the state to Pakistan via the Indus Water Treaty (Gilani 2006).

[14] It became a highly controversial idea which was critiqued both by the separatists as 'diversionary' and by the mainstream parties, particularly the BJP, as 'separatist' (*Greater Kashmir* 2008).

With lines being blurred between the agenda of the PDP and that of the Hurriyat Conference, this party could extend its influence within the electoral and mainstream politics. The party made full use of the political space created by the decline of militancy and the increasing credibility of the electoral politics. And rather than taking position contrary to the separatists, it rather used the separatist discourse within the mainstream politics.[15]

One of the implications of the PDP using the strategy of bringing the separatist agenda to the mainstream space was that the overall discourse of the mainstream politics was changed, and the distance that earlier existed between this politics and the ground situation was significantly reduced.

With this kind of change in the political discourse, the NC was also compelled to follow suit. Until 1999, this party was very strongly opposed to the idea of dialogue with Pakistan, militants or the Hurriyat Conference. Gradually, however, the idea of dialogue started entering the discourse of NC as well. While addressing a two-day conference of International Kashmir Alliance, in 2004, Farooq Abdullah stated that 'I request India that they discuss with every single soul, whether Hurriyat or other parties, and make every effort to see that the discussions are fruitful' (*Daily Excelsior* 2004). A similar statement was made by Omar Abdullah while addressing his party workers in September that year: 'If a long lasting solution to the Kashmir issue is to be found out, then talks should be held with all the groups and without it the whole exercise is futile.' He stated that though 'autonomy' was the stated position of the party, if the people give a different verdict, the party would be ready to accept it (*The Times of India* 2004a).

The 2004 election saw a competitive 'soft-separatism' of both the NC and PDP as each of the two parties sought to outdo the other in taking political positions attributed so far to the separatists. Farooq Abdullah, for instance, changed his stance from 'bombing' of Pakistan

[15] After the three years of Mufti's chief ministership, the PDP became more aggressive about the agenda which was seen as closer to the separatist politics. It particularly chose the issues such as demilitarization, withdrawal of AFSPA and cases of human rights violations. In 2007, there was a standoff between the PDP and Congress over the issue of demilitarization. The PDP members of the coalition started boycotting the cabinet meetings because of this issue.

to entering into dialogue with it. At a time when Government of India had entered into dialogue with the moderates, he suggested that these talks would be meaningless unless hardcore elements like Geelani and militant organizations like Hizbul Mujahideen became a part of it (*The Asian Age* 2004).

The mainstreaming of the separatist agenda by the PDP was to create a major challenge to the separatists who from the beginning were critical of the PDP and its policies. Feeling the brunt of PDP raising issues which were earlier raised exclusively by separatists, they blamed the party for 'hijacking the separatist agenda'. Even the Hizbul Mujahideen was critical about the role of the PDP.[16] Despite the fact that the expansion of democratic space had not in any case weakened the separatist sentiment at the popular level, the separatist organizations felt the impact of the changing situation. While the increasing credibility of the electoral process challenged the exclusive hold of the separatists on the politics of Kashmir; the competitive use of separatist agenda by the mainstream parties restricted the role and relevance of separatist organizations and leaders in this politics. It was in any case a challenging time for the separatists, since the Hurriyat Conference had been split after the 2002 election and different factions of this organization were now going different ways. While the moderates led by Mirwaiz Farooq were engaged in dialogue with the Government of India, the other factions termed it as a compromise of the very separatist position.

SEPARATISM AND EXTENDING DEMOCRATIC SPACE: POST-2002 PERIOD

Since the electoral process was seen as a serious challenge to the separatist politics, the implications were felt during the 2004 Parliamentary election. Even before the mainstream parties started the electoral campaign, the separatists had started the campaign for boycotting the

[16] A few months after the PDP took over the power, it accused Mufti being in league with Indian intelligence agencies and 'killing the freedom movement' in the name of healing touch policy. It critiqued the decisions of the government like reorganization of the SOG and making it part of police as 'a game-plan to involve the State Police in counter-insurgency operations' (Fayyaz 2003).

elections. Touring different parts of the Valley and holding meetings at the level of villages, they talked about the futility of the electoral process and the challenge that it posed to the 'cause' of Kashmiris. Syed Ali Shah Geelani on his own conducted around 90 anti-election rallies during a period of three-and-a-half months (Chowdhary and Rao 2004a, 5455). While there was an aggressive response from the militants and separatists, there was also an intensification of violence. In less than two months' time after the elections were announced, a total of 242 killings took place.[17] In the end, one could see the impact of the violence and mobilization by the separatists. The overall voter turnout was quite lowered. Compared to the voter turnout of 44.67 per cent in Jammu region and 73.27 per cent in Ladakh region, in Kashmir region it was 22.73 per cent. Of the three Parliamentary constituencies, it was only in Baramulla constituency that a reasonable voter turnout (36.07%) was recorded. In the other two constituencies, it was less than 20 per cent (15.12% in Srinagar constituency and 18.57% in Anantnag constituency).[18]

However, despite the boycott being effective in a number of places, what remained a peculiar feature of the 2004 Parliamentary election was that it was a very vibrant election because of intensity of competition between NC and PDP. The electioneering process was quite intense in a large number of areas. On the whole, it was visible that the trust in the electoral process had increased as there were no serious allegations of coercion or rigging or manipulation. And in those areas which were not impacted by boycott politics, there was a genuine interest in the electoral process.

One trend that was clearly reflected in the 2004 elections was that the mainstream politics was gaining space and legitimacy even when

[17] There was a major attack on Mehbooba Mufti's rally in Uri where eight people were killed. There was also an attack on the NC Block President Farooq Ahmed Zargar in which he was killed (*The Times of India*, 2004b).

[18] There were as many as nine Assembly segments where the voter turnout was less than 5 per cent (0.80% in Habbakadal, 2.09% in Tral, 3.09% in Pampore, 3.20% in Zadibal, 3.20% in Amirakadal, 3.30% in Bijbehara, 4.50% in Khanyar, 4.79% in Idgah and 4.81% in Homeshalibugh) and another five segments between 5 per cent to 10 per cent (5.22% in Batmaloo, 5.63% in Pulwama, 6.48% in Anantnag, 8.85% in Srinagar and 9.37% in Kulgam).

the separatist politics continued to assert itself in its own way. The parallel existence of the two spheres of politics was clearly recognizable. However, the two spheres did not remain untouched by each other. The mainstream politics was clearly bringing to its core the separatist issues and agenda and also at the same time acknowledging the relevance of separatist politics.

One of the strategies used by the PDP from the beginning to gain legitimacy for its politics within the overall separatist environment was to draw a distinction between the mainstream and separatist politics, and in the process emphasizing the relevance of each of the two spheres without any contradiction between the two. While the mainstream politics was supposed to deal with the 'day-to-day' issues of 'governance', the separatist politics was to deal with 'long-term' issues linked with the conflict and its resolution. By drawing a self-imposed limitation on the mainstream politics to the issues of 'governance' only and by leaving the sphere of conflict politics open to the separatists, the party was able to chalk a role for itself within the larger context of separatism. This distinction also made it easier for the common people to be involved in the mainstream politics. With no contradiction between their act of voting or getting involved in the electoral politics, on the one hand, and their separatist sentiments, on the other, they could participate in both the spheres of politics and easily switch from one sphere to another. Interestingly, this distinction was accepted by the separatists as well and they would many times acknowledge the extension of the democratic space by arguing that the people needed to fulfil the day-to-day needs related to jobs, roads, water and electricity, etc., and participation in such activities did not mean that the larger 'Kashmir cause' was being sidelined.

This explains the blurring of boundaries between the separatist and the mainstream politics at many places. Such blurring could be seen in the period of elections as the voters would often assert their separatist sentiments while exercising their right to vote. Similarly, the political actors in the mainstream politics also referred to separatism and separatists while being involved in the electioneering process. To give an example from Mehbooba Mufti's election campaign during 2004 Parliamentary elections, she not only referred to Hizbul

Mujahideen's role in Kashmir's politics but also called for dialogue with it on that basis. She stated that it 'is the strongest and local militant organization. Its involvement is imperative for a breakthrough in the solution of Kashmir issue and restoration of the peace with honour' (*Kashmir Times* 13 April 2004, cited in Chowdhary and Rao 2004a, 5455).

The blurring of boundaries was also reflected in the smooth alternation between the two kinds of politics. One could see in the later period as to how the political environment easily could transcend from one sphere to the other. The thriving democratic space, for instance, in the wake of ensuing Assembly poll in 2008 was completely transformed during the Amarnath agitation in the intense separatist mode, and the separatist mood of this agitation gave way to democratic politics when the 2008 Assembly election took place immediately after the agitation.

It was in this context of overlapping roles of the separatist and democratic politics that there was a gradual deepening of democratic politics which was clearly reflected in the 'normalization' of the electoral politics. The 2005 elections for the urban bodies (being held for the first time in 28 years), for instance, were much different from the Panchayat elections held in 2001 in the extreme condition of violence. So enthused was the response of the voters during the 2005 elections that it forced the separatists to issue a boycott call for these. Four separatist organizations, namely the Jammu and Kashmir High Court Bar Association (JKHCBA), Jammu and Kashmir Democratic Freedom Party (JKDFP), JKLF and Jammu and Kashmir Jamiat-e-Ahlihadees (JKAH) issued a joint statement terming the election as a 'useless exercise' and appealed to people to boycott it (*Daily Excelsior* 2005). The militant organizations meanwhile 'had pasted posters warning political leaders and the public of retribution in case of non-compliance with their boycott call' (Ministry of Home Affairs 2005). These elections also witnessed intensified militant violence as many of the candidates contesting election were attacked. These attacks continued after the election as well resulting in the killing of few prominent elected members of the civic bodies. Such was the impact of the militant violence after the elections that there started the 'resignation spree' with elected councillors publicly submitting their 'apologies' for having contested the elections.

Despite the separatist mobilization and militants' threats of violence, there was a very enthusiastic response to the electoral process. Apart from the keen contests, there were also a reasonably fair voter turnout. With the exception of Srinagar district which had 20 per cent voter turnout,[19] other districts registered a fairly high voter turnout. Around 80 per cent voters turnout out to vote (Ministry of Home Affairs 2005).

The electoral enthusiasm was, in no way, seen as a rejection of separatist politics even by the mainstream political leaders. With the boundaries being clearly drawn between the 'politics of governance' and the 'politics of conflict resolution', the mainstream political leaders at no point of time sought to claim the victory over the separatist sphere of politics or to declare its irrelevance.

It was this self-imposed limitation of the scope of the competitive politics that was helping the change in the ground-level response towards the democratic politics. This change was clearly reflected during the by-elections to the Assembly for four constituencies (including three in northern Kashmir—Rafiabad, Pattan and Sangrama) in 2006. Compared to the 2002 Assembly election, there was greater enthusiasm for the electoral process and much higher voter turnout.[20] The positive orientation of people towards the electoral process was reflected from the long queues that they formed in the election booths and their willingness to vote despite the militant violence. In Sangrama constituency, there was a grenade attack and voting was suspended for some time. But not only the people came back to vote but also protested against the militant attack. The same was the situation in Pattan which also witnessed a grenade attack on the day of voting (Chowdhary and Rao 2006, 1965).

[19] Srinagar has had a history of following the boycott, and even in this election, there were a large number of areas where the call for boycott was followed. But even so the 20 per cent vote from here was unprecedented.

[20] While Rafiabad recorded 75.7 per cent voter turnout (as against 52.54%), Pattan recorded 69.23 per cent (compared to 41.55%) and Sangrama recorded 63.83 per cent voters (compared to 22.10%).

By the time the 2008 Assembly election was organized, the democratic space was quite entrenched. This was despite the fact that this election was preceded by a massive separatist upsurge (over Amarnath land issue) that lasted for almost the whole of summer that year. During the period of upsurge, the Valley was swayed towards the separatist politics pushing the democratic politics to the margins. The situation was so grave that mainstream political actors were forced to withdraw from the political scene. As already stated, the situation was reminiscent of the early period of militancy when there was a clear sway of separatist politics with no scope, whatsoever, for mainstream politics. There were similar breakdown of the authority of the state and similar kind of mass response.

The assertion of separatist politics notwithstanding, the democratic space was restored soon after the Amarnath agitation subsided and 2008 Assembly election was announced. The electoral exercise, on the whole, was much more effective than the 2002 Assembly election.[21] There was full-scale electioneering with parties and candidates being active in the public space, and with election rallies, meetings and door-to-door campaigning going on in full steam.[22] The participation of the people in the electioneering process was also quite intense. This was not the situation during the 2002 Assembly election. The CSDS data of the 2002 and 2008 post-poll surveys reveals that the involvement of people in the election process was certainly much higher during the 2008 Assembly election. As per this data, while 25.2 per cent respondents had stated in 2002 that 'during the election campaign any candidate, party worker or party campaigner came to their house to ask for vote', the percentage had increased to 38.5 per cent in 2008. The percentage of respondents in Kashmir who took interest in election campaign had also increased, as against 32 per cent respondents in 2002 to 46.1 per cent in 2008.

With their confidence boosted by the Amarnath agitation, the separatists had given a call for poll boycott; however, no one paid heed to

[21] This was the first such election since 1987 which was not affected by violence. Unlike the earlier elections, the level of violence was quite low.

[22] The extended space for democratic politics was reflected in 2007 itself. In anticipation of the ensuing elections in 2008, Kashmir had become quite vibrant with electioneering process. Parties started organizing huge rallies in all parts of the Valley.

it. As per a news report, more than 400 electoral rallies were held in different parts of the Valley, some of them in the remote areas.[23] The voter participation was also very high (see Table 5.1). With the overall voter turnout of 51.59 per cent compared to the 30 per cent in 2002, the level of participation in all the 10 districts of Kashmir Valley was much higher than that in the 2002 Assembly election. While the districts of Kupwara and Badgam, which had shown higher voter turnout in 2002, significantly improved the percentage of votes cast (68.04% and 62.42%, respectively, as against 53.22% and 45.92%, respectively, in 2002), the districts where there was poor voter turnout in 2002 had also improved the voter turnout very significantly. It was only the erstwhile Srinagar district (now divided into two districts of Srinagar and Ganderbal) which had shown some impact of the boycott call. Here the voter turnout was lowest (28.21%) However, compared to 11.18 per cent votes cast in 2002, this was certainly a much improved situation. There were a number of constituencies within Kashmir

Table 5.1 *Voter Turnout in Kashmir Valley: 2002 and 2008 Assembly Elections*

District	Voter Turnout in 2002 (%)	Voter Turnout in 2008 (%)
Kupwara	53.22	68.04
Badgam	45.92	62.42
Erstwhile Baramulla (Now Baramulla and Bandipur)	39.94	51.20
Erstwhile Anantnag (Now Anantnag and Kulgam)	24.06	63.70
Erstwhile Pulwama (Now Pulwama and Shopian)	23.68	52.73
Erstwhile Srinagar (Now Srinagar and Ganderbal)	11.18	28.21

Source: Election Commission of India.

[23] As reported by the *Statesman*, as many as 406 election rallies were held in Kashmir Valley (*The Statesman* 2008).

where the voter turnout was exceptionally high (ranging from above 80% to above 60%).[24]

One of the reasons offered by the people for their participation was 'voting for governance'. While many asserted voting as their right which needs to be used rather than wasted, there were others who gave the response in the context of basic needs such as roads, water and electricity. With all the difficulties that people were facing in terms of basic infrastructure, it was felt that these problems could be resolved only by the government. Hence boycott was no option at all.[25]

On the whole, the election gained legitimacy. There were no complaints about rigging or intimidation. The CSDS 2008 post-poll data also indicated that in common perception the level of rigging was quite less as compared to the earlier ones. While 40.1 per cent respondents said that they couldn't say anything, 37.2 per cent respondents said there was no rigging at all. Only 6.4 per cent respondents stated that there was large-scale rigging and another 16.3 per cent stated that there was some rigging. On being asked if rigging was more or less than the 2002 elections, only 2.7 per cent said that it was much more than previous elections, while 24.8 per cent in Kashmir said that it was less than previous elections. 11 per cent said that it was same as earlier elections.

To conclude, it can be argued that while separatism continued to sustain itself during the 2002–2008 period, democratic space had also become entrenched. The two spheres of politics—the separatist politics and the mainstream politics—were coexisting side by side without endangering each other. In order to survive, the democratic politics had not challenged the exclusivity of the separatist politics.

[24] Apart from Uri which recorded above 80 per cent voter turnout, there were other constituencies such as Karnah (79.66%), Handwara (75.60%), Khansahib (74.73%), Chrar-e-Sharief (74.58%), Noorabad (74.29%), Gurez (74.02%), Kokernag (70.35%) and Pahalgam (70.25%). There were many other constituencies which recorded more than 60 per cent voter turnout: Doru (69.83%), Shangus (69.29%), Devsar (68.42%), Lola (68.16%), Kupwara (62.44%), Kulgam (61.64%) and Langate (61.34%).

[25] As per a news report in the *Indian Express*, this was one of the responses of a voter: 'We don't have electric poles here—the wires are tied to willows. We have 22 taps in the village, but only two of these function. We want all this.' He added that abstaining from polling is no longer a choice (*The Indian Express* 2008).

Even if the separatist agenda was brought to the democratic space, the separatist sphere of politics was kept intact.[26] This was clearly reflected after the 2008 elections when another phase of separatist assertion started taking shape. Throughout the year 2009 and particularly in the summer of 2010 there was massive separatist assertion. While the alleged murder and rape of two women in Shopian became the reason for the anti-state demonstrations in 2009, the allegations of fake encounters became the basis of upsurge in 2010. The situation of 2010 was quite a repeat of the 2008 agitation and saw the total sidelining of the democratic processes. During the five months when such separatist assertion was taking place, the authority of the state was completely defied. The Valley resounded with anti-India slogans and all routine economic, educational and even governmental activities had come to be totally stalled. It was only by late 2010 and early 2011 that the political order was completely restored and mainstream politics could find a space for itself once more. That this space was not completely lost could be clearly seen during the Panchayati elections that were organized in 2011. Despite severe threats by the militants and killings of candidates, the elections saw more than 80 per cent voter turnout.

References

Ahmad, Mukhtar. 1999, 28 July. 'Mufti Floats New Regional Party in Kashmir'. rediff.com, http://www.rediff.com/news/1999/jul/28mufti.htm (accessed on 8 November 2017).

Ahmed, Aijaz. 2000, 22 July. 'Kashmir Conundrum'. *Frontline* 17 (15). http://www.hindu.com/fline/fl1715/17151090.htm

Behera, Navnita Chadha. 2006. *Demystifying Kashmir*. Washington, D.C.: Brookings Institution Press.

Bose, Sumantra. 2003. *Kashmir: Roots of Conflict, Paths to Peace*. Cambridge, MA: Harvard University Press.

Bukhari, Shujat. 2003, 9 February. 'Geelani's Release, Shot in the Arm for Mufti Govt.' *The Hindu*. http://www.jammu-kashmir.com/archives/archives2003/kashmir20030209c.html (accessed on 31 August 2018).

[26] That the separatist space was intact was clearly reflected in the CSDS data during the 2008 post-poll survey. On being asked whether they will support Hurriyat if they participate in election, 51 per cent respondents in Kashmir said they will support it (11.1% opposed and 17% responded that it makes no difference). Meanwhile, around 60 per cent respondents in Kashmir felt that Hurriyat's decision not to participate in elections was justified (46.1% fully justified and 14.1% somewhat justified).

Bukhari, Shujat. 2006, 28 October. 'PDP Unveils Self-Rule Formula for Kashmir'. *The Hindu*. http://www.jammu-kashmir.com/archives/archives2006/kashmir20061028c.html (accessed on 31 August 2018).

———. 2006a, 22 August. 'Farooq Favours Dialogue with Hizb'. *The Hindu*. https://www.thehindu.com/todays-paper/tp-national/tp-otherstates/farooq-favours-dialogue-with-hizb/article3094459.ece (accessed on 4 November 2018).

Chowdhary, Rekha. 2000, 22–28 July. 'Autonomy Demand: Kashmir at Crossroads'. *Economic & Political Weekly* 35 (30): 2599–2603.

———. 2008, 12 July. 'Electioneering in Kashmir: Overlap between Separatist and Mainstream Political Space'. *Economic and Political Weekly* 43 (28): 22–25.

———. 2014. 'India's Response to the Kashmir Insurgency: A Holistic Perspective'. In *Insurgency and Counter-Insurgency in South Asia*, edited by Moeed Yusuf. Washington, DC: USIP Press Books.

Chowdhary, Rekha, and V. Nagendra Rao. 2003, January–June. 'Jammu and Kashmir: Political Alienation, Regional Divergence and Communal Polarisation in Jammu and Kashmir'. *Journal of Indian School of Political Economy* 15 (1–2): 189–219.

———. 2003a, 4 January. 'Elections 2002: Implications for Politics of Separatism'. *Economic & Political Weekly* 38 (1): 15–21.

———. 2004, 3–10 April. 'National Conference of Jammu and Kashmir: From Hegemonic to Competitive Politics'. *Economic & Political Weekly* 39 (14): 1521–1527.

———. 2004a, 18 December. 'Jammu and Kashmir: Electoral Politics in a Separatist Context'. *Economic & Political Weekly* 39 (51): 5449–5455.

———. 2006, 20 May. 'Jammu and Kashmir: Changed Political Scenario'. *Economic & Political Weekly* 41 (20): 1963–1965.

Daily Excelsior. 1999, 3 September. 'Kashmiris Can't Be Exploited with Green Flags: Umar'. http://www.jammu-kashmir.com/archives/archives1999/99september03.html (accessed on 17 October 2016).

———. 2000, 2 November. 'Mufti Asks PM to Initiate Dialogue on Kashmir'. http://www.jammu-kashmir.com/archives/archives2000/kashmir20001102b.html (accessed on 4 November 2018).

———. 2004, 30 May. 'National Conference Changed Discourse, Farooq Asks Manmohan Govt to Talk to Hurriyat Leaders'. http://www.jammu-kashmir.com/archives/archives2004/kashmir20040530c.html (accessed on 31 August 2018).

———. 2005, 10 January. 'Separatists Appeal for Boycott of Polls'. http://www.jammu-kashmir.com/archives/archives2005/kashmir20050110d.html (accessed on 31 August 2018).

———. 2005a, 30 January. 'Heavy Turnout in Polls Should Be Eye-Opener for Hurriyat: Baig'. http://www.jammu-kashmir.com/archives/archives2005/kashmir20050130b.html (accessed on 31 August 2018).

Donthi, Praveen. 2016, 1 January. 'The Collaborator'. *The Caravan*. http://www.caravanmagazine.in/reportage/the-collaborator-mufti-mohammed-sayeed (accessed on 31 August 2018).

Fayyaz, Ahmed Ali. 2003, 24 January. 'Mufti Killing "Freedom Movement" in the Name of Healing Touch: Hizb'. *Daily Excelsior*. http://www.jammu-kashmir.com/archives/archives2003/kashmir20030124a.html

Gilani, Iftikhar. 2004, 26 February. 'India Tells Kashmir Forces to Exercise Caution in Operations'. *The Daily Times*. http://www.jammu-kashmir.com/archives/archives2004/kashmir20040226c.html (accessed on 31 August 2018).

———. 2006, 30 January. 'PDP Wants Kashmir Fiscal Autonomy'. *The Daily Times*. http://www.jammu-kashmir.com/archives/archives2006/kashmir20060130a.html (accessed on 31 August 2018).

———. 2016, 8 January. 'Mufti Mohammed Sayeed: A Master Politician Who Tried to Nurture a True Indian Constituency in Kashmir'. *DNA*. http://www.dnaindia.com/india/report-mufti-mohammad-sayeed-a-master-politician-who-tried-to-nurture-true-indian-constituency-in-kashmir-2163383 (accessed on 31 August 2018).

Greater Kashmir. 2008, 15 April. 'Mufti's Joint Currency Draws Joint Flak'. http://www.jammu-kashmir.com/archives/archives2008/kashmir20080415c.html (accessed on 4 November 2018).

Indo-Asian News Service. 2006, 18 September. 'Mufti Calls for Time-Bound CBMS'. http://www.jammu-kashmir.com/archives/archives2006/kashmir20060918c.html (accessed on 31 August 2018).

Islah, Mufti. 2002, 30 October. 'They Hope Mehbooba Will Bring Them Justice'. *The Indian Express*. http://www.jammu-kashmir.com/archives/archives2002/kashmir20021030d.html (accessed on 31 August 2018).

Jameel, Muzamil. 2005, 15 February. 'Valley Winners Say Sorry to Militants'. *The Indian Express*. http://www.jammu-kashmir.com/archives/archives2005/kashmir20050215d.html (accessed on 31 August 2018).

Ministry of Home Affairs. 2005. *Annual Report 2004–2005*. https://mha.gov.in/sites/default/files/ar0405-Eng.pdf (accessed on 4 November 2018).

Mody, Anjali. 2002, 10 October. 'Observers Laud Conduct of J&K Assembly Elections'. *The Hindu*. http://www.thehindu.com/2002/10/10/stories/2002101005311100.htm

NDTV. 2008, 19 April. 'Anti-India Rhetorics in J&K Poll Campaign'. http://www.jammu-kashmir.com/archives/archives2008/kashmir20080419b.html (accessed on 31 August 2018).

Reuters. 2004, 1 March. 'Rebels Urge Kashmiris to Boycott Indian Election'. http://www.jammu-kashmir.com/archives/archives2004/kashmir20040301d.html (accessed on 31 August 2018).

SATP. 2002, 27 October. 'Common Minimum Programme of the Congress-I, People's Democratic Party Coalition Government in Jammu and Kashmir'. http://www.satp.org/satporgtp/countries/india/states/jandk/documents/papers/kashmir_CMP.htm (accessed on 8 November 2017).

Swami, Parveen. 2003, 27 September–10 October. 'Death of a General'. *Frontline* 20 (20) http://www.frontline.in/static/html/fl2020/stories/20031010003203400.htm

Syed, Firdous. 2007, 9 September. 'Straight Lines: Real Feelings, False Expressions'. https://www.countercurrents.org/syed090907.htm (accessed on 4 November 2018).

The Asian Age. 2002. 5 November. 'Mufti for Ceasefire during Ramzan'. http://www.jammu-kashmir.com/archives/archives2002/kashmir20021105b.html (accessed on 31 August 2018).

———. 2004, 28 April. 'Farooq Speech Leaves J&K Speechless'. http://www.jammu-kashmir.com/archives/archives2004/kashmir20040428b.html (accessed on 31 August 2018).

The Hindustan Times. 2002, 4 December. 'Strict Action against Custodial Death: Mehbooba'. http://www.jammu-kashmir.com/archives/archives2002/kashmir20021204d.html (accessed on 31 August 2018).

The Indian Express. 2002, 13 November. 'Mufti to Go Ahead with Release of Prisoners'. http://www.jammu-kashmir.com/archives/archives2002/kashmir20021113d.html (accessed on 31 August 2018).

———. 2003, 20 August. 'PM Opening Hurriyat Door: Mufti'. http://www.jammu-kashmir.com/archives/archives2003/kashmir20030820d.html (accessed on 31 August 2018).

———. 2005, 14 February. 'Fear of Death Has J&K Councillors Refuse Their Jobs'. http://www.jammu-kashmir.com/archives/archives2005/kashmir20050214c.html (accessed on 31 August 2018).

———. 2008, 17 December. 'Militancy, Boycott No Deterrent, 64% Cast Vote'. http://www.jammu-kashmir.com/archives/archives2008/kashmir20081217b.html (accessed on 31 August 2018).

The Statesman. 2002, 27 October. 'Mufti Prefers Unconditional Talks to Guns'. http://www.jammu-kashmir.com/archives/archives2002/kashmir20021027c.html (accessed on 31 August 2018).

———. 2008, 12 November. '862 Rallies Ahead of Polls in J&K'. http://www.jammu-kashmir.com/archives/archives2008/kashmir20081112d.html (accessed on 31 August 2018).

The Times of India. 2002, 15 August. 'Full Text of Prime Minister's Independence Day Speech'. https://timesofindia.indiatimes.com/india/Full-text-of-Prime-Ministers-Independence-Day-speech/articleshow/19165614.cms (accessed on 7 November 2017).

———. 2004, 1 February. 'J&K Govt Okays Rehab Policy for Militants'. http://www.jammu-kashmir.com/archives/archives2004/kashmir20040201d.html (accessed on 31 August 2018).

———. 2004a, 8 September. 'NC Ready to Drop Autonomy Demand if There's Acceptable Solution'. http://www.jammu-kashmir.com/archives/archives2004/kashmir20040908d.html (accessed on 31 August 2018).

———. 2004b, 30 December. 'NC Block President, BSF Man, 2 Ultras Shot Dead'. http://www.jammu-kashmir.com/archives/archives2004/kashmir20041230d.html (accessed on 31 August 2018).

6

Competitive Politics in Jammu and Kashmir

The democratic politics of the state, for a very long time, was defined by a very restrictive nature of competition. With a single party dominating the power politics, there was not much space for articulation of discontent. From the perspective of conflict situation, this had serious implications, especially for Kashmir region where separatist politics had become entrenched right in the early 1950s. In the absence of any oppositional space within the mainstream politics, the separatist politics was also substituting for the oppositional parties and in the process it was legitimizing and extending itself.

With Sheikh Abdullah joining power in 1975, there was a shift in the nature of politics. The separatist sphere of politics was pushed to the margins and there was expansion of the democratic political space. At the level of the state, the element of competition was introduced and apart from the NC, there were other parties like the Congress and the Janata Party that made the 1977 Assembly election quite vibrant. However, the nature of competition was more at the interregional level. Within Kashmir region, the hegemonic control of the ruling party was maintained. The NC remained the only choice for the people during the election. It was only in 1999 that the hegemony of the NC was challenged with the emergence of the PDP as another Kashmir-based regional party.

By 2002, the paradigm of the party politics was substantially changed both at the state and regional levels. While the NC lost its dominance in the Assembly election, the electoral space became highly competitive. With people finding an effective choice between the two regional parties, that is, the NC and PDP, the democratic space in

Kashmir region became sufficiently vibrant. This also had implications for the competitive politics at the state level as well, where, besides the NC, the PDP and Congress also started making claims for political power. By 2014 Assembly election, the BJP had also become an effective stakeholder in the power politics.

The paradigm shift in the competitive politics since 2002, therefore, not only made the regional politics of Kashmir more democratic but also brought in greater regional parity at the state level. As no single party could win clear majority, the coalition governments that were formed reflected regional representations. All coalitions since 2002 have represented an alliance between a Kashmir-based political party and a Jammu-based political party.

THE PARTY AND ELECTORAL POLITICS PRIOR TO 2002

NATURE OF THE PARTY POLITICS

The competitive politics prior to 2002 was defined by the dominance of the NC at the state level. Revived in 1975 following the Indira–Sheikh Accord, this party exercised a hegemonic control over the regional politics of Kashmir. While some space for oppositional politics started evolving in post-1975 phase, it was located mainly in Jammu region. In Kashmir's mainstream politics, there was complete monopoly of the NC. Dominating the politics of the state as a whole it also remained the only viable party in the power politics of the state (Chowdhary and Rao 2004).

However, the party politics as it existed in post-1975 differed a lot from the one that was available in the pre-1975 period, characterized as it was by the total absence of the opposition and no basis for electoral competition. However, despite the dominance of the NC during the 1977 Assembly election, there was a multiplicity of political parties. Besides the Congress which was a vibrant party in Jammu region, there were other parties like the Janata Party which also occupied a significant space in that region. It is because of these parties that both the 1977 and 1983 Assembly elections were quite competitive. However, the competition was at interregional level and it neither affected the hegemonic role of NC in Kashmir region nor its dominance in the power politics. The NC continued to dominate the power politics of the state up to the 1996 Assembly election. By this time, many other political parties had captured the electoral space in Jammu region: BJP, BSP, Janata Dal and Jammu Kashmir Panthers Party (JKPP).

What therefore remained the peculiarity of the party politics of the state was that the two major regions of the state followed altogether different patterns. While Kashmir continued to reflect a hegemonic control of the single party, Jammu's party politics reflected a multiplicity of parties and fragmentation of the electoral space. One of the major implications of these differences was that despite the competition, the dominance of the NC party was sustained. Its hegemonic control over Kashmir's regional politics, on the one hand, and Jammu's fragmented politics, on the other, helped it to continue holding power without any challenge.

Another implication of this kind of party politics was lack of parity between the two regions. Since the NC's access to power emanated mainly from its control over Kashmir's electoral politics, electoral equation from Jammu region did not matter that much, and for that reason, the political elite of this region nursed a major grievance of 'political neglect' and 'deprivation' from power politics. All this was to change with the 2002 Assembly election.

Electoral Politics in 1970s and 1980s: 1977 and 1983 Assembly Elections

In the history of the state politics of J&K, the Assembly election of 1977 is seen to be politically very significant. This was the first such election which developed the reputation of being fair. This reputation had more to do with the nature of competition rather than with the actual management of the election. The election had been organized in the background of the political bitterness between the NC and Congress. The Congress that had taken the initiative to support the minority NC government following the Indira–Sheikh accord in 1975 had withdrawn its support in March 1977 and forced the mid-term polls. The keen competition between the NC and Congress therefore was one of the major features of this election. Competition had become much more intense with the newly floated Janata Party (that had swept the national election only a few months back) joining the fray (Verma 1994, 127).

The intensity of competition was matched by the enthusiasm of voters, especially in Kashmir Valley. The Congress party's withdrawal of support to the Sheikh-led NC government earlier was seen as an act of 'betrayal' against the Kashmiris as a political community.[1] The NC therefore could sweep this region winning as many as 39 of the 42 Assembly seats. It also emerged as the dominant party of the state winning as many as 47 of the 76 seats.

What was peculiar about the 1977 Assembly election was that despite the dominance of the NC, for the first time there emerged a solid opposition. On the whole 25 seats were captured by the opposition parties: Janata Party (13), Congress (11) and Jamaat-e-Islami (1). However, rather than being spread all over the state, the opposition was mostly located in Jammu region. Thus of the 25 seats, only three seats were obtained in Kashmir region. (Of these three seats, two went to Congress and one to Jamaat-e-Islami.)

As against the hegemonic control of the NC in Kashmir, Jammu's electoral space had become quite fragmented: Janata Party (11), Congress (10), NC (7) and Independents (4). The two seats of Ladakh were also equally divided between the NC and the Congress.

The 1977 Assembly election set the trends for the party politics of the state for the next two decades. Despite the multiplicity of parties and increased competitiveness, there was a dominance of a single party in the power politics.

The 1983 Assembly election was also highly competitive with a very bitterly organized campaign both on the part of the NC and the Congress party (Singh 1995, 25–35). Like the 1977 Assembly election, the nature of competition was interregional—between the NC with its stronghold in Kashmir and Congress with its base in Jammu region.

[1] Following the Indira–Sheikh Accord, the support of Congress was pledged to the NC. This party had only four members in the Legislature.

The bitterness that had developed between the two parties during the 1977 Assembly election had intensified by this time, specifically after Farooq Abdullah, who had succeeded Sheikh as the leader of the NC, had refused to have any kind of electoral alliance with the Congress. As a result, in Kashmir, the NC invoked the Kashmiri identity and sought people's support to fight the 'intrusive' tendencies of the Centre; in Jammu, the Congress party mobilized voters around the issue of 'extremist' and 'separatist' tendencies of the NC. It was in this process that a regional-cum-communal polarization was created between 'Muslim Kashmir' and 'Hindu Jammu'. In Jammu especially, there started a process of consolidation of 'Hindu constituency' (Ganguly 1997, 83). All earlier attempts to carve such a Hindu constituency by the Bharatiya Jana Sangh had failed. This party, despite its claim to represent Jammu Hindus, had failed to make a mark in the electoral arena and could not extend its influence beyond a point and could never win more than three seats. However, the Congress, during this election, using its religious and nationalist card, could win as many as 22 seats (Chowdhary and Rao 2003, 202).

The logic of the electoral campaign of the NC was equally communal. To counter the influence of Congress party in Hindu-dominated constituencies, it sought to extend its influence among the Muslim-populated areas of Jammu region. As a consequence, the political response of this region got polarized on communal basis. While the Congress got its maximum support in this region from predominantly Hindu-populated areas, the NC got its share of seats from the areas with large Muslim population (Puri 1987, 836). Thus Haveli and Mendhar (Poonch district), Rajouri (Rajouri district), Inderwal, Banihal (Doda district) and Gulabgarh (Udhampur district)—all constituencies with overwhelming Muslim population—went to the NC (Verma 1994).

Despite the intensity of competition during the 1983 Assembly election, the overall nature of the state's politics continued to be defined by the dominance of the NC. Notwithstanding the solid opposition within the Legislative Assembly (Congress having its presence with one-third of the total strength of the Assembly), there was a massive presence of the NC. This was mainly due to the fact that the electoral space of Kashmir region was totally controlled by this party. The implication of such a control of the NC on the politics of Kashmir was that it was able to win massive majority within the state and continue its dominance over the state politics.

Muslim United Front and 1987 Assembly Election

The emergence of MUF in 1986 had thrown up the possibility of an alternate regional party of Kashmir which could have given some challenge to the hegemony of the NC in this region. It was a conglomeration of a number of parties that was led by Jamaat-e-Islami and had been formed in the context of the political vacuum created due to the NC's alliance with the Congress. The NC till now had represented the most credible anti-Centre voice in Kashmir. With its joining force with the Congress in 1986, following the Rajiv–Farooq Accord, it could no longer represent that voice. Seeking to fill this vacuum, the Jamaat had taken the initiative to organize the MUF.

Jamaat had its presence in Kashmir since 1942 but it could not find much space in Kashmir's politics. In 1971, in the face of the possibility of Plebiscite Front participating the Assembly election through its proxies, it was encouraged by the Congress-led Central Government to contest the election (Puri 1987, 835). While the Plebiscite Front was banned and could not participate in the elections, the Jamaat was able to win five Assembly seats. However, once the NC was revived, the electoral space of Jamaat was restricted and it could not register its presence in more than one seat during the 1977 Assembly election. However, in the context of the deep discontent in Kashmir owing to NC's alliance with Congress in 1986, the Jamaat was able to extend its political space. It took the lead first to form the United Muslim Front but later named it as MUF. Apart from the Jamaat, the other components of the MUF were Ummat-e-Islam, Anjuman-Ittehad-ul-Muslimeen the Islamic Study Circle, the Muslim Education Trust, the Muslim Welfare Society, Islamic Jammat-i-Tulba, Majlis Tahafuzul-ul-Islam, Mahaz-i-Azadi, Jamiat-ul-Hadis, Shia Rabita Committee and Idara Tahquiqat Islami (Verma 1994, 76). Many of these organizations were affiliated with the Jamaat itself.

What was peculiar about the MUF was that in providing an alternative to the NC, it made the use of religion and brought it to the centre of Kashmir's political discourse. Its constitution clearly specified that it would not involve itself with any 'non-Muslim political activity' (Swami 2006, 159). Among various concerns shown by the party, many were related to the moral and religious culture of Kashmir. Political consolidation of Muslims within the state was its major agenda and it had Jammu Muslims as its special focus, and therefore made various demands on their behalf including those related to their social and educational upliftment (Chowdhary and Rao 2003, 193).

Entry of MUF in the regional politics of Kashmir animated the political environment in the Valley.[2] Facing the NC–Congress alliance, this conglomerate along with the People's Conference and Awami National Conference (these two organizations backed MUF while remaining out of it) targeted the discontent at the ground level to mobilize people in their favour. While issues such as unemployment particularly of educated youth, lack of opportunities of economic development, corruption and discrimination against the Muslim youth in matters of admissions to educational and professional institutions marked the agenda of campaign of this organization, it also focused on issues related to conflict situation. Its manifesto 'stressed the need for solution to all outstanding issues according to the Simla Agreement. It also assured the voters that it will work for Islamic unity and against political interference from the Centre' (Schofield 2000, 137).

Contradictory to the popular perceptions of a higher number of electoral returns of the MUF, the conglomerate could win only four seats in Kashmir compared to 38 seats by the NC–Congress alliance (32 for NC and 6 for Congress). This was despite the fact that it was successful in making a huge dent in the share of votes of the NC. As against the 60 per cent vote-share of the NC, the MUF and its associates could get around 38 per cent share of votes in Kashmir.

[2] While the emotions and expectations were raised, the overall level of participation was very high. This was one of those elections which saw higher voter turnout in Kashmir (74%) as compared to Jammu region (69%). There were as many as 22 constituencies where the voter turnout was still higher—more than 80 per cent.

The mismatch between the popular expectations about the performance of the MUF and the formal outcome of the elections resulted in huge disappointment and anger in Kashmir. In a situation in which the political emotions of people were highly surcharged, the election result led to lot of anger. There were charges of rigging and manipulation. As the election data would show, there were certain glaring anomalies[3] (Chowdhary et al. 2007).

At the state level, the NC–Congress alliance had dominated the electoral scene with 66/76 seats being captured by it and more than 2/3 share of votes. At a regional level, the Congress emerged as the biggest party of Jammu region with 20 seats, followed by the NC which got seven seats and BJP which got two seats. Of the two seats of Ladakh, one was captured by the NC and the other by the Congress. What was peculiar about this election in Jammu was that apart from Congress and NC, BJP had increased its vote share from 8.21 per cent in 1983 to 12.37 per cent in this election. Meanwhile, there was also the entry of Panthers Party. Its total share of votes in the region was 2.61 per cent.

It was the disappointment with the electoral outcome in Kashmir valley that ultimately gave way to militancy and separatism. The election got the infamous reputation of being highly rigged. It was after this election that democratic space got completely eroded and for the next one and half decade or so, the electoral process continued to suffer from the acute legitimacy crisis. One of the reasons for such legitimacy crisis was the absence of real competitive spirit in Kashmir region. More the electoral politics was controlled by one party, less was the connect between the political parties and the voters. Despite the fact that the NC was sweeping the elections with massive mandate and huge majorities, it failed to enthuse the voters. On the part of the

[3] While there were certain constituencies with as low a margin of victory as 100, 122 and 336 votes (Bijbehera, Wachi and Shopian, respectively—all NC victories), there were a number of constituencies where there was very high proportion of invalid votes (6.7% in Doru; 5.6% in Chrar-e-Sharief; 4.9% in Homeshalibug; 4.8% in Wachi; 4.8 per cent in Sangrama; 4.5% in Amirakadal; 4.2% in Handwara). What was further intriguing a fact was that in most of the constituencies where the margin of victory was very small, there was higher number of invalid votes. Thus for a 100 margin victory in Bijbehera, 1,177 votes were declared invalid; for 122 margin victory of Wachi, 1,806 votes were declared invalid; and for 136 vote margin victory in Shopian, 1,122 votes were declared invalid (Chowdhary and Rao 2003, 194).

NC, it was in such a comfortable position without any competition that it failed to invest its politics on building grassroots support base. In the absence of any other party, it could easily take its electoral support for granted. Its major concern remained managing its relationship with the Centre.

The party politics as it operated in Kashmir therefore had a lot to contribute to the political discontent and alienation as it got manifested in post-1980 period. The absence of a really competitive politics had not only created the disconnect between the people and the democratic politics but also had allowed the dominant party to degenerate from a progressive pro-people and policy-oriented party to a corrupt and power-seeking one that stopped being sensitive to popular responses.

As compared to Kashmir region, the politics of Jammu region had acquired competitiveness, with political space being shared by the Congress, NC, BJP and other parties. Such competitiveness was, in a significant way, a reflection of Jammu's complex pluralities. Since the decade of the seventies, the electoral politics had started reflecting the internal heterogeneity and faultiness along the subregional, religious, caste and tribal lines with different patterns of voters' responses. The most visible divide in this region was between the predominantly Hindu-dominated, relatively more urbanized districts of Jammu (now Samba and Jammu), Kathua and also Udhampur (partially, at least), on the one hand, and the peripheral and backward Muslim-majority districts of Doda (now Doda, Kishtwar and Ramban) and bordered districts of Poonch and Rajouri, on the other. Besides the subregional and religious identities, the logic of the politics of this area is defined by the strong caste (Rajput vs Brahmin and Dalit) and tribal (Gujjar vs Pahari) identities.

However, despite such competitiveness, there was a different kind of discontent in this region which had much to do with its fragmented electoral outcome, on the one hand, and the token presence of regional political elite in power politics, on the other. With the dominant party having a comfortable position due to its full control of the political space in Kashmir, it could always form government without needing the support from Jammu region. Hence, the general refrain in Jammu regarding the electoral politics has been its 'Kashmir-dominated' nature.

Like Jammu, the electoral politics of Ladakh has also been impacted by the regional discontent. This discontent articulated by Ladakh Buddhist Association and later by the political parties operating from the region having taken the form of the demand of separation from the state with a UT status has often been reflected in the electoral politics as well.

1996 Assembly Election

The 1996 Assembly election, which was held after a long break of seven years, continued with the tradition of the single-party dominance at the state level. Like earlier elections, the NC had its hegemonic control over the electoral space in Kashmir and a dominant position within the State Assembly (see Table 6.1).

The NC that had been approached by the Central Government to reclaim its political space in Kashmir and even promised autonomy to facilitate its re-entry in Kashmir's politics contested the election on the 'autonomy' plank. Conscious of the popular anger against it, the party also promised effective governance, pro-people administration,

Table 6.1 *Performance of Parties at State Level: 1996 Assembly Elections*

Name of the Party	*Percentage of Votes Polled*	*Total Number of Seats*	*Percentage of Seats*
NC	34.78	57	65.51
BJP	12.13	08	09.19
INC	20.00	07	08.04
Janata Dal	10.87	05	05.74
BSP	6.43	04	04.59
Panthers Party	2.25	01	01.14
CPM	0.95	01	01.14
JKAL	**	01	01.14
Congress (T)	0.70	01	01.14
IND	9.30	02	02.29

Source: ECI, Statistical Report on General Election, 1996, to the Legislative Assembly of Jammu & Kashmir.

corruption-free government, employment and development. It also committed betterment of its record on human rights (Chowdhary and Rao 2003, 198).

As stated above, the NC emerged as the dominant party of the state polling 34.78 per cent votes and capturing two-thirds of the total seats in the Assembly (57/87). The opposition meanwhile was quite fragmented. Thus polling 20 per cent of the total votes Congress had got seven seats; BJP with 12.13 per cent votes had eight seats; the Janata Dal with 10.87 per cent votes had five seats and BSP with 6.43 per cent votes had four seats.

The dominance of the NC was reflected not only because it was the largest party of the state, but it had also emerged as the largest party of each of the three regions—40/46 seats (with 48.15% votes) in Kashmir region, 14/37 seats (with 23.72% votes) in Jammu region and 3/4 seats with (46.63%) votes in Ladakh region.

The performance of parties other than the NC was quite dismal in Kashmir, especially in terms of share of seats (see Table 6.2). While the Congress got two seats, Janata Dal, CPM and Jammu and Kashmir

Table 6.2 *Performance of Parties in Kashmir Region: 1996 Assembly Election*

Name of Party	*Total Number of Seats*	*Percentage of Votes Polled*	*Percentage of Seats*
NC	40	48.15	86.95
BJP	–	0.98	–
INC	02	18.18	4.34
Janata Dal	01	15.84	2.17
BSP	–	0.79	–
Panthers Party	–	2.05	–
CPM	01	2.11	2.17
JKAL	01	**	2.17
Congress (T)	–	0.25	–
IND	01	5.84	2.17

Source: ECI, Statistical Report on General Election, 1996, to the Legislative Assembly of Jammu & Kashmir.

Awami League (JKAL) each got one seat. In terms of share of votes, while the share of votes Congress in this region was 18.18 per cent and that of Janata Dal was 15.84 per cent.

One major reflection of the 1996 Assembly election on the Jammu region was the loss of the space that the Congress party had occupied since 1983 (see Table 6.3). By creating a Hindu constituency the party had captured a bulk of seats in that election—a feat that it could maintain during the 1987 Assembly election. However, by 1996, this constituency seems to have shifted slightly towards BJP.

As a clear implication of seven years' militancy on the electoral politics, one could see that there was a significant extension of space for the BJP in Jammu region. Though the electoral space for BJP had been extending since the 1980s, in this election, it had substantial gain both in terms of seats as well as its vote share. The Parliamentary election that preceded the Assembly election had already indicated the extended space for this party since it was able to register its victory in one of the two parliamentary seats of the region. Its share of votes was also increased from 13.09 per cent in the 1989 Parliamentary election to 31.07 per cent in the 1996 Parliamentary election. The party

Table 6.3 *Performance of Parties in Jammu Region: 1996 Assembly Election*

Name of the Party	*Total Number of Seats*	*Percentage of Votes*	*Percentage of Seats*
NC	14	23.72	37.83
BJP	08	21.10	21.62
INC	04	20.02	10.81
Janata Dal	04	07.83	10.81
BSP	04	11.19	10.81
Panthers Party	01	02.55	02.70
CPM	–	0.14	–
Congress (T)	01	–	02.70
IND	01	12.03	02.70

Source: ECI, Statistical Report on General Election, 1996, to the Legislative Assembly of Jammu & Kashmir.

continued with its spate of improved performance during the 1996 Assembly election as well. A party that generally had not been able to capture more than three Assembly seats till the 1980s was able to capture eight seats with 12 per cent votes at the level of the state. In Jammu region, its share of votes had increased to 20 per cent votes. In three predominantly Hindu districts of Udhampur (present-day Udhampur and Reasi), Jammu (present-day Jammu and Samba) and Kathua districts, its share of votes was still higher—28.14 per cent, 24.87 per cent and 22.62 per cent, respectively. This way it had become one of the three important competing parties of the region, along with Congress and NC.[4]

The implications of militancy could also be seen in the polarized electoral responses in the region. Apart from the indications about the carving of the Hindu constituency by the BJP, there were pointers towards consolidation of Muslim votes by the NC in some of the predominantly Muslim-populated districts. However, notwithstanding this kind of polarization by the BJP and NC, there was a significant central space that was filled in by parties such as Janata Dal, Congress, BSP and Panthers Party. Even the NC formed a part of this central space since it could win many constituencies of the Hindu heartland, including Akhnoor, Marh, Nagrota and Vijaypur.

Another important highlight of this election in Jammu region was the influence of the BSP. The party was able to win four seats from the region. All these seats had a large number of SC population and two of these seats were reserved. However, the reason that this party was able to have such an influence in this election was due to the efforts of the local BSP leader Sheikh Abdul Rehman. With his leaving the

[4] Although BJP won eight seats of Ramban, Udhampur, Chananni, Hiranagar, Gandhi Nagar, Jammu East, Jammu West and Suchetgarh, it lost four more seats of Akhnoor, Chhamb, Billawar and Marh by a very narrow margin of a few hundred votes. In four other constituencies of Raipur Domana, Reasi, Baderwah and Kishtwar its candidates were placed in second position. Besides registering its presence in the three Hindu dominated districts of Kathua, Jammu and Udhampur it could also demonstrate its strength in Doda district. In Udhampur and Jammu, it emerged as the largest party polling 28 per cent and 27 per cent votes, respectively. In the third Hindu-dominated district of Kathua, it stood second to the Congress party polling 23 per cent votes here. In Doda district, the BJP could poll as high as 30 per cent of the total votes (Chowdhary and Rao 2003, 205–206).

Table 6.4 *Performance of Parties in Ladakh Region: 1996 Assembly Election*

Name of Party	*Total Number of Seats*	*Percentage of Votes*	*Percentage of Seats*
NC	03	46.63	75.00
INC	01	39.01	25.00
BJP	—	05.84	—
IND	—	8.20	—

Source: ECI, Statistical Report on General Election, 1996, to the Legislative Assembly of Jammu & Kashmir.

party, the space for BSP was reduced significantly and it could win only one seat in the next assembly election in 2002.

Like Jammu, the 1996 Assembly election was keenly contested in Ladakh as well (see Table 6.4). Apart from the issue of the UT status, it was the intraregional divide bordering on the communal divide that informed its electoral politics. With the assertion of Buddhist identity of Leh as against the Muslim identity of Kargil, the party competition was also intensified. While the NC identified with the Muslims, the Congress identified with the Buddhists. In the end, the NC emerged as the dominant party of Ladakh winning three of the four seats (two of Kargil and one of Leh district). However, in terms of vote share, the competition between the two parties was quite strong—in Leh district the Congress polled around 51 per cent votes, while the NC got around 35 per cent votes. In Kargil district, the Congress polled 31 per cent votes and the NC got around 55 per cent votes.

What was particular about this election in Ladakh was the entry of the BJP. The party succeeded in polling 5.84 per cent votes. In Buddhist-dominated Zanskar, its vote share was around 15 per cent. In Leh, it was 7.63 per cent.

SHIFT IN ELECTORAL AND PARTY POLITICS

The 2002 Assembly election reflected a major shift in the party politics in the state. The central point of this shift was the emergence of an alternative regional party of Kashmir that challenged the hegemonic role of the NC and made the electoral space highly competitive. The NC that had been monopolizing the electoral space and sweeping the successive elections since 1977 could not continue its winning streak. Although it still emerged as the largest party of the state as well as of Kashmir region, however, it could not attain majority of seats. Its loss of the hegemonic space of Kashmir region therefore also led to its loss of dominance in the politics of the state. It was a fragmented verdict in 2002 Assembly election—besides the three large parties including the NC, Congress and PDP, there was presence of a number of other parties including the BJP, the Panthers Party and the CPM.

The end of the dominance of a single party led to the new patterns not only of electoral verdict but also of power sharing. Every election since 2002 has thrown a fragmented verdict which has had its implications for regional balance of power. Regional imbalance that was a reflection of the party politics in the pre-2002 era (mainly due to the hegemonic control over the electoral space of Kashmir region in the hands of one party) now gave way to a parity between the regions. Since the electoral verdict in Kashmir region got to be fragmented between two or more parties, there started the process of coalition governance, with an alliance of a Kashmir-based party with a party based in Jammu region.

The mandate, on the whole, was quite fractured and no party could win the majority of seats (see Table 6.5). While NC got a total of 28 seats, Congress could capture 20 seats. The new entrant, the PDP, was able to win 16 seats. Panthers Party got four seats; two seats were captured by the CPM; one seat each went to the BJP, BSP, JKAL and DM. Despite being the largest party both in terms of share of seats and share of votes, the NC failed to cross the half-way mark. It could capture only one-third of the total seats of the Assembly. In terms of the share of votes, 28.23 per cent votes were polled by the NC, 21.38 per cent by the Congress, 9.4 per cent by the PDP, 8.57 per cent by the BJP, 4.68 per cent by the Panthers Party and 4.5 per cent by the BSP.

At the state level, the NC was the biggest loser. From 57 seats in the 1996 Assembly election, its strength was reduced to almost half, that is, 28. Its share of votes was also reduced from 35 per cent in 1996 to 28.23 per cent in this election. Congress though maintained its share of votes (21% as compared to 20% in 1996), and it was also a major

Table 6.5 *Performance of Political Parties at State Level: 2002 Assembly Election*

Name of Political Party	*Total Number of Seats*	*Percentage of Seats*	*Percentage of Votes*
NC	28	32.18	28.23
INC	20	22.98	21.38
PDP	16	18.39	09.04
Panthers Party	4	4.59	04.68
CPM	2	2.29	0.53
BJP	1	1.14	8.57
BSP	1	1.14	4.5
JKAL	1	1.14	**
DM	1	1.14	**
IND	13	14.94	26.2

Source: ECI, Statistical Report on General Election, 2002, to the Legislative Assembly of Jammu & Kashmir.

gainer in terms of seats. It got the advantage of fragmentation of votes and improved its tally from 7 in 1996 to 20 in 2002.

BJP was another loser in this election. From eight seats in 1996, its share of seats was reduced to one in 2002. Its share of votes was also reduced from around 12 per cent at the state level to 8.57 per cent. One reason for its loss was the fragmentation of votes in its core constituency in Jammu region. Here Jammu State Morcha representing the same ideological base as the BJP contested independently. Although it could win only one seat, however, due to the fragmentation of votes between the Morcha and BJP, the latter had to face huge loss and its share of votes in this region were reduced from 21 per cent in 1996 to 12 per cent in this election. The advantage of this certainly went to the Congress party. Another party to gain from the fragmentation of votes between the BJP and State Morcha was the Panthers Party. From one seat in 1996, it could increase its tally to 4 seats. Its share of votes was also increased from around 2 per cent to nearing 5 per cent.[5]

[5] Among others whose performance was worse than the 1996 elections were the Janata Dal and the BSP. The Janata Dal which had five seats in 1996 failed to win a

Table 6.6 *Performance of Political Parties in Kashmir Region: 2002 Assembly Election*

Name of Party	*Total Number of Seats*	*Percentage of Seats*	*Percentage of Votes*
NC	18	39.13	35.67
INC	05	10.86	14.43
PDP	16	34.87	24.51
Panthers Party	0	–	0.3
CPM	2	4.24	1.64
BJP	0	–	1.6
BSP	0	–	0.11
JKAL	1	2.17	–
DM	0	–	–
IND	4	8.69	13.2

Source: ECI, Statistical Report on General Election, 2002, to the Legislative Assembly of Jammu & Kashmir.

The fragmentation of electoral space of Kashmir region was the peculiarity of this election (see Table 6.6). While the NC got 18 seats with around 36 per cent votes, the PDP got 16 seats with around 25 per cent of the votes. Five seats were captured by the Congress party with around 15 per cent votes, the CPM got two seats and JKAL got one seat. In four constituencies, independent candidates succeeded.

As a party that had been in existence only for three years, the performance of the PDP was quite impressive. Since it competed mainly in Kashmir, its vote share of around 25 per cent in comparison to 35.67 per cent of NC in this region was quite high. Its performance was much better in South Kashmir—39.09 per cent votes (4 seats) in Pulwama district and 33.22 per cent votes (6 seats) in Anantnag district. In Central Kashmir, it got 37.93 per cent votes (2 seats) in Budgam district and 25.99 per cent votes (1 seat) in Srinagar district. In north, it polled 19.87 per cent votes (3 seats) in Baramulla

single seat in 2002 elections. The BSP which had won four seats in 1996 could win only one seat in 2002. Its share of votes of more than 11 per cent was reduced to 6.83 per cent in 2002.

district. Apart from these 16 seats which it won, it was runner up in seven constituencies—two constituencies in North Kashmir (Langate, Kangan), four constituencies in Central Kashmir (Hazratbal, Sonawar, Batmaloo, Chrar-e-Sharief) and one constituency in South Kashmir (Wachi). Its performance in Jammu region was negligible even though it fielded its candidates in around 30 constituencies. It polled less than 2 per cent votes and lost in all the constituencies.

Other than the PDP, it was the Congress and People's Conference that gave a good fight to the NC in Kashmir region. The Congress got five seats with around 14 per cent vote share. It could get a reasonably high percentage of votes in some districts—21.98 per cent in Baramulla, 18.51 per cent in Anantnag and 17.79 per cent in Pulwama. It was runner up in as many as eight constituencies, namely Karnah, Rafiabad, Bandipora, Pattan, Khanyar, Tral, Pampore and Shangus.

The People's Conference contested the election through its proxy candidates and two of these candidates succeeded in getting elected. However, more than the victory of the candidates, it was the participation of this party—a key constituent of the separatist conglomeration, the APHC—that had important implications for the 2002 Assembly election. The participation of this party not only invigorated the electoral environment of the North Kashmir districts of Handwara and Kupwara but also led to a very high voter turnout here.

The electoral space of Jammu region was already fragmented—a trend that continued in this election as well (see Table 6.7). The Congress emerged as the leading party of the region with 15 seats, followed by the NC which had nine seats and Panthers Party which got four seats. While one seat each was captured by BJP, BSP and Jammu State Morcha, five seats were won by the Independents. In terms of the vote share, 29.79 per cent votes were polled by the Congress, 24 per cent by the NC, 12 per cent by the BJP, 7.02 per cent by the Panthers Party and 6.83 per cent by the BSP.

The Congress was the biggest gainer in the region as it could increase its tally of seats from four in 1996 to 15 in this election. Its share of votes had also increased substantially—from 20.02 per cent

Table 6.7 *Performance of Political Parties in Jammu Region: 2002 Assembly Election*

Name of the Party	Total Number of Seats	Percentage of Seats	Percentage of Votes
NC	09	24.32	23.94
INC	15	40.54	29.79
PDP	–	–	1.76
Panthers Party	4	10.81	7.02
CPM	–	–	–
BJP	1	2.70	12.3
BSP	1	2.70	6.83
JKAL	–	–	–
DM	1	2.70	–
IND	5	13.51	31.8

Source: ECI, Statistical Report on General Election, 2002, to the Legislative Assembly of Jammu & Kashmir.

in 1996 to 29.79 per cent.[6] NC and BJP suffered loss in this election. From 14 seats in 1996, the share of NC's victory in the region went down to nine seats. However, the bigger loss was that of BJP—from eight seats in 1996, its tally was reduced to one seat.

In Ladakh, especially in Leh district, there was an altogether different electoral scenario (see Table 6.8). In pursuance of the demand of UT status for Ladakh, all political parties operating in this district (including the NC, Congress and BJP) had dissolved their local units prior to election and merged themselves into a newly floated Ladakh Union Territory Front (LUTF), which won both the seats of this district without any contest. Apart from various political parties, support was

[6] Of the 15 seats that the Congress won, eight were in Jammu district, three in Kathua district, two in Doda district and one each in Udhampur and in Rajouri district. It was runner-up in eight constituencies at this region. What was interesting about the performance of Congress in this election was that it was able to make a comeback in the Hindu-dominated areas. Thus it won Nowshera, Chhamb, Akhnoor, Raipur Domana, Suchetgarh, R. S. Pura, Jammu West, Jammu East, Gandhi Nagar, Hiranagar, Basohli, Bani, Baderwah and Inderpal. Clearly the loss of BJP was gain for the Congress party.

Table 6.8 *Performance of Political Parties in Ladakh Region: 2002 Assembly Election*

Name of the Party	*Number of Seats*	*Percentage of Seats*	*Percentage of Votes*
NC	01	25	44.55
INC	–	–	05.62
IND	03	75	49.4

Source: ECI, Statistical Report on General Election, 2002, to the Legislative Assembly of Jammu & Kashmir.

extended to this Front from the Buddhist organizations as well as also from the Muslim organizations located in Leh. The Ladakh Muslim Coordination Committee (Leh) extended its support to LUTF.

The LUTF, however, did not have support in the Kargil district of Ladakh region. Politics here is influenced by two semi-political organizations, namely the Imam Khumani Memorial Trust (IKMT) and Islamia School. The NC and Congress generally affiliate themselves with one of the two organizations and field their candidates accordingly. In this election, one NC candidate supported by Islamia School and one Independent candidate won the election.

Loss of Dominance/Hegemony of NC

The loss of the dominant position of the NC was the most important outcome of the 2002 Assembly election. As one can see from Table 6.9, the NC had been generally capturing more than 60 per cent of the total seats of the Assembly. In 1996, its share of seats was as high as two-thirds of the total strength of the Assembly. However, in 2002, its number was drastically reduced. It could win only a total of 28 seats which was one-third of the total number of seats.

While the NC lost its dominant position at the state level, its loss at the regional level in Kashmir was much more severe. It lost its hegemonic status here. As Table 6.10 shows, the NC had been single-handedly controlling the electoral space of Kashmir region capturing as high as 93 per cent of the seats in 1977 and 90 per cent in 1983. In 1987 when it contested the election in alliance with the Congress, it could register its victory in 76 per cent of the total seats.

Table 6.9 *Performance of NC in the State Assembly Elections: 1977–2002*

Year of Election	*Total Number of Seats in the Assembly*	*Number of Seats Obtained by NC*	*Percentage of Seats Obtained by NC*
1977	76	47	61.84
1983	76	46	60.52
1987	76	40	52.63
1996	87	57	65.51
2002	87	28	32.18

Source: Election Commission of India.

Table 6.10 *Seat Share of NC: 1977–2002 Assembly Elections*

Year of Election	*Total Number Seats*	*Number of Seats Obtained by NC*	*Percentage of NC's Seats*
1977	42	39	92.85
1983	42	38	90.47
1987	42	32	76.19
1996	46	40	86.95
2002	46	18	35.67

Source: Election Commission of India.

(The combined strength of the NC–Congress alliance, however, was much higher—88%.) In 1996, the NC was able to register its victory in as many as 40 of the 46 seats from the Valley (87%), leaving only six seats for other parties (two for Congress and one each for CPM, Janata Dal and JKAL). From such a situation of controlling most of the electoral space, the strength of NC was reduced to that of one-third of the total seats in the Assembly.

In the 2002 election, the NC faced tough contest for the first time. The PDP made a huge dent in its support base winning a large chunk of 16 seats with around 25 per cent share of votes going to this party. With election becoming intensely competitive between these two parties, the Congress could also gain with 14 per cent vote share and five seats. In South Kashmir, the NC lost much of its space as it could get elected only on two of the 16 seats here (Anantnag and Tral). It got most of its seats from Central Kashmir where poll boycott was strictly enforced. However, even when it could get elected in a large number of seats in North Kashmir, it got a tough competition from the proxy candidates of the People's Conference with two of them winning the election as well.

The NC not only suffered a loss of seats in Kashmir but also in Jammu region. In 1996, it had emerged as the largest party of the region with 14 seats in its favour; however, this time its strength was reduced to 9. However, its vote share remained intact. As against 23.72 per cent votes in 1996, it could get a vote share of 23.94 per cent in 2002. The situation was similar in Ladakh also. From three seats in Ladakh, its strength was reduced to one seat with a slight reduction in its vote share from 46.63 per cent in 1996 to 44.55 per cent in 2002.

From a dominant party at the state level and a hegemonic party at the regional level, the position of the NC was changed to that of the largest party at both the levels. For the first time in the history of the state's politics, the party was to occupy the opposition benches in the Legislative Assembly. The sense of defeat of the party was sharpened due to personal defeat of Omar Abdullah himself.

However, in the situation in which no party got the majority at either level, the NC still emerged as the largest party of the state as well as in Kashmir region. It was also the party that had significant presence in all the three regions (see Table 6.11). Hence, apart from Kashmir region where it got 18 seats, it had registered its victory in nine seats in Jammu region and one seat in Ladakh region. In Jammu region, it had almost complete control in the Poonch district and had a fairly good representation in Rajouri district. Its share of votes (24%) was almost comparable to that of the Congress party (25%), which had emerged as the largest party of Jammu region. In Ladakh also its share of votes was significant (45%).

There were various reasons for the decline of the NC many of which had roots in the long history of the party. For one thing, the party had become truncated as early as in 1953 when it lost Sheikh Abdullah to separatist politics. Engrossed in conflict politics, it lost its ideological roots and even when it was revived in 1975, it did not have much to offer except its history of progressive past. Sheikh Abdullah had some vision about governance and when he came back to power politics,

Table 6.11 *Comparative Performance of NC Region-wise: 1996 and 2002 Assembly Elections*

	Kashmir Region			*Jammu Region*			*Ladakh Region*		
Year of Election	*Percentage of Votes*	*Number of Seats*	*Percentage of Seats*	*Percentage of Votes*	*Number of Seats*	*Percentage of Seats*	*Percentage of Votes*	*Number of Seats*	*Percentage of Seats*
1996	48.15	40	86.95	23.72	14	37.83	46.63	03	75
2002	35.67	18	39.13	23.94	9	24.32	44.55	01	25

Source: Election Commission of India.

he sought to bring about changes particularly in the fields of education and administration. His emphasis on decentralized planning and administration was quite forward-looking. But his successor, Farooq Abdullah, lacked vision and was more casual in his approach towards governance. Under his leadership, the state not only lost social direction but also got entrapped in a corrupt bureaucratic and political regime. The NC also had to face the consequences of its changed approach towards the Centre in the post-1984 period. The popular response had started turning hostile against the NC right in 1986 when the party had entered into alliance with the Congress party. It was the shift of the popular base from the NC to MUF that was clearly reflected during the 1987 Assembly election. The debacle of the 1987 election had further turned people away from the NC towards the separatist politics. Not only the NC but even Sheikh Abdullah, by this time, had lost popular appeal. His political judgements and decision were now openly challenged and he was blamed for his post-1975 politics. Meanwhile, Farooq Abdullah had developed the reputation of being a non-serious leader who was more inclined towards power rather than interest of people. His approach of political convenience in the post-1996 period, particularly alliance with the NDA, had made the NC highly unpopular in Kashmir. The continuation of this alliance even after the NC government was snubbed by the Central Government over its Autonomy Resolution increased resentment against this party.

THE 2008 ASSEMBLY ELECTION

The 2008 Assembly election that immediately followed the Amarnath agitation during which there was massive separatist upsurge in Kashmir was an intensely competitive election. With very high stakes for the competing political parties, the electioneering had started almost a year before the election. Political rallies were organized since the middle of 2007 in different parts of the Valley not only by the local parties but also by the national parties. However, with the Amarnath land row, all electoral activities were halted and for a prolonged period of five months there was a complete withdrawal of mainstream political processes from Kashmir Valley. However, as soon as the election schedule was announced, the hectic political environment was restored.

Table 6.12 *Performance of Political Parties at State Level: 2008 Assembly Election*

Name of Political Party	Total Number of Seats	Percentage of Seats	Percentage of Votes
NC	28	32.18	23.07
INC	17	19.54	17.71
PDP	21	24.13	15.39
Panthers Party	3	3.44	3.33
CPM	1	1.14	0.80
BJP	11	12.64	12.45
JKDPN	1	1.14	1.38
PDF	1	1.14	1.38
IND	4	4.59	16.34

Source: ECI, Statistical Report on General Election, 2008, to the Legislative Assembly of Jammu and Kashmir.

Like the 2002 Assembly election, the 2008 Assembly election also produced a fragmented mandate, with seats being shared by the NC, Congress, PDP and BJP (see Table 6.12). Although way behind the majority mark, the NC emerged as the largest party both in terms of seats and share of votes at 23.07 per cent. While it was able to retain its seat share of 28 as in 2002, its overall share of votes was somewhat reduced. The NC was followed by the PDP which had improved its seat share from 16 in 2002 to 21 in this election. Its share of votes was also increased from 9.04 per cent in 2002 to 15.39 per cent this time. At third number was the Congress party with 17 seats and 17.71 per cent of vote share. Compared to 2002, this party had lost both in terms of seats and share of votes (in 2002, it had 20 seats and 21.38% votes). At the fourth place stood the BJP which got 11 seats with 12.45 per cent votes. In terms of seats, this party was the biggest gainer since from its tally of one seat in 2002, it was able to get 11 seats in this election (see Table 6.13). Panthers Party got three seats with a 3.33 per cent share of votes. CPM, Jammu & Kashmir Democratic Party Nationalist (JKDPN) and PDF got one seat each.

At the regional level, there was an intense competition between the NC and PDP in Kashmir (see Table 6.14). While the NC won 20

Table 6.13 *Comparative Performance of Political Parties: 2002 and 2008 Assembly Elections*

Name of Political Party	Share of Seats in 2002	Share of Seats in 2008	Percentage of Seats in 2002	Percentage of Seats in 2008
NC	28	28	28.23	23.07
INC	20	17	21.38	17.71
PDP	16	21	09.04	15.39
Panthers Party	04	3	04.68	3.33
CPM	2	1	0.53	0.80
BJP	1	11	8.57	12.45
JKDPN	–	1	–	1.38
PDF	–	1	–	1.38
IND	13	4	26.2	16.34

Source: Election Commission of India.

Table 6.14 *Performance of Political Parties in Kashmir Region*

Name of Party	Number of Seats	Percentage of Seats	Percentage of Votes
NC	20	43.47	27.51
INC	3	6.52	10.48
PDP	19	41.30	27.41
Panthers Party	0	–	0.78
CPM	1	2.17	–
BJP	0	–	0.96
IND	4	8.69	13.2

Source: ECI, Statistical Report on General Election, 2008, to the Legislative Assembly of Jammu and Kashmir.

seats with a vote share of 27.51 per cent, the PDP got 19 seats with a vote share of 27.4 per cent. The rest of the seats were divided among Congress (3 seats with 10.49% votes), CPM (1 seat) and Independents (4 seats).

The PDP improved its performance in Kashmir region. Compared to 16 seats in 2002, it was able to win 19 seats in this election. It also increased its share of votes from 24.51 per cent to 27.41 per cent. The NC, though increased its share of seats (from 19 in 2002 to 20 in 2008), had a decreased share of votes. From 35.67 per cent votes in its favour in 2002, its share was reduced to 27.51 per cent. It was the Congress party that had lost its political space in Kashmir both in terms of seats and share of votes. As against five seats in 2002, its total strength was reduced to 3, and as compared to its vote share of 14.53 per cent in 2002, in 2008, it was reduced to 10.48 per cent.

In Jammu region, the level of competition was much higher (see Table 6.15). While the major competitors here were the Congress, NC and BJP, the Panthers and PDP were also serious contenders in some parts of the region. Panthers had its hold in Udhampur district and PDP was seriously contesting in the Muslim-majority Doda belt and the twin districts of Poonch and Rajouri.

The major competition, however, was between the Congress and the BJP and though Congress got a larger number of seats (13) and share of votes (23.99%), the BJP was quite close to it with 11 seats and 22.9 per cent votes. Compared to its tally of one seat in 2002, the BJP had made a tremendous come back with an increase of 10 seats. Its share of votes was also doubled, from 12.3 in 2002 to 22.9 in 2008.

The NC lost both in terms of its share of seats (from nine in 2002 to six in 2008) and share of votes (from 23.94% in 2002 to 14.3%

Table 6.15 *Performance of Political Parties in Jammu Region*

Name of Political Party	*Total Number of Seats*	*Percentage of Seats*	*Percentage of Votes*
NC	6	–	19.31
INC	13	–	22.97
PDP	2	–	6.59
Panthers Party	3	–	5.45
BJP	11	–	21.98
IND	2	–	–

Source: ECI, Statistical Report on General Election, 2008, to the Legislative Assembly of Jammu and Kashmir.

Table 6.16 *Performance of Political Parties in Ladakh Region*

Name of Political Party	*Total Number of Seats*	*Percentage of Seats*	*Percentage of Votes*
NC	2	50	28.44
INC	1	25	27.31
BJP	–	–	0.67
Panthers Party	–	–	0.37
PDP	–	–	0.54

Source: ECI, Statistical Report on General Election, 2008, to the Legislative Assembly of Jammu and Kashmir.

in 2008). The strength of the Panthers Party was also reduced from four in 2002 to three in 2008 and its share of votes was also slightly decreased from 7.02 per cent in 2002 to 5.69 per cent in 2008.

In Ladakh region, the NC was able to win two seats with a total share of 28.44 per cent votes (see Table 6.16). The Congress got one seat with 27.31 per cent votes and the fourth seat was won by an independent candidate. The two seats that the NC won were from the Kargil district. The Congress won the seat from Leh constituency. The fourth seat of Nubra went to the independent candidate. The LUTF that had won both the seats of Leh without contest in 2002 was nowhere in the scene.

Since the 2008 Assembly election took place immediately after the Amarnath agitation which had jolted the whole of the state, its reflection could be seen in the election results. The shadow of the unprecedented regional and communal polarization that had afflicted the state during this agitation was to be seen in the electoral outcome, particularly in the performance of PDP and BJP.

Before the Amarnath agitation, the PDP was facing the anti-incumbency factor and was not in a very comfortable position in Kashmir. However, as the agitation honed the Kashmiri regional and separatist sentiments, PDP's gain was ensured. In the regionally polarized politics where Jammu's right-wing forces were provoking anti-Kashmir sentiments, PDP was projecting itself as the redeemer of the Kashmiri sentiment. Its leader Mehbooba Mufti was vociferously campaigning against the 'economic blockade' of Kashmir by Jammu's agitators. In this context of regional communal polarization, the PDP's increase in popularity was clearly reflected during the Assembly election.

The electoral polarization on the communal basis was more clearly established in the Jammu region. In the context of militant violence, the BJP could succeed in extending its constituency in the post-1989 period. However, as the violence level came down, the influence of the BJP also started weakening. During the 2002 Assembly election, therefore, this party could manage to win only one seat.

The constituency of BJP's politics was in any case shrinking due to the changed nature of power politics of the state. The extreme politics of regional discontent on which the popularity of this party depends was getting blunted in the context of coalitional power sharing. For the first time in the political history of the state, Jammu had a fair share of power in the state after the 2002 Assembly election. However, the Amarnath agitation provided space and opportunity for the BJP and other like-minded organizations to mobilize the Hindu constituency. The massive mandate in favour of the BJP in Jammu's Hindu-dominated districts indicated that the region was now getting communally polarized.

The fact that the PDP could register its victory in two Muslim-dominated constituencies of the Jammu region provided additional reason to believe that impact of communal polarization was growing. Being a Kashmir-centric party which has been seeking to legitimize its politics by emphasizing its 'pro-Kashmir' orientation with a pro-Muslim bias, PDP's entry into the Muslim pockets of Jammu and its success in two predominantly Muslim constituencies was an indication of the communal polarization that was taking deeper roots in the state.

To Conclude

The last two decades saw a significant change in the nature of competitive politics of the state. From a very static party politics in the pre-2002 period, it assumed a highly dynamic character. With the hegemonic role of the NC in Kashmir region being challenged by the PDP, the party politics witnessed an overall vibrancy. It was a multi-party system that emerged in 2002 with at least four political parties having serious stakes in the electoral area—the NC, PDP, Congress and BJP. In the context of the fragmented verdict that the Assembly faced, a few smaller parties including the Panthers and CPM also counted. In this multiplicity of parties, what emerged as an important factor was the increasing regional divide in the party politics. The major players of Kashmir's politics were the NC and PDP and in Jammu region the Congress and BJP. However, despite this being a general trend, there were a number of exceptions. For instance, despite its declining influence in Jammu region, the NC continued to have its presence here. In fact, this was one party that had its presence in all the three regions of the state not only in 2002 but also in 2008. In a smaller way, the same could be said of the Congress as well. Although it remained the leading party of the Jammu region, however, it could register few victories in Kashmir and Ladakh. PDP which had started as an exclusively Kashmir-centric party in 2002 was struggling to extend its constituency in Jammu region by 2008, albeit in predominantly Muslim districts. Its success in this effort could be seen in the victory on two seats in the region. The BJP, however, remained primarily a Jammu-based party though it started making some dent in the Leh district of Ladakh.

The intensity of competition that defined the post-2002 period electoral politics had the implications not only of making electoral space of Kashmir region very competitive but also of changing the interregional equations. For the first time in the electoral history of the state, a Kashmir-based political party had started depending on a Jammu-based political party for forming the government. Meanwhile, an effective oppositional space also emerged within the state. Until the time there was dominance of a single party within the politics of the state, the opposition not only remained fragmented but also ineffective. However, now in the era of coalition governments, oppositional space has also been invigorated.

References

Chowdhary, Rekha, Avineet Prashar, and Paawan Vivek. 2007. *Elections in Jammu and Kashmir: A Commentary*. Jammu: Kashmir Times Publications.

Chowdhary, Rekha, and V. Nagendra Rao. 2004, 3–10 April. 'National Conference of Jammu and Kashmir: From Hegemonic to Competitive Politics', *Economic & Political Weekly* 39 (14): 1521–1527.

Chowdhary, Rekha, and V. Nagendra Rao. 2003, January–June. 'Jammu and Kashmir: Political Alienation, Regional Divergence and Communal Polarisation'. *Journal of Indian School of Political Economy* 15 (1–2): 189–219.

Ganguly, Sumit. 1997. *The Crisis in Kashmir: Portents of War, Hopes of Peace*. New York and Washington, DC: Cambridge University Press, co-published with Woodrow Wilson Center.

Singh, Tavleen. 1995. *Kashmir: A Tragedy of Errors*. New Delhi/New York: Viking.

Puri, Balraj. 1987, 30 May. 'Fundamentalism in Kashmir, Fragmentation in Jammu'. *Economic & Political Weekly* 22 (22): 835–837.

Schofield, Victoria. 2000. *Kashmir in Conflict: India, Pakistan and the Unending War*. London: I. B. Tauris.

Swami, Praveen. 2006. *India, Pakistan and the Secret Jihad: The Covert War in Kashmir, 1947–2004*. London: Routledge.

Verma, P. S. 1994. *Jammu and Kashmir at the Political Crossroads*. New Delhi: Vikas Publishing House.

7 Governance in Jammu and Kashmir

Governance has always been problematic in the state of J&K. The conflict situation led to a lag both in the democratization and institutionalization processes. The internal political contestation by the Plebiscite Front from 1953 to 1975 so shifted the focus of the national and state politics that governance became the major casualty. The period reflected poorly on the political and administrative processes with many undemocratic tendencies creeping in the system. Thus from the beginning there was personalized and arbitrary basis of power politics, absence of boundaries between the party and government, and nepotism and lack of accountability. Corruption was almost legitimized with the bureaucratic and political class emerging as the major beneficiaries along with the class of contractors, forest lessees, traders, etc. In the process of favouring a pro-Indian sociopolitical elite, the Central Government not only looked the other way but also in many ways contributed to the fragility of the governance processes.

GOVERNANCE ISSUES IN THE PRE-MILITANCY PERIOD

The distortions that emerged in the immediate post-1953 period, under the regime of Bakshi Ghulam Mohammed, were quite blatant and to the knowledge of the Central leadership. These were tolerated for the singular reason that Bakshi and his successors were seen to be representing the 'national interest' in Kashmir. It is in this process that throughout the period of 1953–1975 when the legitimacy of the state's accession as well as the power of the successive local governments was challenged by the Plebiscite Front, the state became an exception in the story of Indian democracy. There were not many mechanisms that made the power holders accountable for their actions of omission and commission (Puri 1968).

On his return to power politics in 1975, Sheikh Abdullah encountered an altogether different Kashmir. Rather than the hopeful mass that was bred on ideals of 'New Kashmir' that lapped up the land reforms and other progressive government policies during his earlier stint of power in immediate post-Accession period, he was now confronted with Kashmiris who had become thoroughly critical not only of the Central Government but also the local political elite. They had lost their faith in governance and were sceptical of the mainstream political processes per se. Most sceptical were the middle classes who ironically were also the beneficiaries of the largesse of the 'developmental' politics and economy in the post-1953 period (Punjabi 1992).

However, notwithstanding this scepticism and some undercurrents of bafflement linked with Sheikh's decision to take a U-turn in his politics, he continued to enjoy the support of people. His government did not suffer from the kind of crisis of legitimacy that his predecessors faced. On the contrary, the massive turnout and emotional response in favour of the NC during the 1977 Assembly election proved his continued popularity and his hold on Kashmir's politics. This election not only earned the reputation of being the first 'free and fair election' in the history of Kashmir but denoted legitimacy to the mainstream politics. Sheikh Abdullah, in turn, made a few attempts to improve the process of governance. He introduced certain path-breaking reforms. Of these, the most innovative one related to the development planning. Known as Single Line Administration, this was a system of decentralizing planning from the state to the district level. The idea was 'to draw into the vortex of developmental policies and strategies, the representatives of the people' (Shafi 1990, 33). The single line administration was a mechanism for decentralization of planning. Its objective 'was to secure a mechanism for developing the planning process at the district level to take full account of the resource endowments, the potentialities and needs structure and also to initiate a process of equitable development of various areas within the district' (Chowdhari 1990, 240). Under this system, planning boards for each district were constituted, which were given the power to formulate and supervise implementation of the plans (Sultan 1994, 91). Sheikh also constituted a Development Review Committee with L. K. Jha as its convenor, which came out with various recommendations for 'revamping the policies and strategies related to various aspects of development administration' (Pandit 2009). He also made efforts to take the state out of its structural dependence on the Centre by taking the bold decision of discontinuing the subsidized rations for the state and doing away with other concessions.

However, though he had a broader vision of politics and governance, Sheikh's personal orientation towards power was quite authoritarian. That he would not tolerate any dissent within his party and felt insecure vis-à-vis his close associates was reflected when he ousted his long-trusted friend and lieutenant, Mirza Afzal Baig, from the party in 1978 (Kak 1978). Fearing that he and others in the party might desert the party, he even got the anti-defection bill passed by the legislature. It was during the same year that his government got the Public Safety Act legislated. Meant to deal with timber smugglers, this was to become one of the most oppressive laws to be used in Kashmir during the period of militancy.

Notwithstanding these limitations, this tenure of Sheikh Abdullah provided a sanctity to institutions of governance in the state. He was also able to assert the political autonomy of the state and specifically keep the Central Government away from intruding in the politics of the state. This was despite the fact that the Congress as the ruling party in the Centre was quite ambitious about sharing power and was putting a lot of pressure on the state for this reason. It was the sheer weight of Sheikh Abdullah's stature that Congress could not succeed in this process. Even when there were moments of tension between the Centre and the state, the state's relationship with the Centre was quite smooth. With no assertive separatism on the surface, the political environment of the state was peaceful. Although Sheikh continued to mobilize Kashmiris around the issues of identity politics, via the politics of autonomy of the state, yet this politics did not disrupt the governance in any way.

It was, however, in the period after Sheikh's death that governance again became a serious casualty in the state. Farooq Abdullah, his successor, was quite easy-going in his approach to governance, but even before he could establish his credentials as CM of the state, he was removed from power. This not only started a phase of political uncertainties but also of accumulation of political discontent. Farooq's party had been earlier given a massive mandate in Kashmir in the face of a severe challenge by the Congress party during the 1983 Assembly election. Failing to win the election, the Congress in 1984 had manoeuvred defections within the NC and installed the G. M. Shah government that included all the defectors as ministers. By the time Shah was ousted from power in 1986, there were serious allegations of corruption, nepotism and arbitrary actions against his government. There were numerous complaints and even court cases with regard to government jobs which were distributed to the kins of the ministers and others without following the proper rules. Serious allegations of irregularities were also levelled which included the charge of government 'pushing financial assistance to the Tycoons group of industries owned by the chief minister's second son Muzaffar' (Chawla 1985). The political environment also deteriorated under Shah's government. So grave was the situation that his government was ill-famed as 'curfew government' due to the frequency of imposition of curfew. Sumantra Bose noted that 'for 72 of first 90 days of the new government the Kashmir Valley was under curfew orders to prevent protests' (Bose 2013, 43).

Shah's replacement by Farooq Abdullah in 1986 did not help the process of governance. By this time, Farooq had lost much of his credibility and, in any case, he did not pay much attention to the process of governance. This tenure of Farooq Abdullah followed the unpopular alliance of the NC with the Congress and faced acute legitimacy crisis.

After the 1987 Assembly election, turbulence overtook the state. There was a huge mass resentment that started being reflected on the streets of Kashmir. A large number of youth who had been mobilized by the MUF and who had actively participated in the election were disillusioned with the election result. However, rather than addressing the popular resentment, the Farooq government detained many of the youth in jails (Bose 2013, 47).

Meanwhile, the government did not offer anything to the common people. Unemployment and corruption continued to remain the major problems. As his style was, Farooq did not seem to be taking governance seriously and approached the issues with a very casual approach. He, in fact, allowed Kashmir to slip away towards the separatist mode as he neither acknowledged the troubles at the ground level nor did he take any concrete action to stop the process. As many political analysts have reported, when situation was actually deteriorating and needed his assertive presence, he was found to be involved in some trivial activity elsewhere in or outside the country. From 1987 to 1989, the situation in Kashmir continued to deteriorate with governance taking the major brunt. Much before Farooq Abdullah submitted his resignation in January 1990, the government had miserably failed in maintaining the law and order in the Valley.

PERIOD OF MILITANCY AND GOVERNANCE

With massive separatist upsurge on the ground, it became increasingly difficult to enforce the writ of the state. So much so that even imposition of curfew did not help restore the order as it was defied by people. Meanwhile, the 'civil curfew', which was a name given to the call for shut down by any militant organization, was seriously observed. On the whole, the normal life was completely disrupted with not much economic activities taking place; educational institutions being closed for long durations; movement on the road totally stalled; and even public offices not functioning for most of the time. The impact of militancy and separatism on the governance continued to be felt for more than a decade. The administration was severely impacted. Sudhir S. Bloeria, who served as the chief secretary of the state, describes the situation:

> By the beginning of 1990 the administration in Srinagar and some other towns of the Valley had almost collapsed. Within a couple of months, efficacy of the government almost hit the rock bottom. With great difficulty a semblance of essential services and supplies was attempted and that too with unexpected disruptions for indeterminate periods. (Bloeria 2016, 36)

Worst were the first few months of 1990 when besides the collapse of law and order situation and shattering of peace and public order, there was a lot of uncertainty. Describing the period as the 'most trying' and 'difficult', Bloeria notes the 'collapse of administrative machinery' and 'destabilisation of political structures'. To quote him:

> Large-scale targeted kidnappings and killings took place, wanton destruction of government institutions and buildings was resorted to, efforts made to undermine Indian support structure; especially targeting J&K police and the Intelligence Bureau, Central government establishments like Accountant General's Office, BSNL, Post and Telegraph departments, and even some banks, virtually became defunct under terror threats. (Bloeria 2016, 36)

One major implication of this situation was that many institutions either became dysfunctional or were severely distorted. So much so that 'it became difficult to collect user charges and sales tax revenue' (Planning Commission 2003, 353). Bloeria refers to the calls given by the militant groups for not paying the sales tax and threats received by some of the Excise and Taxation Officers (ETOs).

Incapacity of the concerned institutions to operate effectively during the period of peak of militancy, especially during the first 10 years, led to various long-term implications. By the time there was some semblance of law and order, much of the civil administrative system had been distorted and there were signs of anarchic conditions throughout the Valley. More particularly, there was devastation of state resources and massive encroachments. The forests particularly were severely impacted. To quote Arun Joshi:

> Forests were the first victims. Militancy spurred building constructions all across the Valley. People believed that whatever Kashmir's status, the property would remain an asset. Trees were ruthlessly cut and militants smuggled timber at a time when the vigilance system in forests had collapsed. Trees were felled and sold at dirt-cheap rates. The security forces were no less guilty. Trucks of precious wood were smuggled out of the Valley. Walnut furniture and timber were the special attraction. This loot and the failure to preserve forests resulted in a denudation of forests. A rough estimate is that over 100 km of forest cover was lost in the initial years of militancy. (Joshi 2001)

Even before the militancy, the state did not have a good record of forest preservation. During the decades of the 1960s and 1970s, there was already a plundering of timber as a particular class of forest contractors grew extremely wealthy under the state patronage. Most of the rules made to preserve forest were deliberately ignored. However, during the period of militancy, 'even the symbolic checks disappeared. The forest guards would not go into the remote areas controlled by militants and plundering of forest wealth began ... by paying off the militants' (*The Hindu* 2004). Records of five years of peak of militancy from 1992 to 1997 reflected that 'state underwent tremendous deforestation' in these years 'losing some of its most virgin cover, comprising rich coniferous tress like spruce, pine, fir and woodlands of deodar cedar, walnut, willow, elm and polar' (Vashishtha 2015). Deforestation further has had implications for wildlife and environment. As Jha notes, deforestation and poaching over the last few decades has made the wildlife extinct in Kashmir. The Hygam Weyland, he states, 'once home for many migratory birds, has shrunk to only 4.5 sq. km, the rest having been transformed into grazing ground for cattle' (Jha 2014, 147).

The riverbeds as well as the lakes were adversely affected. Not only the Dal Lake got shrunk and hugely polluted but even the river Jhelum was affected. There were thousands of encroachments in Dal Lake during the very early period of militancy. These encroachments, however, continued till the later period. In the process, massive farming tracts, residential places and hotels were constructed, and even shopping areas came up in and around the lake. The interiors of the lake have become concrete spaces and much of the lake has been converted into landmass. Meanwhile, due to the lack of governmental attention 'catchment areas were not preserved and irrigation canals or nullahs were not distilled. The rising mountains of silt soon stopped the flow of water. The silt soaked the water that used to flow in these nullahs and the farms got parched' (Joshi 2001).

1996–2002: PICKING UP THREADS OF GOVERNANCE: FAROOQ ABDULLAH'S GOVERNMENT

There were a lot of expectations from the Farooq Abdullah government that took over the power after six years of governor's rule. Political governance, for many, was a relief from the administrative rule, but governance at this time was not a very easy task for many reasons. Most importantly, it was the overall environment of violence where will of the state was at best enforced through coercion only. Politics had not much space and the authority of the government was still to be established. Another problem which the NC government faced was of legitimacy as the 1996 Assembly election was generally perceived to be conducted with the help of surrendered militants and security forces, and coercion rather than free will of people was seen to be the basis of election. More than governance, it was the legitimacy of the government that was the major issue at that time.

Although the writ of the state was established in the major towns of Srinagar and adjoining areas, there were still the remote areas which were under the influence of militants and were not 'safe' for free movement of civil population or the political class. Militancy was still at its peak and even the political class could not move freely within the Valley.

During the peak years of militancy, no development work could be undertaken. This along with the fact that militancy led to the massive damage to the infrastructure created a peculiar situation. Hundreds of schools and health centres were burnt, numerous bridges were exploded and a large network of roads was destroyed. The first major task before the Farooq government was therefore to provide basic infrastructure. And this was one thing that his government offered as its achievement after six years of being in power. As per a statement made by the then Works Minister, Ali Mohammed Sagar, the NC government had during first four years of its government reconstructed 50 per cent of the 401 gutted bridges (including 116 major and 52 minor bridges) and another 30 were in the process of completion. Around 27 educational institutions had been reconstructed. Many health centres were in the process of reconstruction. Meanwhile, there was addition of 400 kilometres of road and availability of additional 110 lakh gallons of potable water (*The Asian Age* 2000).

Beyond the reconstruction of the infrastructure, the Farooq government did not have much to offer. There were the usual complaints about the corruption, maladministration, high-headedness of senior bureaucrats. The feudal style of functioning of the CM and the spread of corruption under his government was a constant point of critique offered by his distractors. One serious charge floated against him was his non-serious approach to governance. The way Farooq Abdullah was caricatured by his rivals reflected this non-seriousness. In one such incident, a FIR was lodged in one of the police stations in Delhi about him being 'missing' when he was taking a break in London during a crucial political timing of the arrival of President of Pakistan in India. The idea underlying the FIR was to emphasize the implication of such absence on the day-to-day administration in the times of militancy (*The Indian Express* 2001). The general impression about the NC government was that it was internally corrupted and morally debauched and was not interested in resolving basic problems of day-to-day needs. On the whole, its performance was abysmal.

There was financial pressure on the government and the state was in debt. The financial situation of the state was quite fragile when Farooq Abdullah took over reins of government. There was recurring deficit that was accumulated over the period. On the whole, as the Planning Commission noted, there was 'erosion of the tax base, increase in expenditure, destruction of infrastructure and various other factors related with disturbed law and order'. The deficit therefore was significantly increased as there was 'continued tax and non-tax revenue shortfalls and heavy pressures on expenditure'. While in 1990 the fiscal deficit was 1338 crores that was increased by 40% to ₹1873 crores in 2000–01 (Planning Commission 2003, 353–354). Apart from other reasons, the security expenses also contributed to the deficit. Bhat notes that a 'a major chunk of the financial resources available to the State, which could have been otherwise utilised for the growth and development of the State economy, have been actually consumed by the security related expenditures' (Bhat 2012, 115). Although the security-related expenditure incurred by the state was reimbursed by the Central Government, however, there remained a gap between the expenses incurred and the amount compensated. Thus, as per Abdul Rahim Rather, the then Finance Minister of the state, between 1990 and 2000, the state government had incurred an expense of ₹2,949.20 crore. However, only ₹1,648.24 crores was reimbursed (*The Indian Express* 2001a).

Due to fiscal deficit, there was huge pressure on the government as there was not much money available due to the large service debt that the state was to pay. Although the government had been asking for writing off the debt, however, the Centre not only refused it but also refused releasing funds. And this led to the government going in for more debt and thus pushing the state virtually into a debt trap. As per the Human Development Report of the Planning Commission:

> The problem of large and persistent revenue and fiscal deficits is serious. In fact, the increasing fiscal deficit of the state government over the years and the adverse financial indicators point to improper fiscal management. While the state government needs enough resources for discharging its legitimate functions effectively, the finances of the state have been under considerable stress particularly during the last few years. (Planning Commission 2003, 353–354)

The government faced another pressure because of the expectations regarding the state employment. However, the government could not do anything in this direction as the Central Government had barred the state from filling in vacant positions.

The fact that the Farooq government on the whole failed to make much impact on the ground gets reflected from the CSDS data. The data collected during the 2002 election survey reveals that a large number of people in Kashmir (80.6%) said that they were not satisfied with the work done by the NC government (52.9% 'not at all satisfied' and 27.7% 'not satisfied'). The level of dissatisfaction was much higher in Kashmir as compared to that in Jammu (73.6%) and Ladakh (74.2%).

Apart from the negative opinion about the NC, there was negativity attached with Farooq Abdullah as the leader. As per the post-poll survey of 2002 Assembly election, an overwhelmingly large number of respondents (76.3%) had a negative opinion in Kashmir (that he was a bad leader). (Only 13% respondents found him OK, 6% said that he was good and 2.3% said that he was very good). Interestingly, compared to Farooq Abdullah, Omar Abdullah had a better response in Kashmir. Only 55.9 per cent had negative opinion about him.

However, one can see that the negativity attached with the NC was so widespread that it was not only linked to Farooq Abdullah but was also attached with Omar Abdullah. This becomes further clear when one notes that there was quite less negativity attached with Mehbooba Mufti in Kashmir region (26.3%).

Farooq was unpopular in Jammu and Ladakh as well. 56.3 per cent in Jammu, 54.6 per cent in Ladakh said that Farooq was a bad leader. As in Kashmir, there was lesser negativity about Omar Abdullah in Jammu (27%) and Ladakh (5.2%).

The negative image of the party and the leader has had its reflection in the overall lack of trust in government. As per the 2002 post-poll survey, 72.9 per cent respondents in Kashmir said that they had no trust at all in the state government (meanwhile only 19.8% said that they had somewhat trust, and 4.4% said that they had somewhat trust in the state government). Compared to that, 50.6 per cent respondents in Jammu and 48.5 per cent in Ladakh stated that they had complete lack of trust in government.

POST-2002 PERIOD: COALITION GOVERNANCE

Difficult Coalitions and Implications for Governance

In the process of formation of governments in the state, there was a major shift after the 2002 Assembly election. This election ended the hegemonic role of the NC in the party politics of the Kashmir Valley and brought an alternative competitive party to the scene. For the first time in the history of J&K politics, no political party was able to single-handedly form the government and hence a coalition government partnering Congress and PDP and other minor partners came into existence. The Assembly elections of 2008 and 2014 repeated the situation and a NC–Congress coalition and a PDP–BJP coalition, respectively, were formed.

Regional partnership has been one of the major features of the coalition governments. Since 2002 all coalitions have reflected an alliance between a party that had its stronghold in Kashmir region and a party that had won the larger share of its seats from Jammu region. Thus in 2002 while PDP had won all its 15 seats from Kashmir region, the largest share of seats of Congress had come from Jammu region (15/20). In 2008 while NC had the major share of seats from Kashmir region (20/28), Congress had 13/17 seats from Jammu region. In 2014, while BJP won all of its 25 seats from Jammu region, the PDP got 25/28 of its total seats from Kashmir region. This regional representation while opening new opportunities for governance also created new challenges for the coalition governments. For the first time, a regional balance was created in the state's government and instead of a token representation, the share of Jammu region in the government formation was on equal basis and even Ladakh was to have a reasonable presence. This has been a major requirement of the state politics since the internal politics of the state has been defined by regional grievances in Jammu and Ladakh regions. There has been a persistent feeling that in the process of governance, the interests of these two regions have been ignored as the successive governments since 1951 were comprised of Kashmir-based political elite. There is no more any basis of this grievance in the era of coalition governance.

However, the regional partnership in coalition politics has generated its own problems. Since the political logic of the two regions has remained different, exclusive and even at cross-purposes, the coalitions have been facing the problems arising out of lack of ideological cohesiveness. This has serious implications for governance since the energies of coalition partners are at many points diverted away from the process of governance towards meeting the ideological expectation of the respective regional constituencies. While this problem has persisted right from PDP—Congress to Congress–NC government, however, the problem became much more acute in the PDP–BJP government due to a history of strong ideological differences between the two parties. Acknowledging the ideological differences and political incompatibilities, the successive coalition governments have sought to develop some minimum principles of governance and also sought to provide for a mechanism for sorting out the differences. However, following the commonly accepted principles and the common agenda has not been an easy task. Most of the time, the differences between the two sides are so wide that even when for the sake of coming together, the parties agree on the minimum, the coalition partners remain pressurized not to cross the lines beyond the accepted party positions. Beyond ideology, there are certainly issues such as employment, corruption, development where the coalition partners can show a sense of coherence and work together. However, for a state where conflict situation remains alive and where political parties are forced to take stand on emotive issues, much of the energies of the partners get wasted in assuring their respective constituencies that they have not compromised on their basic agenda. In the context of intensified conflict in the last three decades, the ideological gap has increased and respective positions have been hardened. With no consensus on issues such as Article 370, human rights violations, role of security forces, AFSPA, peace process, India–Pakistan relations—any issue can assume an emotionally volatile nature. Even while the coalition partners would like to underemphasize the political and ideological differences for the sake of sustaining power, this may not be possible due to the different expectations of constituencies they represent and the basic contradiction in the political logic of the two regions.

With this kind of problem, the coalitions in the state have remained fragile throughout the period of their existence. Thus during the PDP–Congress government in the 2002–2008 period, the PDP which was a new party with all seats from Kashmir was keen on diluting the effects of conflict and emphasizing on issues such as demilitarization and removal of AFSPA, which would best be avoided by the Congress party. PDP's position on self-rule throughout remained problematic for the Congress party. With many in the opposition terming the concept of self-rule as extreme and going beyond nationalist lines and BJP being very critical about it, the Congress was under severe pressure to distance itself from the political lines of its coalition partner. The situation actually turned volatile when PDP members started referring to 'joint currency' as an imaginative future process of cross-LoC relations between the Indian- and Pakistan-administered parts of the state. The two partners were also on different notes around the issue of PRC for women. While seeking to cater to the Kashmiri constituency, the PDP sought to overcome the implications of the decision of High Court declaring the invalidity of the practice of denying state subject to women married outside the state, the Congress was not very comfortable with it. There were similar strains within the NC–Congress government over the issue of AFSPA, with Omar Abdullah seeking the removal of AFSPA and the Congress being not fully committed to it. The PDP–BJP government started on a volatile note right from the beginning when Mufti Sayeed seeking to address his constituency in Kashmir thanked the militants and Pakistan for a peaceful 2014 Assembly election. The PDP–BJP government throughout remained vulnerable as various issues were publicly raised by affiliates of the BJP, making the PDP quite uncomfortable. Among the issues raised by these affiliates included those related to Article 370 and Article 35A, and even the legal route was followed in a complete embarrassment to the PDP. In Kashmir, these articles are matters of faith and any possibility of tinkering with these can lead to very emotive response. The issues such as the return and rehabilitation of Kashmiri Pandits and the minority status to the non-Muslims, particularly the Kashmiri Pandits, put both the coalition partners in a difficult position.

The Congress–PDP Government: 2002–2008

Although the Congress and PDP were major partners, the coalition also included the Panthers Party and the CPM, besides a few independent MLAs. With different political stances, the coalition partners had agreed upon a CMP. A Coalition Coordination Committee (CCC) was also constituted to deal with the differences among the coalition partners. The CMP was comprised of 30 points and carried matters from the manifestos of all the parties. It was mainly divided into three kinds of issues: those emphasised by the PDP, mainly the policy of healing touch, those that emanated from Congress programme keeping Jammu and Ladakh in consideration and those that were linked with development and welfare.

Thus keeping in view the concerns of PDP, the CMP talked of healing the physical, psychological and emotional wounds inflicted by militancy, and approaching the Government of India for a dialogue for the sake of restoration of peace and reviewing cases of detainees. Although the AFSPA and PSA were not named, commitment however was made for reviewing all such laws that 'deprive people of their basic rights to life and liberty' and also promised investigation of 'all cases of custodial killings and violation of human rights'.[1]

Reflecting the concerns of the Congress and Panthers Party, the CMP referred to the commitment of return of Kashmiri Pandits, of providing adequate financial assistance for relief and rehabilitation of migrants from various disturbed areas of Jammu and Ladakh, and compensation to border people affected by conflict, among other things. It also emphasized equitable share of resources to all the three regions and for that purpose establishment of a state finance commission with a statutory status. It also referred to inclusion of Dogri in the Eighth Schedule of the Constitution and called for full powers to Autonomous Hill Councils of Ladakh.

The issues of development incorporated in the CMP related to ridding the state administration of corruption and nepotism; establishment of Accountability Commission; preparation of employment-oriented, medium-term development plan with special attention for youth employment; development of power resources of the state; provision of basic minimum needs such as safe drinking water, sanitation, rural roads, primary health care, etc.; Panchayati Raj institution; special welfare programme for women; and protection to minorities and safeguarding their interests (CMP 2002).

The CMP, however, remained in paper, and there was no debate around it and never was it referred to while taking the governmental decisions (Choudhary 2008, 14–15). Both the major partners were guided by their own slogans: 'healing touch' for PDP and 'Khushal Kashmir' for Congress. Further, even while the Coalition Coordination Committee (CCC) was constituted with 11 members and Ghulam Nabi Azad as its chairman, barring the two meetings soon after the formation of government, it was not brought in picture even to sort out differences during the moments of severe internal tensions between the coalition partners.

[1] It also talked of strengthening of State Human Rights Commission; formulating a comprehensive relief and rehabilitation package for families affected by militant violence; scheme to rehabilitate former militants; reaching out to the children, widows and parents of the deceased militants; and disbanding of SOGs, among other things.

As per the arrangement among the coalition partners, the positions of CM and deputy CM were rotated between the PDP and the Congress. During the first three years, the government was headed by Mufti Mohammed Sayeed of PDP with Mr Mangat Ram Sharma of Congress as the deputy CM. In the next three years, Ghulam Nabi Azad of Congress headed the government with Muzaffar Baig of PDP as the deputy CM.

During the first three years under Mufti Sayeed's chief ministership, the emphasis of government remained on implementing its 'healing touch' policy. On the whole, it succeeded in easing the pressure of the security forces. At the time when Mufti took over the reins of government, common people felt harassment because of security checks, security cordons and the movement of the security forces or the presence of the security camps. It was because of the intervention of Mufti and his personal rapport with the army officials that that environment changed a lot. Lt General Syed Ata Hasnain, former General Officer commanding the Srinagar-based Chinar Corps, who served as Commander of Uri Brigade during Mufti's first tenure as CM, said, he (Mufti) wanted no civilian should be harassed during the anti-militancy operations. 'We carried out many anti-militancy operations during those days, but at the same time we were ordered to ensure that no innocent faces inconvenience' (Yusuf 2016). One of the promises made by Mufti government related to disbanding of the SOG of Police which was dealing with the militancy and was involved in the largest number of cases of human rights violations. These complaints ranged from 'custodial killings, disappearances and extortion to forcible occupation of civilian property'. SOG was so powerful that it was seen as a law unto itself. In 2003, the government took the decision of merging the SOG with the police. It was decided that there would be no independent counter-insurgency wing of the state police and that it would be under the supervision of the district superintendent of police that the anti-militancy operations would now be planned and executed (Pandit 2003).

The PDP–Congress coalition was able to introduce certain innovations in the structures of administration and governance. Among these included the institution of Additional District Development

Commissioner (ADDC) with the objective of better monitoring the development task at the ground level. Also, a public grievance system was introduced with government officials holding public darbars at tehsil, block and district levels. To root out the corruption, the measures taken by the government included introduction of a new provision to the Corruption Act which was related to the attachment of the property of public servants with disproportionate income (Ahmad 2015, 44). The government also suggested the institutionalization of an accountability commission with public offices including those of the chief minister, cabinet ministers and legislators under its scrutiny. One of the first few acts of the Mufti government was to constitute the Accountability Commission by the Jammu and Kashmir State Accountability Commission Act, 2002. Its function was to 'inquire into grievances and allegations against public functionaries and for matter connected therewith'. In March 2003, the government set up a three-member committee headed by senior bureaucrat S. D. Singh to recommend premature retirement of tainted officers and to suggest action under the law against those involved in corrupt practices. The decision was purportedly taken to rid the administration of officers responsible for swindling public funds (*The Times of India* 2003). Meanwhile, the state vigilance bureau was activated to take actions against the corrupt officials. When Ghulam Nabi Azad took over as the CM of the state after three years of Mufti's tenure, the emphasis of government was changed to development. Using the slogan of 'Khushhal Kashmir', his main focus was on infrastructural development, construction of roads and bridges and various projects including tourism development authorities in various parts of the state. Much before he became the CM of the state, Azad had been promising jobs to youth in areas such as consumer affairs, rural development and tourism.

Despite the fact that controlling corruption was one of the major commitments of the PDP–Congress government, however, not much could be accomplished in that direction. The state, in fact, got the infamous status of being the second most corrupt state of India after Bihar, by Transparency International in 2004. Notwithstanding the institutional arrangements put in place, the government on the whole failed to curb the practice of corruption. With the exception of one IAS officer (who was arrested for a scam in 1999 but was honourably reinstated during Azad's tenure), most of the times, action was taken against low-level officials only. Around 60 such officials were ousted from their jobs.[2] Most of those who got trapped in the anti-corruption net could get relief by taking political patronage and joining sides with the powerful political groups. Choudhary gives the example of Syed Asghar Hussain, Director of Rural Development Department, during Azad's time, against whom action was taken. Hussain, however, joined PDP and became its organizing secretary (Choudhary 2008, 15–16).

Besides corruption, the issue of exploitation of state resources, particularly the land, under the political patronage, assumed important proportions during the period of Congress–PDP government. There were reported cases of encroachment of large parts of state's agricultural land, including farms and nurseries in many districts of Kashmir including Srinagar, Badgam and, Anantnag. Such encroachers enjoyed the patronage of both the politicians and powerful officials. Much of the horticultural and sericultural lands had also been encroached and the authorities had failed to get them vacated.[3]

To what extent the PDP–Congress government created satisfaction among the people? The 2008 post-poll survey data of CSDS showed that though there was mixed responses of people in Kashmir, the

[2] Referring to the superficiality of the PDP–Congress government around the issue of controlling corruption, Choudhary thus noted:

> When Azad took over in 2006, he did not talk about anything else except his war against corruption. The Vigilance Organisation moved randomly against the officials more on the basis of complaints and less on basic investigations. Amidst a tremendous fear psychosis among the government officials, the rate of bribe to be paid for every petty work skyrocketed as officials openly admitted to the rising 'risk factor'.

He refers to the whole campaign being trivialized with senior ministers in the cabinet accusing the Vigilance Organisation for targeting a particular community only, or accusing the minister of coalition partners as being highly corrupt (Choudhary 2008, 15–16).

[3] Such is the power of Land Mafia that it has not been dissuaded from encroaching the areas where it was legally and formally forbidden. For instance, much of the land in famous tourist resort Pahalgam has been encroached. Construction of residential areas, huts and hotels has been going on in total violation of the law that restricts such constructions.

performance of this government was certainly more appreciated than that of the earlier Farooq Abdullah government. The data recorded that a larger percentage of people were satisfied by the work done by this government (51.3%, out of which 38% somewhat satisfied and 13.3% fully satisfied) as compared to the people who were dissatisfied (37.4%, out of which 24.6% fully dissatisfied and 12.8% somewhat dissatisfied). It is a different matter, however, that the level of scepticism in Kashmir still was higher since the level of satisfaction was higher in Jammu region. On the whole, 59.4 per cent expressed their satisfaction with this government as against 19.5 per cent who were dissatisfied.

As regards the response of the people who were asked to rate the development—whether it has improved or deteriorated during this government, again a larger number of people within the state said that it had improved (37.7%) as compared to the number of people who said that it deteriorated (14.3%). However, 35.1 per cent stated that it remained the same. On the specific questions of supply of electricity, condition of roads, price rise, situation of employment, corruption, security of common people and human rights violations, a larger percentage of the respondents felt that the situation either remained the same or it had deteriorated.

However, despite this perception, there was generally a positive response towards the PDP–Congress government, especially for the three years of Mufti's chief ministership.[4]

THE NC–CONGRESS GOVERNMENT: 2008–2014

The NC–Congress coalition started on a good note of massive participation of people. With Farooq Abdullah deciding to leave the political space for Omar Abdullah, there was sufficient excitement about the

[4] As against 31.9 per cent respondents who expressed their dissatisfaction with Mufti's government as many as 76.6% respondents expressed satisfaction. Compared to that only 45.2 per cent% respondents expressed satisfaction with Azad's government. 41.7 per cent expressed dissatisfaction. On being asked to compare the governments led by Mufti Sayeed, Ghulam Nabi Azad and Farooq Abdullah, a larger number of people (47.4%) in Kashmir clearly rated that of Mufti being the best.

impact of generational change. As the youngest CM who had earned sufficient popularity during his stint as Union Minister of State for Foreign Affairs, there were lot of expectations from his leadership. Youth particularly identified with Omar Abdullah and expected that the NC which had lost its dynamism in the last few decades would be reinvigorated.

As per the coalition arrangement, Congress as the coalition partner had not insisted on rotation of chief ministership and therefore Omar Abdullah had been designated as CM for the full term of six years. This provided a sense of political stability to the government. However, despite all these positives in his favour, Omar Abdullah had to face quite rough times for the first two years as Kashmir was overtaken by popular protests and separatist upsurge. With massive demonstrations, bandhs, hartals and curfews throughout 2009 and 2010, governance was totally paralyzed and the major challenge before the government was to restore the normalcy. It was only by the end of the year 2010 that the government could pay attention on the task of governance. In 2014 also, this government had to face the challenge of unprecedented flood situation which inundated large parts of Kashmir Valley. Government was once more paralyzed at that time.

There was a pressure of very high popular expectations from Omar Abdullah when he took over as the chief minister of the state. Apart from the fact that as a junior minister in the NDA government in the Centre, he had established a reputation of being a straightforward, no-nonsense, serious politician who was ready to take position on issues related to Kashmir, his young age inspired the youth who expected that with him there will be a fresh approach to governance and that he would be able to resolve problems faced by them, including those related to employment for educated youth and corruption. The negativity attached to Farooq Abdullah was not attached to Omar Abdullah.[5]

[5] The CSDS post-poll survey of 2008 clearly reflected the relatively greater popularity of Omar Abdullah in Kashmir as compared to Farooq Abdullah. On a question as to who should lead the NC, in Kashmir 43.4 per cent stated Omar Abdullah and only 9.3 per cent stated Farooq Abdullah. 39.5 per cent respondents, however, stated that it made no difference. In Jammu, the opinion was different—while 32.3 per cent were

However, the government failed in fulfilling the expectations of the youth. Although it had launched a scheme with lot of fanfare to deal with the problem of unemployment of the educated youth, it failed to bring about any change in the ground situation. On the contrary, it generated lot of resentment and critique because of the suggested drastic cut of emoluments during the first five years.[6] Launched under the name of Sher-i-Kashmir Employment and Welfare Programme for Youth (SKEWPY) this policy was withdrawn by the government in the sixth year, following the debacle of the NC–Congress coalition in the 2014 Parliamentary election.

On the whole, the record of the government on the employment front remained very poor. It also failed to fill in thousands of gazetted and non-gazetted jobs that were available. To begin with, it was due to the political upsurge, but later, it was the poor management of the government. It postponed the process of recruitment till the last year to get the maximum political mileage. However, this proved to be a bad decision. The government was handicapped in 2014—first due to the Parliamentary election and the code of conduct being put in place, and later due to the situation of flood.

Where the government faired very poorly was on the count of corruption. Despite the public pronouncements of both the NC and Congress regarding their commitment to revival of State Accountability Commission (SAC) and empowering State Vigilance Commission, not much was done in that direction. On the contrary, the government actually diluted the powers of the SAC. The lack of commitment of this government to these institutions was clearly reflected from the fact that for a long period both the Accountability Commission and the Vigilance Commission remained headless or without other members. In July 2014, following a public interest litigation (Sheikh Mohammad Shafi and Another Versus Union of India and Others), the Division

in favour of Farooq Abdullah, 9.8 per cent favoured Omar Abdullah and 36.8 per cent said that it made no difference.

[6] As per this scheme, all non-gazetted employees were to get monthly salary equivalent to 50 per cent of the basic pay for the first two years, and fixed salary of about 75 per cent of the basic pay in the next three years.

Bench of State High Court asked the government to take immediate steps for appointment of chairperson and members of the SAC. Earlier, the High Court had intervened for providing investigating wing to the Accountability Commission and necessary staff to the State Vigilance Commission (Verma 2014). On the whole, in common perception the NC–Congress government was more corrupt than the preceding governments. So deep-rooted was this perception that even the coalition partners blamed each other for being corrupt. However, despite this mutual blaming, the cases were not seriously pursued and even the very serious charges made against the government members were generally overlooked.[7]

Among the claims made by the Omar Abdullah ministry about improving the administrative set-up, one was related to the Jammu and Kashmir Public Services Guarantee Act, 2011. This Act provided delivery of public services within a specified limit and made provision for holding the concerned designated officer accountable in this process. Around 80 basic services from 13 departments were brought under the ambit of the Public Services Guarantee Act. These included matters related to issuance of ration cards, state subject certificate, reserved category certificate, dependent certificate, driving licence, birth and death certificates; electricity and domestic water connection; some land and property related matters; NOC for house construction, etc. However, this Act did not make much impact on the delivery of public services and notwithstanding this Act, the functioning of public offices remained as inefficient as it was earlier.

Towards the tail end of the tenure of the government, specifically after the 2014 Lok Sabha polls in which the coalition partners were defeated in all the six seats, Omar Abdullah sought to introduce some populist measures to win back the public support. Among the measures introduced included the increase in the retirement age of

[7] For instance, there was a corruption charge against the State Congress President and Minister for Education, Peerzada Muhammad Sayeed. An independent MLA floated a charge of paying the minister for transfer of his sister. Similarly, there were corruption charges against another minister as well from the Congress party, Taj Mahiuddin, but no action was taken.

the government employees, removing the internet ban on the mobile phones and reversing the recruitment policy.

One major issue that confronted the NC–Congress government in the last leg of its tenure was its complete failure in managing the situation during the massive floods in September 2014. Around 1.4 million people got affected and apart from the 300 deaths, there was a huge financial loss. However, as the disaster approached, the state was conspicuous by its absence. With all communication lines broken, people remained struck up in odd situations and waited for days to be rescued. The intervention came either from the Central Government or from the locals.[8]

How the popular response in Kashmir was reflected around the question of disaster management gets revealed from the 2014 post-poll survey of CSDS. On the question in which opinion was sought about the rescue, relief and rehabilitation work done by the state government during and after the floods, as against 28.7 per cent respondents who said that they were satisfied, 41.6 per cent respondents said that they were dissatisfied. Compared to Kashmir, the level of dissatisfaction in Jammu region was substantially lower (21.7%). In the perception of larger number of people in Kashmir, the help came mainly from the local volunteers, ordinary people and villagers or friends and relatives. (While 41.5% respondents stated that the help came from the local volunteers, 28.2% stated friends and relatives.)

On the whole, the NC government's image about its development activities, particularly in Kashmir region, was very poor. Thus of all the respondents covered in Kashmir, around half of them (49.6%) believed that during NC–Congress tenure, the situation of development deteriorated;[9] 48.9 per cent respondents believed that the supply

[8] The warning signals were being given by various agencies and the Central Government had also sanctioned money for preparing a plan for meeting this situation. However, these warnings were ignored and as the situation evolved the government itself collapsed.

[9] As against this, 24.6 per cent stated that it improved, 19.8 per cent stated that it remained the same. In Jammu the response was: 43.3 per cent stated that it improved, 38.5 per cent stated that it remained same and only 14.6 per cent stated that it deteriorated.

of electricity deteriorated;[10] and as high a percentage as 57.9 per cent believed that the condition of roads had deteriorated.[11]

On the issue of corruption, there was a general feeling of disappointment both in Jammu and Kashmir regions. Thus 80.3 per cent respondents in Kashmir region and 69.7 per cent respondents in Jammu region believed that the corruption had increased during the six years' tenure of NC–Congress government.[12] Similar was the sense of despondency about the situation of employment. 50.7 per cent respondents in Kashmir region and 37.2 per cent in Jammu region believed that the employment opportunities had decreased during this period.[13]

The survey found that there was a huge dissatisfaction against the government in both the regions—51.9 per cent respondents in Kashmir[14] and 40.2 per cent[15] in Jammu stated that they were dissatisfied with this government. It is with reference to this dissatisfaction when asked to compare the PDP–Congress government with the NC–Congress government that larger percentage of respondents (44.4% in Kashmir and 28% respondents in Jammu region) said that the former was better. As against this, 18.8 per cent respondents in Kashmir and 16.7 per cent in Jammu region felt that the NC–Congress government was better.

[10] For 24.6 per cent it was improved, and it remained the same for 19.8 per cent. In Jammu only 14.6 per cent said that the supply of electricity deteriorated, 43.3 per cent stated that it improved and 38.5 per cent stated that it remained same.

[11] 17.6 per cent stated that it improved and 16.7 per cent stated that it remained the same. In Jammu region, only 21.5 per cent stated that it deteriorated, 42.6 per cent stated that it improved and 31.3 per cent stated that it remained the same.

[12] For 9.5 per cent respondents in Kashmir, it remained the same and for 3.1 per cent it was decreased. In Jammu, it remained the same for 8.9 per cent and decreased for 1.4 per cent respondents.

[13] Situation was still much better in Jammu region where 17 per cent respondents stated that such opportunities were increased. 36.2 per cent stated that these remained the same. As against this, for 13.7 per cent respondents in Kashmir region such opportunities were increased and for 23 per cent these remained the same.

[14] 38.5 per cent fully dissatisfied and 13.4 per cent somewhat dissatisfied.

[15] 22.1 per cent somewhat dissatisfied and 18.1 per cent fully dissatisfied.

This reflected poor opinion about the leadership of Omar Abdullah. The general opinion about him as the CM was quite contrary to the higher expectations with which he had started. Thus in Kashmir region more than half the respondents had expressed dissatisfaction (39.9% fully dissatisfied and 11.6% somewhat dissatisfied). In Jammu region, 19.9 per cent stated that they were fully dissatisfied and 25.4 per cent stated that they were somewhat dissatisfied.[16]

In sum, the fragility of governance continued throughout the tenure of NC–Congress government. Besides other issues, what made the people resentful about this government were the continued incidences of human rights violations. The cases of 'fake encounter' not only came to be highlighted during this period but there were massive protests around this issue as well. Omar Abdullah throughout the period of six years of his government remained vocal about the revocation of AFSPA but could not get any result in that direction. The home minister reportedly had moved amendments in the law but could not succeed because of opposition of the defence minister. The army also opposed the idea of withdrawal of AFSPA and it 'argued that a withdrawal even if partial would hamper counter-insurgency efforts because of the legal shield the Act provides to the troops' (Bhan 2013, 161). As the CSDS data revealed for 44.9% respondents in Kashmir, there was increase in the incidences of human rights violations during the NC–Congress government. (For 15.9% these remained the same and for the 11.8% these had decreased.)[17]

LACK OF INSTITUTIONALIZATION

Lack of institutionalization remains as one of the major problems of governance in the state. Many institutions which are crucial to governance process remain dysfunctional for one reason or the other.

[16] In Jammu region 25.2 per cent respondents stated that they were somewhat satisfied and 13.5 per cent stated that they were fully satisfied. In Kashmir 25.2 per cent somewhat satisfied and 13.5 per cent fully satisfied.

[17] This was despite the fact that as high a percentage as 27.5 per cent recorded the response 'Can't say'.

The lack of government's commitment towards these institutions gets reflected from the fact that many of these are either not properly constituted or not properly supported by the state. When it comes to the crucial institutions such as the State Women's Commission, State Information Commission (SIC), Vigilance Commission, SAC, State Human Rights Commission and even Public Service Commission, for long periods these remain headless or without adequate members. The State Commission for Women, for instance, throughout the Congress–PDP government remained headless. The non-seriousness of the successive governments in making these institutions functional gets reflected from a response to a question in State Legislature in 2015 when the then CM Mufti Mohammed Sayeed revealed that 'All positions in the Jammu and Kashmir Public Service Commission, Jammu and Kashmir Accountability Commission, Jammu and Kashmir State Human Rights Commission, Jammu and Kashmir State Commission for Women, including that of the chairman are vacant' (*The Economic Times* 2015).

It was in acknowledgement of the problems related to accountability and transparency of the administration that the Prime Minister's Working Group on Good Governance made a number of recommendations in its report in 2007. These included the appointment of Chief Information Commissioner and other members of the commission, encouraging people to use the Right to Information, introduction of e-governance particularly digitization of land record, treasury operation, IT-enabled single-window payment, simplification of rules and regulations, deregulation and file movement. Among other suggestions made by the Working Group included those related to the arbitrary transfers and what is generally known in the state as the 'transfer industry'. It called for a new transfer policy. It also called for reduction in the amount of discretion in appointments by Public Service Commission. It also recommended preparation and publication of Citizen's Charter by every department with a mechanism of periodic review. It also called for institutional strengthening, people's participation especially through public–private partnerships, social audits, performance management, fiscal management and such others.

Right to Information (RTI)

The central RTI legislation was not extended to the state as the state under Article 370 had the option of being excluded from its jurisdiction or having its own legislation. The state chose to have its own law. Jammu and Kashmir Right to Information Act was passed by the State Legislature in December 2003 and was notified in *Government Gazette* on 7 January 2004. However, the law was found to be quite deficient and compared to the Central law did not provide enough protection to the citizens to use the RTI. However, it was in 2009 that another Act was passed that superseded the earlier legislation and removed the lacunas in the exercise of the RTI in this state. It was only in 2011 that the process of constitution of the State Information Commission could be started.

Despite its delayed initiation, the RTI in the state seems to have enforced some amount of accountability in the functioning of government. As per the Annual Report of the Commission 2013–2014:

> The use of RTI by the people is witnessing a growing trend over the past several years. Almost all the public authorities/departments have become focus of the people while using their right to information, so to say, from block level offices to Chief Ministers Secretariat, from small government entities to Governors' Secretariat and from sub-district level civil courts to Hon'ble High Court asking for varied information about the different facets of public authorities and for resolving day-to-day problems. (J&K State Information Commission 2014, 6)

However, in general perception there is no follow-up mechanism after RTI. The information made available is of no use because of lack of accountability. To quote an activist:

> The real journey starts after receiving the information and the data from the public authorities, most of the citizens do not know what to do after getting the information. However in personal RTI pleas the appellants after getting the requisite information approach the court of law for getting the justice but in case of mass corruption, huge land scams, irregularities and deviation of stipulated rules by the officers and the departments, the information seekers remain helpless. As of now, the citizens remain confused as there is no such institution in the state where they can go with

> the information in their hands for seeking action against the defaulters and remedial measures. (Sharma 2012)

The problem of accountability after receiving the information has been raised by the SIC itself. In its Annual Report of 2013–2014, it stated that:

> The general refrain about not so effectiveness of the legislation is emanating from the reason that there is nothing under the statute which hold any government agency responsible for taking follow up action on the disclosure which are made under RTI on some serious cases of corruption and irregularities committed by the public authorities. There is a perception in the public circles in the State as well as outside State that there is no mechanism under the Act or under administrative provisions which will compel the authorities to take notice of the serious discourses affecting financial and administrative health of the State. (J&K SIC 2014, 48)

Panchayati Raj Institutions

Despite the fact that state had passed the Panchayati Raj Act in 1989, the Panchayati Raj institutions have remained quite weak and powerless in either providing for grass-roots democracy or working as third tier of federal structure. With lot of gaps between the state Act and the 73rd Amendment Act, the PRIs which are operational only at the village level, are neither financially empowered nor given functional autonomy. These bodies, like the urban local bodies, have been constituted in a half-hearted manner and their existence remains subject to the governmental control. Rather than constitutional bodies which derive their power from the higher law of the land, these institutions in J&K are constituted by the government in an arbitrary and ad hoc manner.

The state enjoys constitutional autonomy under Article 370 and hence the provisions of 73rd Constitutional Amendment do not apply to the state. Panchayats as envisaged in the State Act fall much short of being the institutions of democratic self-governance. Unlike the 73rd constitutional amendment and the Model Panchayat Act, the panchayats at all the three levels are not democratically structured. The principle of direct election of panchayats, for instance, is applied only at the village level, neither the block-level panchayat nor the district-level panchayat comprise the directly elected representatives of the people. It is only the chairman of the Block Development Council who is elected, but the process of election is not direct but indirectly done by the Electoral College constituted of the panches and sarpanches within that block. Similarly, there is no provision for direct election in the District Planning and Development Board. It is only the vice-chairperson of the Board who is elected, the Electoral College being constituted of the members of the Board itself.

What hampers the democratic structuring of panchayats at the three levels is the presence of the government officials. The secretary panchayat at all the three levels is a government official, the Gram Sevak at the level of the Halqa Panchayat, the block development officer at the Block Development Council level and the deputy commissioner at the level of District Planning and Development Board.

Actually, the concept of panchayats, in the sense of institutions of self-governance, cannot be applied at all to the block or district levels, since these levels are comprised more like the administrative extensions of government rather than autonomous bodies of self-governance. This is more so in case of the District Planning and Development Board. Besides, the secretary, the chairperson of the District Planning and Development Board is also a nominee of the government. As the practice has been, the government generally nominates a senior minister to be the chairperson of the board. Also as per the practice, the meeting of the Board is attended by many senior ministers, including the CM and the senior bureaucrats. The presence of such high-powered government officials and ministers cannot in any case allow the panchayat at this level to be a democratic body autonomous of governmental control and influence.

The structure of the District Planning and Development Board actually is more in line with the single line administration system that was introduced in the state in the mid-1970s rather than in line with Panchayati Raj institution. The idea underlying the single line administration was to decentralize planning to the level of the district, and at the time when it was introduced, it was quite a forward-looking idea. However, under the scheme of Panchayati Raj institutions, the concept of decentralized planning remains incomplete without its democratic structuring. The idea is to decentralize planning through democratic rather than the administrative structures.

There is a degree of arbitrariness in the constitution of panchayats in the state. Despite the fact that the Act provides for the continuity of panchayats by mandating that before the expiry of the term of panchayats, the next elections are to be conducted, it has been possible for the governments to ignore this provision and not conduct the elections before the expiry of the term of panchayats. After 2006, for five years, there was a vacuum with no elected panchayats in place. In another manner, the arbitrariness was reflected. Although the Act provides for the three tiers of panchayat, the government while holding the elections for the village panchayats has not been under any obligation to constitute the Block Development Council. The Block Development Council therefore was never constituted.

At the operational level, the biggest issue remains the powerlessness of the panchayats. From 2001 to 2006, though the Halqa Panchayats were the only democratically constituted layer of panchayat, these were not empowered. While the powers mentioned in the Act were not operationalized, additionally notified powers (in 2003) were also not made available. If panchayats remained functional, these were only in relation to the Centrally sponsored schemes, for which it was mandatory that the panchayats be involved. If there was anything more pathetic than the powerlessness of the panchayats, it was the absence of funding. Again, the only funding that was available to the panchayats was that which was tied with some Centrally sponsored schemes. Other than that neither the panchayats were provided basic funding by the state nor were these directed to raise their own resources.

While much of the problem of the powerlessness of panchayats rests with the unwillingness of the parallel administrative and higher governmental structures to transfer real powers to the panchayats, there is a structural problem in the Act as well. The PRIs in the state are not structured on the basis of federal principles. The principle of devolution of powers between the state and panchayats is not reflected in the Act in any manner. The Act provides the powers of the three tiers of the panchayat, but it does not in any case guarantee that there is no overlapping of functions and powers between the administrative and field agencies under the control of the state government and the panchayats.

The devolution of powers besides demanding that there be a clear specification of the powers in the Act requires that there be no conflict between the powers of the panchayat and those of the administrative agencies. Since many of the functions assigned to the panchayats are already in the sphere of the field administration, it is important that with the specification of powers of panchayats, there be simultaneously withdrawal of powers from the administrative agencies. This means that the process of empowerment of panchayats also requires fundamental changes in the administrative set-up in the rural areas.

It seems that due to the conflict situation of the state, the institutionalization of Panchayati Raj has not taken place according to a cohesive logic. The decision to institute Panchayati Raj rather than having its own logic appears to be based on exterior compulsions rather than internal logic. There is a general feeling in the state that the panchayats have been constituted mainly under the pressure of the Centre. That it is out of fear of the loss of the Central grants that panchayats are constituted. This lack of a cohesive logic gets reflected at many points. For instance, there has been a slow recognition and acceptance that seats through direct elections be reserved for women and other marginal classes. However, when an amendment was introduced for that purpose in 2004, such reservation was limited to the level of panches and was not extended to the level of sarpanches. Similarly, when the provision for Gram Sabha was incorporated in the Act, the powers of the Gram Sabha were not detailed.

THE STATE OF ECONOMY

There is a paradox that defines the economy of the state. While the state performs much better in terms of the living standards and levels of poverty, the economy of the state remains quite backward and crisis ridden. As per the *Digest of Statistics*, J&K, the poverty figures for this state in 2011–2012 was 10.4 per cent which was much lower than the all-India poverty figure of 21.9 per cent.[18] One factor that has contributed to the lower levels of poverty in the state is the land reforms that took place in the 1948–1950 period. More particularly, this is a reflection of the ceiling laws and the successful acquisition of surplus land by the state and the land redistribution to the tillers. As per the SECC data, 78 per cent of the rural households in this state have their own land. This percentage is quite higher when seen in the context to the national percentage of 44 per cent. The SECC data also shows that compared to many other states, the state is much better placed in many other areas as well. For instance, the percentage of people whose economic survival is dependent on casual and manual labour, though quite large, is still below the national level. While for the rest of rural India, for majority of the households (51.14%) the source of living is through casual or manual labour, in case of this state the percentage of such households is 37.28. 30.12 per cent have cultivation as the main source of living.[19]

Assessed from the perspective of the income level, the state presents a relatively better picture compared to many other states. The SECC data shows that while at the all-India level 74.49 per cent rural households fall in the income bracket of less than ₹5,000 per month, the percentage of such households in the state is 67.45. 14.52 per cent rural households have a monthly income between ₹5,000 and 10,000 per month. What is significant, the percentage of those who have a monthly income of more than ₹10,000 is much higher in the state than at the national level. At the national level only 8.29 per cent people fall in this bracket, but in J&K, as many as 18.03 per cent of the households in the rural areas have a monthly income of more than ₹10,000.

The state also ranks much higher in the case of salaried jobs. As compared to the all-India level where only 9.68 per cent of rural households have someone with salaried jobs, in case of J&K, the

[18] While the rural poverty level was 11.5 per cent for the state compared to 25.7 per cent at the all-India level, the urban poverty level was 7.2 per cent compared to 13.7 per cent at the all-India level.

[19] Curiously, the percentage of those who earn their livelihood by being domestic servants (4.46%) is relatively higher than the national average of 2.5 per cent.

percentage is as high as 22.37 per cent. Of these the largest number, that is, 19.95 per cent are employed in the government sector. Again this is much higher than the national average. At the all-India level, only 5.02 per cent rural households have someone with government jobs.

Notwithstanding these factors reflecting the relatively better economic situation of people in the state, the state is paradoxically placed in a very poor situation in many areas, especially in matters of social welfare. For instance, the state's performance with regards to the literacy levels is very dismal. This is despite the fact that after 1947 the state went ahead in acknowledging the right of free education for all up to the university level, a concept that was incorporated in the state's Constitution.[20] Compared to many other states in India, this state has a very high rate of rural illiteracy (39.52%). If we add those who are literate but educated up to primary level to this number, we will see that it will add to almost half of the population of the state. Which means that half of the households in this state are either illiterate or literate to the level of below primary. The only states which are worse than J&K in this case are Rajasthan and Bihar. In terms of education, only 3.24 per cent of the rural population has been able to reach up to the level of graduation and 6.09 per cent have been educated up to the higher secondary level (11.58% up to the secondary level and 15.49% up to the middle level).

The situation is not very positive as regards the overall quality of life of people in rural areas. Although the housing situation is slightly better than the national level, where 44.52 per cent people reside in *kuccha* houses and 55.38 per cent in *pucca* houses), it is a matter of concern that only 59.63 per cent of the rural households have *pucca* houses to live. As many as four of the 10 households in the rural areas are still the *kuccha* houses.

The poor quality of life of people in the state was noted in the Human Development Report of the Planning Commission. It stated:

[20] Even in the pre-1947 period, the concept of *Jabri* schools (compulsory or forced schools) was in vogue, especially during the time of Maharaja Hari Singh.

> [The state] ranks among one of the bottom-line states with respect to socio-economic development indicators like literacy rate, infant mortality rate, death rate, birth rate, status of children and women, power consumption, industrial and infrastructure development.

The Report concludes that the state 'falls behind most of the developed states in India'. It found poor infrastructure in literacy, education and health care. On social indicators such as literacy, infant mortality rate, death rate, birth rate, status of children and women, and rural development, it found the state to be doing quite badly (Planning Commission 2003, 43).

Although agriculture continues to be the major source of livelihood in the state, yet this sector remains the most constrained one, for many reasons. Despite the fact that the land reforms made it possible for a large number of the people to hold land and yet the average landholding is very small, almost the lowest in the country with the exception of Kerala[21] (Planning Commission 2003, 44). Further, there remains the issue of productivity due to lack of irrigation sources. As per the SECC data, 53 per cent of rural land is unirrigated and only 25 per cent of the rural household have assured irrigation for two crops. This is much below the national level where 37 per cent rural households are assured irrigation for two crops. Further, the process of cultivation is quite backward. This is reflected from the fact that only 1.72 per cent rural households here have mechanized three- or four-wheeler agricultural equipment.

While agriculture remains backward, the state is not industrially developed as well. To quote the report of the Planning Commission, 'The state does not have a strong industrial base, because geographical location of the state is such that the setting up of large industries with a large capital base is not feasible, besides adverse environmental consequences' (Planning Commission 2003, 92). One of the major

[21] As per the data quoted by the Planning Commission report, marginal landholders—those having land holdings below 0.05 to 1.00 hectares—formed the 77.97 per cent of the total population. While the small- and middle-range farmers comprised 18.77 and 2.63 per cent, respectively, the number of farmers with high landholding was below 1 per cent.

problems is the location disadvantage of the state and hence much of the industrial policy is dependent on central packages and concessions. From time to time, such packages have been announced and tax incentives are offered to those willing to invest in industrial development in the state. However, the state has not been able to benefit from the tax incentives offered by the Centre, since similar kinds of incentives are offered to other neighbouring states such as Himachal Pradesh. While the private sector is reluctant in investing in this state, the condition of the public sector industries is not very good. To quote the Planning Commission, 'Most of the public sector undertakings of the state have been running into losses continuously. Despite their poor performance and complete erosion of their paid-up capital, the state government continued to provide financial support to these loss-incurring companies' (Planning Commission 2003, 362).

Backward Economy

On the whole, the Planning Commission has defined the economy of the state as quite backward. It identified the characteristics of backwardness as 'predominance of agriculture sector', 'low degree of urbanization', 'inadequately developed infrastructure', 'widespread illiteracy' and 'low levels of investment'. Reaffirming this situation, the Task Force, constituted by the prime minister and headed by Dr C. Ranganathan, referred to a 'backwardness trap' that the state has been struck in. This trap keeps the state in a condition of 'low employment and low-income generation'. The Report of the Task Force referred to the 'unique economic disadvantages' that the state has due to its remoteness and poor connectivity, hilly and often inhospitable terrain, vulnerability to natural disasters, a weak resource base, poor infrastructure, sparse population density, shallow markets and most importantly a law and order situation threatened by militancy (Government of India 2006, 1).

A number of factors can be identified that have resulted in the poor and backward state of economy. Bhat classifies these factors in four categories. First, the topography and climatic factors. These factors 'do not allow agricultural activity to be conducted along the modern mechanized and scientific lines and consequently keeps the agriculture growth at a low level'. Second, there is the issue of poor physical infrastructure, 'which does not give a fillip to the investment activity in the State'. Third is the problem of 'lack of flow of private capital to the State' which he clarifies is 'mainly due to the non-economic reasons'. Finally, he identifies, 'rather continued heavy dependence on Government sector to generate growth', 'when the higher growth of the national economy and the better performing state economics in the last decade or so is mainly attributable to the private initiatives'. In addition to these factors, he attributes to the turmoil situation the reason for backwardness of economy[22] (Bhat 2012, 112).

One of the reasons that the Task Force identified for inability of the state to fight back its backwardness is the disinterest of the private sector in investing in this state. Its indifference is

> in part due to low supply and demand linkages and in part because of inhibition of the private sector on account of restrictive legislations. This private sector perspective was compounded by security concerns. Consequently, the burden of generating economic activity has had to be borne almost exclusively by the public sector. (Government of India 2006, 1–2)

In such a situation of low economic activity, the situation of employment is the most adversely impacted one. There are not many work opportunities and even when there is expansion of the middle class and a large population of educated within this class, there are no available jobs for this class. The Economic Survey of 2011–2012 revealed that the state of J&K had the highest unemployment rate of 5.3 per cent compared to other neighbouring states—while Punjab had 4.5 per cent, Himachal Pradesh 2.8 per cent, Delhi 2.7 per cent and Haryana 2.6 per cent (the all-India figure for unemployment is 2.6%) (Hakoo 2012). It also noted that the number of registered unemployed had crossed the mark of six lakh. Of these six lakh, the highest number was that of those who were educated.

[22] Task force has identified inherent problems of the state in the process of scaling up the production—small internal market, unfeasibility of export to market outside the state due to poor connectivity, high costs of service delivery because of high costs of inputs and poor private sector (Government of India 2006, 1).

With not many jobs being created in the industrial or service sectors, there has been extra burden on the state for providing the jobs. Further, there is 'the reluctance of many educated youth to move outside the State for exploring various employment opportunities there' (Bhat 2012, 113). In the absence of jobs in the industrial sector, the state youth are not ready to take advantage of the rich tradition of handicrafts and other cottage industries. The educated youth would rather go for a low-level government job rather than these avenues of work. Hence, the meagre jobs provided by the state become the most coveted ones. However, due to lack of availability of state jobs, what the state has been engaging, the highly trained professionals on contract basis; or on reduced salary for a number of years before they are properly regularized. There are schemes such as Rehbar-e-Taleem, Rehbar-e-Sehat, Rehbar-e-Zerat, etc., which work under the principle of contract and low wages.

Impact of Militancy on Economy

As the period of liberalization coincided with militancy the state could not take advantage of it—on the contrary, the economy of the state had to face adverse implications and therefore economic reversals. To quote the Report of the Task Force, 'Even as the India growth story is the global toast, much of the positive benefits of this are bypassing J&K.' It identified, 'the negative investor perception about security situation in the state' as one of the major reasons for this[23] (Government of India 2006, 3–4).

Right from the beginning of the period of militancy there was slowing down of the economic processes. With the law and order situation going haywire and the Valley losing its normalcy, there was loss of working days for the economy to go on its normal speed. As Dabla notes, militancy impacted the whole economy as the number

[23] The other two reasons identified by the Task Force Report included competition among states for attracting both domestic and foreign investment which is very fierce and J&K is handicapped in joining this competition because of its poor infrastructure situation and remoteness from markets and the land ownership issue which prohibits non-state subjects from owning property in the state (Task Force Report 2006, 3–4).

of working days were reduced due to the continuous shutdowns or the curfews. The existing economic infrastructure was 'reduced to rumbles' (Dabla 2012, 71–72). Of all the sectors of economy, it was the tourism which was the worst hit because of the security situation. Bhat notes that 'Many households, which had a long history and tradition of deriving their sustenance from tourism and allied sectors, had to switch over to some new, alien and less remunerator occupations.' Even after the late 1990s, this sector, according to him had a 'cyclic behaviour' and 'being a highly security sensitive sector, behaved as per the security perception at various points of time during the last decade or so'[24] (Bhat 2012, 113).

Among those who suffered the most included not only those dependent on tourism, mostly the 'taxi-transport operators, shikarawallas, retail sellers, footpath vendors, handicraft and other shopkeepers, and other seasonal-occupational personnel', but also the artisans and workers including the handicraft workers and the peasants. Dabla also traces the long-term implications for the agriculture as he has noted shifting of large-scale agricultural–horticultural land towards the 'construction of houses and other establishment' (Dabla 2012, 71–72).

However, more than other classes, these were the marginal classes which felt the impact of the situation much more. The destruction of the state's assets like schools have had implications for the education of the poorer sections who are mainly dependent on the state resources. There has been a silent migration of middle- and upper-class Kashmiri Muslims from the valley as the avenues of normal life started getting affected there. They sent their children to all parts of the state for educational purposes. However, the poor people could

[24] One can see the impact of such security-related sensitivity on the tourism sector in the last few years. With the initiation of the peace process in post-2000 period, this sector picked up relatively. However, right through the peak season of 2008, there was massive agitation which lasted for a number of months and thereby this sector witnessed a retreat. 2009 also was affected but through the 2010 summer there was another massive phase of unrest which led to the total decline of tourism that year. With a brief interval from 2011 to 2015 when things seemed to be picking up, tourism was again affected by the massive unrest in Kashmir in 2016 following the killing of Hizbul Mujahideen's Burhan Wani.

not do so and hence had to face the brunt of discontinuities in normal life. As Bhat notes:

> The education of the poorer segment, particularly of rural society, became the main casualty, as the better-off households sent their children outside the State for (better) education and those belonging to poor households got derived of even basic literacy and elementary education and became illiterates for lifetime. In the disrupted atmosphere, the parents from poor socio-economic background lost the enthusiasm to send their children, particularly the girls to school (Bhat 2012, 118).

Besides education, it was the health sector which was adversely impacted by the situation of militancy. There have been many studies which have shown higher level of psychological and stress-related diseases in Kashmir during the period of militancy. As per these studies, the conflict situation in general and the increased level of violence and militarisation since 1989 in particular, has led to psychological trauma among people of all ages. The number of people who have been diagnosed with post traumatic stress disorders and anxiety is very high.

The economy was impacted in many ways. The Planning Commission has noted as to how there was 'erosion of the tax base, increase in expenditure, destruction of infrastructure and various other factors related with disturbed law and order'. It also noted that 'because of continued tax and non-tax revenue shortfalls and heavy pressures on expenditure, the deficit has been increasing significantly.... The fiscal deficit increased from ₹1338 crores in the year 1999–00 to ₹1873 crores in 2000–01, registering an increase of 40 per cent' (Planning Commission 2003, 353–354). The economy on the whole came to halt as there was loss of working days due to bandhs and curfews.

Since the state has not been able to generate additional revenue from its own sources, fiscal and revenue deficit has been increasing. Besides other issues, there has been the problem of financial mismanagement. The CAG has often raised the issue of fiscal mismanagement. It reported that the state's overall fiscal liabilities having increased from ₹9,224 crore in 2000–2001 to ₹16,801 crore in 2005–2006. It also reported that the fiscal deficit had risen from ₹1,311 crore in 2002–2003 to ₹2,643 crore in 2005–2006. The state, according to the CAG, also had a serious primary deficit, which increased from ₹216 crore in 2002–2003 to ₹1,528 crore in 2005–06 (Talib 2007). This situation has led the state to a position of debt trap as 'borrowed funds or grants from the Centre are being increasingly used to meet revenue expenses and not used for productive purposes'. There is a very high level of debt servicing. As the Planning Commission has noted, 'The state is in debt trap on account of central loans, market borrowings and other loans besides the bank overdrafts.' There are also huge losses on power purchase (Planning Commission 2003, 359–360).

The security-related expenses formed one of the major burdens on the state's economy. 'A major chunk of the financial resources available to the State, which could have been otherwise utilised for the growth and development of the State economy, have been actually consumed by the security related expenditures' (Bhat 2012, 115).

To Conclude

This chapter has focused on issues related to the governance in J&K and emphasized as to how the state has suffered from various problems, many of which emanate from the conflict situation. The issue of governance was a prominent one even before the period of militancy, however, militancy aggravated the situation. The violence that was unleashed in the initial period not only led to loss of 'normalcy' but also resulted in devastation of the infrastructures. Much of the energies of the successive governments that came into power in the post-1996 period were therefore exhausted in rebuilding the infrastructure rather than investing in new projects. In the last few years, it has been the situation of popular separatist upsurge that has often resulted in paralyzing the whole government process. The period of 2008–2010 was one such period when the process of governance was seriously impacted by the massive protests which lasted for months together. 2016 also witnessed another period of prolonged upsurge during which there was almost a total collapse of the process of governance.

Seen in the long terms, the conflict situation has led to the institutional lag. Often being stuck up in situations in which governance becomes a secondary issue and establishing the law and order and asserting the authority of the state becomes the primary one, it is the institutionalization of governance that remains the issue. The state therefore suffers from the fragility of the institutions, particularly those related to provide checks and balances in the process of governance.

It is because of the long-term impact of the conflict situation that some of the problems faced by the state have seeped into the system. The problems related to accountability, employment, corruption, economic backwardness, for instance, have been so deep-rooted that these have continued to impact the state irrespective of the changes in the government.

References

Bhan, Ashok. 2013. '"Positive Peace" in Jammu and Kashmir'. In *Armed Conflicts in South Asia 2012: Uneasy Stasis and Fragile Peace*, edited by D. Suba Chandran and P. R. Chari. London: Routledge.

Bhat, R. L. 2012. 'Impact on Economy'. In *Conflict in Jammu and Kashmir: Impact on Polity, Society and Economy*, edited by V. R. Raghavan, 112–121. New Delhi: Vij Books.

Bloeria, S. S. 2016. *The Men Who Served Jammu and Kashmir*. New Delhi: Vij Books.

Bose, Sumantra. 2013. *Transforming India: Challenges to the World's Largest Democracy*. Cambridge, MA: Harvard University Press.

Bukhari, Shujaat. 2014, 22 July. 'Jammu and Kashmir: The New Battle'. IPCS #4579. http://www.ipcs.org/comm_select.php?articleNo=4584 (accessed on 5 November 2018).

Chawla, Prabhu. 1985, 31 May. 'Jammu and Kashmir: Tarnished Image'. *India Today*. http://indiatoday.intoday.in/story/j&k-cm-ghulam-mohammed-shah-faces-charges-of-large-scale-nepotism-and-corruption/1/354182.html (accessed on 4 September 2018).

Choudhary, Zafar. 2008, August. 'Good Riddance'. *Epilogue* 2 (8), 14–16.

Chowdhari, Sushma. 1990. 'Does the Bill Give Power to People?' In *Panchayati Raj in Jammu & Kashmir*, edited by George Mathew. New Delhi: Concept Publishing House.

CMP. 2002. 'Common Minimum Programme of the Congress-I, People's Democratic Party Coalition Government in Jammu & Kashmir'. http://www.satp.org/satporgtp/countries/india/states/jandk/documents/papers/kashmir_CMP.htm (accessed on 4 September 2018).

Dabla, Bashir Ahmad. 2012. *Social Impact of Militancy in Kashmir*. New Delhi: Gyan Publishers.

Daily Excelsior. 2016, 4 June. 'RTI Act Helped in Bringing Transparency, Accountability in Govt Deptts: SIC'. http://epaper.dailyexcelsior.com/epaperpdf/2016/june/16june04/page11.pdf (accessed on 6 September 2018).

Government of India. 2006, November. *Development of Jammu and Kashmir Growth Generating Initiatives: Report of the Task Force on Development of Jammu and Kashmir*. http://eac.gov.in/reports/rp_jk.pdf (accessed on 6 September 2018).

Hakoo, Sumit. 2012, 3 March. 'Highest Unemployment Rate of 5.3% among Northern States'. *Greater Kashmir*. http://www.greaterkashmir.com/news/news/jk-has-6-lakh-jobless-youth/114847.html (accessed on 26 November 2017).

Jammu and Kashmir State Information Commission. 2014. *Annual Report (2013–14)*. http://jksic.nic.in/Annual%20Report%202013-14%20.pdf (accessed on 6 September 2018).

Jha, U. C. 2014. *Armed Conflict and Environment Damage*. New Delhi: Vij Books.

Joshi, Arun. 2001, 28 March. 'Kashmir on the Brink of an Eco-Disaster'. *The Hindustan Times*. http://www.jammu-kashmir.com/archives/archives2001/kashmir20010328d.html (accessed on 6 September 2018).

Kak, B. L. 1978, 30 November. 'Kashmir: Status Quo'. *India Today*. http://indiatoday.intoday.in/story/j&k-cm-sheikh-abdullah-rejects-move-for-rapprochement-between-him-and-mirza-afzal-beg/1/434977.html (accessed on 17 November 2017).

Lone, Shabir Ahmad. 2015, January. 'Working of Peoples Democratic Party (PDP) and Congress Coalition Government in Jammu and Kashmir 2002–2008'. *International Journal of Research* 2 (1): 38–47.

Planning Commission of India. 2003. *Jammu and Kashmir Development Report*. http://planningcommission.nic.in/plans/stateplan/sdr_jandk/sdr_jkch5.pdf (accessed on 6 September 2018).

Pandit, M. Saleem. 2003, 25 February. 'Mufti Government Disbands SOG'. *The Times of India*. http://timesofindia.indiatimes.com/india/Mufti-government-disbands-SOG/articleshow/38504593.cms (accessed on 6 September 2018).

Puri, Balraj. 1968. 'Jammu and Kashmir'. In *State Politics in India*, edited by Myron Weiner. Princeton, NJ: Princeton University Press.

Pandit, Muhammad Shafi. 2009, 5 November. 'Governance in Jammu & Kashmir: A Historical Perspective: 1'. *Greater Kashmir*. http://www.greaterkashmir.com/news/gk-magazine/governance-in-jammu-kashmir-a-historical-perspective-i/63116.html (accessed on 17 November 2017).

Pargal, Sanjeev. 2009. 'The Toothless SVO-Delayed Probe: Half of Tainted Officers Retire'. http://kashmirforumorg.blogspot.in/search?updated-min=2009-01-

01T00:00:00-08:00&updated-max=2009-12-20T09:34:00-08:00&max-results=50&start=20&by-date=false (accessed on 6 September 2018).

Planning Commission of India. 2003. *Jammu and Kashmir Development Report*. http://planningcommission.nic.in/plans/stateplan/sdr_jandk/sdr_jkch5.pdf (accessed on 6 September 2018).

Punjabi, Riyaz. 1992. 'Kashmir: The Bruised Identity'. In *Perspectives on Kashmir*, edited by Raju C. Thomas. Boulder, CO: Westview Press.

Shafi, Mohammad. 1990. 'Revival of a Democratic Tradition'. In *Panchayati Raj in Jammu & Kashmir*, edited by George Mathew. New Delhi: Concept Publishing House.

Sharma, Raman. 2015, 24 March. 'J&K RTI Act Lot Has Been Done, More Is Required'. *State Times*. http://news.statetimes.in/jk-rti-act-lot-has-been-done-more-is-required/ (accessed on 6 September 2018).

Sharma, Raman. 2012, 13 February. 'After RTI? Transparency Is Okay, but What about Accountability!' *Greater Kashmir*. https://www.greaterkashmir.com/news/opinion/after-rti/113476.html (accessed on 5 November 2018).

Sultan, Mohammad. 1994. 'Jammu and Kashmir'. In *Status of Panchayati Raj in the States of India 1994*, edited by George Mathew. New Delhi: Institute of Social Sciences.

Talib, Arjimand Hussain. 2007, 23 December. 'Fiscal Challenges in J&K: A Pre-budget Review'. KashmirForum.org. http://kashmirforumorg.blogspot.in/search?updated-min=2007-01-01T00:00:00-08:00&updated-max=2008-01-01T00:00:00-08:00&max-results=22

The Times of India. 2003. 'J&K Sets up Panel to Retire Corrupt Officials', 9 March. https://timesofindia.indiatimes.com/india/JK-sets-up-panel-to-retire-corrupt-officials/articleshow/39759064.cms (accessed on 11 November 2018).

The Asian Age. 2000, 17 October. '4 Years On, Abdullah Tom-Tom's Successes'. http://www.jammu-kashmir.com/archives/archives2000/kashmir20001017b.html (accessed on 6 September 2018).

The Economic Times. 2015, 6 April. 'Five Out of Six Commissions "Headless" in Jammu and Kashmir'. https://economictimes.indiatimes.com/news/politics-and-nation/five-out-of-six-commissions-headless-in-jammu-and-kashmir/articleshow/46828226.cms (accessed on 5 November 2018).

The Hindu. 2004, 27 June. 'Eco Time-Bomb'. http://www.thehindu.com/thehindu/mag/2004/06/27/stories/2004062700130200.htm (accessed on 6 September 2018).

The Indian Express. 2001, 5 July. 'Farooq "Missing," FIR Lodged to Hunt Him Down'. http://www.jammu-kashmir.com/archives/archives2001/kashmir20010705c.html (accessed on 6 September 2018).

———. 2001, 22 March. 'JK Spent over ₹2900 Cr on Security'. http://www.jammu-kashmir.com/archives/archives2001/kashmir20010322c.html (accessed on 6 September 2018).

Vashishtha, Akash. 2015, 17 April. 'Deforestation Continues in Jammu and Kashmir Despite Floods'. *India Today*. http://indiatoday.intoday.in/story/jammu-kashmir-floods-deforestation-deodar-cedar-trees/1/430610.html (accessed on 6 September 2018).

Verma, Mohinder. 2014, 16 August. 'Accountability Commission All Set to Be Defunct from Aug 20'. *Daily Excelsior*. http://www.dailyexcelsior.com/accountability-commission-set-defunct-aug-20/ (accessed on 6 September 2018).

Yusuf, Shabir Ibn. 2016, 7 January. 'Mufti's "Healing Touch" Policy Changed JK's Security Scenario'. *Greater Kashmir*. http://www.greaterkashmir.com/news/kashmir/story/206385.html (accessed on 6 September 2018).

Interregional Relations and Politics of Jammu and Ladakh Since 1990

8

As we have already seen in the second chapter, the interregional tensions have defined the internal politics of the state right from the early post-Accession period and have been manifested in various forms ranging from day-to-day protests to prolonged mass agitations. These agitations though mostly articulating the feeling of 'regional imbalances' or 'regional discrimination' have reflected the deep political gulf that exists among the three regions of the state. This gulf that arose due to the distinct historical–political trajectories of each of the regions, on the one hand, and the exclusive nature and logic of the identity politics of these regions, on the other, was widened in the post-Accession period and was often manifested in the form of agitational politics. The political discourse in Jammu and Ladakh, meanwhile, got to be shaped around the idea of 'Kashmir's domination'. It was the perpetual sense of 'political deprivation' in the context of power politics as well as the lack of negotiability and political invisibility of these regions that generated a psyche of political neglect in these regions.

The gulf that exists between Kashmir on the one hand and Jammu and Ladakh regions on the other was further widened during the period of militancy and separatism. As the process of assertion of Kashmiri nationalism was intensified during this period, the internal political divergence within the state was also clearly reflected. While separatism overtook the Valley's politics, there was sharpening of regional assertions in Jammu and Ladakh.

REGIONAL POLITICS OF JAMMU PRIOR TO THE PERIOD OF MILITANCY

The decades of the 1980s saw the sharpening of regional identity of Jammu mainly due to the regional divide that was getting reflected in the electoral politics of that time. The 1977 Assembly election introduced the dimension of regionally competitive politics in the state. Prior to this, the electoral politics didn't reflect any regional difference since this politics was dominated by a single party in all the three regions of the state—the NC prior to 1965 and the Congress from 1965 to 1975. (The NC was merged with the Congress in 1965.) However, the merger of the NC with the Congress in 1965 had some implications for the regional equations. Despite the fact that the top positions of this party continued to be filled in by the same Kashmiri leaders who were earlier part of the NC, the Congress gradually started taking roots in Jammu region. Being the 'national' rather than a regional party based in Kashmir, the popular response to this party was much more positive in this region. What helped the party to get rooted in this region was increase in the influence of a few Jammu-based Congress leaders. These leaders included Pandit Tirlochan Dutt and Pandit Girdhari Lal Dogra, who were associated with the NC earlier, but with the party now directly linked with the national Congress leadership, their access to the central leadership made them quite powerful at the state level.

The presence of Congress as the dominant party of the state also helped in blunting the sharpness of Jammu's regional politics. However, it was with the revival of NC following the Indira–Sheikh Accord that the regional politics started becoming sharper once again. It was in pursuance of this Accord that the ruling Congress was forced to shun power to make space for the newly revived NC.

As Kashmir's politics came to be under the complete control of the NC, the sphere of influence of the Congress party came to be confined mostly to Jammu region. It was in this context that regionally polarized politics between Kashmir-based NC and Jammu-based Congress came to take shape. The 1977 Assembly election reflected this polarization to some extent. In this keenly contested election between NC, Congress and the newly formed Janata Party, the NC swept the political space in Kashmir winning as many as 39/42 seats. The Congress and Janata Party captured 21/32 seats of Jammu region (11 for Janata Party and 10 for Congress).

In many ways, the regionally polarized politics in the state also led to the initiation of communal divide. Competing with the Jammu based parties, the NC sought to extend its political constituency to Muslims of Jammu and Ladakh. Meanwhile, the Congress also sought to redefine its politics on the basis of a religious-cum-regional divide. It sought to carve Jammu as a Hindu constituency—a trend that became much more intensified in the subsequent years.

The regional gulf started increasing as political parties started pulling the politics of the state in different directions after the 1977 Assembly election. Sheikh Abdullah's stint in power politics after 1977 was also a period of assertion of Kashmiri identity vis-à-vis the Centre. Conscious of the Kashmiri response to his changed stance from 'Plebiscite politics' to 'power politics', he did not want to project himself as subservient to the Central Government and used the political space in Kashmir to assert his political autonomy vis-à-vis the Centre. It is a different matter that in the given situation in which the state was totally dependent on the Centre for its financial survival, there was not much space for assertion of such autonomy and he had to take reconciliatory steps after each such situation of assertion. However, as Schofield has noted, a number of statements made by Abdullah in which he demanded safeguards to Article 370 resulted in the strains in the relationship between the state and the Central Government now led by Janata Party. She notes that he continued to make provocative statements even after Congress under Mrs Gandhi came back to power in 1980. These statements like 'Kashmiris not being the slaves of either India or Pakistan' (Schofield 2003, 125) resulted in strong reactions in Jammu region, sharpening the regional-cum-nationalist sentiments. Traditionally, it was the Hindu right parties and organizations that had sought to interpret the Kashmiri emphasis on autonomy in the binary of nationalist/anti-nationalist discourse and to assert 'nationalist' basis of Jammu's regional identity. However, during this period, it was the Congress party that contributed to this process. As this binary continued to define the regional politics of Jammu for the times to come, assertion of 'nationalism' became a major component of the regional identity politics here.

However, apart from the 'nationalist' manifestation of regional identity politics, there were purely regional issues that were raised during this time. In the context of Sheikh's powerful position in the politics of the state and his political assertions, the perceptions about 'Kashmiri domination' were intensified in Jammu region. In 1978, a major regional agitation erupted here. The agitation was started at a local level in Poonch district with complaints about irregularities in appointment of school teachers. However, a few months later, this transformed into a major regional agitation spreading to all major towns of the region. Although the students took the lead, the agitation had the support of various sociopolitical organizations. An all-party Jammu Action Committee was formed to give a direction to the agitation. This committee identified the continued regional neglect as the basis of the ongoing discontent and popular unrest. Apart from highlighting the lower share of the region in state employment, the general refrain during the agitation was that the state government was not paying attention to the demands of Jammu people and that the recommendations made by Gajendragadkar Commission were not implemented. 'The Committee adopted a unanimous resolution on 26th December 1978, demanding statutory, political and democratic setups at regional, district, block and *panchayat* level' (Behera 2012, 171). The issues raised during the agitation caught the attention of the Central Government which sent a delegation of five MPs to ascertain the situation and later appointed a Commission of Inquiry headed by Justice S. M. Sikri. This Commission pointed out that 'there existed discrimination and favouritism in the context of different regions, which was giving rise to irritations and tensions among the people of the state' (Singh 2007, 139). It recommended the setting up of a State Development Board and made suggestions regarding financial allocations for regions (Behera 2012, 173).

The regional sentiments were further sharpened when Sheikh Abdullah introduced the Resettlement Bill in the State Legislative Assembly in March 1980. The Bill sought to grant permission for settlement to those Pakistani nationals who had migrated to Pakistan from J&K between 1947 and 1954.[1] This Bill was severely opposed in Jammu region not only because it was seen from the prism of religious affiliation of those who would be benefitted by the policy but also because of the reason that it affected the material interest of many of those residents of Jammu region, particularly the refugees who had been allotted the property (whether agricultural land or residential houses) of those who had migrated to Pakistan. A large number of Hindu PoK refugees located in Jammu region apprehended that this would lead to the dispossession of their land, since they settled on this land without the propriety right which still remained in the name of original owners.

The Resettlement Bill which later on became a law generated an intensely polarized politics within the state. While most of the political organizations and parties based in Kashmir supported it, those located in Jammu region stood against it.[2] The Congress party, identifying itself with the regional politics of Jammu, strongly opposed it.

The regional-cum-communal divide continued to inform the politics of the state throughout the decade of the 1980s. The 1983 Assembly election was particularly regionally and communally very polarized. While the NC asserting the Kashmiri identity politics sought to woo the Muslims of Jammu region, the Congress mobilized the Hindu voters of this region by playing both the regional and nationalist card. The discourse of nationalism was invoked by the Congress as it critiqued the 'autonomy' politics of the NC and characterized it as 'anti-national'. In the end while the NC dominated the electoral space of Kashmir region capturing bulk of the seats there, Congress got as many as 26/37 seats from Jammu region, mostly from Hindu-dominated constituencies.

[1] As per the provisions of the Bill, those persons who were valid state subjects before 14 May 1954, and had migrated to the 'territory now in Pakistan' after 1 March 1947, could return and resettle in the state of J&K.

[2] After the Governor reserved his assent to the Bill, it was given mandatory approval when it was passed again by the Legislative Assembly; however, it was sent for presidential reference to the Supreme Court, but after 19 years it was returned unanswered by the Supreme Court. On the basis of a plea, it was stayed by the Supreme Court.

Since the Congress and NC formed a pre-poll alliance during the 1987 Assembly election, this election did not reflect the tendency of these two parties to regionally or communally polarize the politics of the state. However, the communal polarization did take place in this election as the MUF invoked religion in its electoral campaign.

Soon after the 1987 Assembly election, the regional sentiments were sharpened in Jammu region. There was a spontaneous protest against the Farooq Abdullah government's decision to stop the practice of annual 'darbar move'. As per an old practice going on since the pre-Accession period, the whole government moves from Kashmir to Jammu in the winter months and from Jammu to Kashmir in summer months. This practice has often come under severe criticism not merely for financial implications but also for the reason that it stalls the process of governance for a number of weeks, twice a year. However, the very practice of 'Darbar Move' has come to have political connotations, especially for regional politics of Jammu. The shifting of the whole government from Kashmir to Jammu brings a sense of parity to the region since the city of Jammu is given the status of capital for six winter months (along with Srinagar which becomes the capital city during the summer months), with not only the political class and bureaucracy being stationed here but the winter Legislative Assembly session also taking place here. The financial implications notwithstanding, the decision to stop the practice generated fears about the loss of the political status of Jammu region and the parity that it enjoyed with Kashmir on this issue. The agitation that lasted for more than a month ended only after the decision was reversed with the intervention of Boota Singh, the then Home Minister of India. Although initiated by the Jammu Bar Council, the agitation was supported by various sociopolitical organizations. So complete was the popular support to the agitation that members of the ruling Congress based in Jammu also joined it. As a consequence, the government was forced to withdraw the decision. However, this led to a reaction in Kashmir region and soon enough Kashmir erupted over the issue. Interestingly, the ruling NC members were part of the agitation in the Valley.

This agitation was followed by another agitation, though at a smaller scale. This was the Reasi agitation around the demand for implementation of the Wazir Commission Report that had recommended the creation of three more districts in Jammu region—Reasi, Samba and Kishtwar. The Commission had been constituted in the early 1980s following an agitation in Jammu region demanding reorganization of the districts following a decision of the government to create three districts in Kashmir Valley (Badgam, Pulwama and Kupwara) and one more district of Ladakh (bifurcation of Ladakh into the two districts of Leh and Kargil). It was the non-implementation of the recommendation of the Wazir Committee Report that led to a renewed agitation in 1988. The agitation was supported by Jammu-based political parties and organizations including BJP, Janata Party, Panthers Party, Shiv Sena as well as Jammu Bar Council and traders. All these organizations supported the agitation launched under the banner of Citizen's Action Committee. Although the intense agitation was located in Reasi only, it had its impact on the whole of Jammu region.

On the basis of above analysis, one can say that before the period of militancy, the regional sentiments were quite sharpened in the two major regions of the state. Regionalism, on the whole, informed the electoral politics of the state in a big way and in certain ways also came to be communalized. Many a times, in Jammu region, this politics also took the agitational mode. Most of these agitations emanated out of a perception that that there is an imbalance in the power politics of the state and that Jammu region being marginalized in power politics is also 'discriminated against' in terms of policy matters. The various commissions appointed by the Central and the state governments to go into the question of imbalances and discriminations, particularly the Gajendragadkar Commission, remained the point of reference during these agitations. There remained a persistent feeling in Jammu region that the recommendations, on the whole, were being ignored and when it came to distribution of development resources, employment in state services, administrative reorganization, educational and other resources, Jammu was being 'neglected'. These perceptions were shared across the party and organizational lines and though the Hindu rightist organizations and parties, particularly the Bharatiya Jana Sangh earlier and the BJP later, appropriated the regional politics of Jammu, the Jammu-based political leaders belonging to other parties equally shared this perception. That is the reason why within the political parties particularly like the Congress and Janata Party (and even at times within the NC), there remains a regional divide.

REGIONAL POLITICS OF JAMMU: THE PERIOD OF MILITANCY AND AFTER

It was during the period of militancy that political divergence between Kashmir and Jammu came to be clearly reflected. Mainly rooted in Kashmir, militancy got extended to the Jammu region. But compared to Kashmir, it had altogether different nature and implications here. Unlike Kashmir region where there was a linkage between militancy and popular separatism, in Jammu region that linkage was missing. Although there were parts of the region which became infested with militancy, however, the popular separatist politics that accompanied militancy in Kashmir was not reflected in any form. Many parts of the region, in fact, got caught up involuntarily in the situation of militancy. For example, in a city like Jammu, where there were a number of incidents of militant violence, there were explosions in public transport, militant attacks during the weddings and public functions, and huge loss of life and damage to public infrastructure. There were of course areas which became infested with militancy with local recruits joining in. However, even in these cases, there were clear cut distinctions in the nature of militancy.

The erstwhile district of Doda which now comprises the three districts of Doda, Kishtwar and Ramban was the first one to be affected with a huge number of militants located in Kashmir seeking refuge in the difficult hilly terrain here and also a number of locals joining the militancy. This was not only because of the geographical proximity but the ethnic affinity of this area with Kashmir. As Luv Puri notes, about this belt:

> The main linkage of the district with the Kashmiri militancy lies in the fact that approx. 40% of the population is of Kashmiri origin and speak Kashmiri or some of its dialects. Historical accounts show that many centuries ago people from Kashmir valley, more specifically from its Anantnag district migrated to Doda district on account of break out of a famine in

> the area. Some of them still maintain relations with the people on the other side of mighty Pir Panjal. (Puri, 2002)

The ethnic Kashmiri-speaking people in this belt have from the beginning a strong sense of identification and emotional attachment with Kashmir. This attachment extends to politics as well. Right from the early post-Accession period, the Muslims of this belt had come under the influence of the NC and, thereafter, the Plebiscite Front, when it was formed. During the period of militancy also, there was a general sense of identification with the Kashmiris. However, despite such identification, the separatist politics did not impact this area in the manner in which it had impacted the Kashmiris. Unlike Kashmir, there were no anti-India demonstrations here and there was not much presence of separatist organizations like the Hurriyat. Militancy was also of different nature. Despite the fact that there were local recruits, there were no local militant organizations. Even JKLF didn't have any presence here. A large number of militants who were operative here were foreign militants.

The other part of the region where militancy had huge impact was in the twin border districts of Poonch and Rajouri. Despite the fact that Poonch and Rajouri districts are located on the border and provided an easy route to entry in the state to the militants,[3] it took pretty long time for militancy to be localized here. However, as Suba Chandran notes:

> While the Muslim population initially sympathised with the cause of azadi and backed the militancy, that support could not be sustained for the lack of physical, economic, cultural and political connections. As the militant movement became violent, the fault lines became apparent, leading to the decline. (Chandran 2007)

He further notes the reality of the mixed community life in this belt that prevented the deepening of the impact of militancy in these two districts. To quote him:

[3] The region offered five transit routes along the mountain ridges, all of them converging either at Choru Sira, a village at the base of the Pir Panji Gali mountain range, or near the Rad Khad, a river at the base of the mountains. As a trek through these routes took 15 to 20 days, the militants took shelter in villages on the way, sometimes after forcing their residents into submission (Swami 1999).

> The substantial presence of minority communities and the history of their living together have also contributed to the decline of militancy in these two districts. Besides the Muslims, these two districts also have Hindus and Sikhs, who have lived here for a long time. Unlike the Kashmiri Pandits of the Valley, these minority groups stayed back in these districts. There were migrations in the last ten years, but there was no exodus.... The presence of the 'other' and the confidence in each other added to the communal harmony in these two districts. (Chandran 2007)

As we can see, the situation of Kashmir was replicated neither here nor in the Doda belt. Despite all the odds, the mainstream political space remained intact and the political parties and political leaders maintained their relevance. There were many local issues and concerns and the political parties and leaders were quite involved in these. In fact, it was during the period of militancy that the issues of backwardness and underdevelopment of these areas were articulated and raised. These included the demand for Chenab Valley Hill Council in Doda belt, the demand for Peer Panchal Hill Council in Poonch–Rajouri districts and the demand for ST status for Paharis at par with Gujjars.

Other than these areas, in the rest of the region, there was a feeling of being caught involuntarily in the situation. The militant attacks generated a counter response leading not only to the assertion of regional but also nationalist identity. This response was more intensified as there were series of provocative attacks in which a large number of people were killed and injured, prominent among these included the attacks within the city of Jammu region—for instance, the explosions during the Republic Day Parade in Jammu's Bakshi stadium (1995), fidayeen attack in Raghunath Temple (March 2002 and November 2002) and fidayeen attack in Jammu's railway station (2001 and 2004). Much provocation was provided meanwhile by the 'selective communal killings' in the Doda belt after 1993. Here there were series of militant attacks in which the Hindus were identified and killed by the militants (Sarthal in 1993, Barshalla in 1996, Kamlari in 1997, Kudh Dhar in 1998). To quote Praveen Swami:

> From 1998, communal massacres gathered momentum and in scale. In 1998, 132 civilians died in six massacres conducted across the State and in adjoining Himachal Pradesh. After a lull in 1999, the massacres resumed

> in 2000. In 2001, 108 people were killed in 11 major incidents, while 83 people were killed in five incidents in 2002. Most of these killings targeted desperately poor communities in the State's more remote mountain regions. (Swami 2006a)[4]

In the situation as it evolved during this period of militancy, there was certainly a realignment of political forces. The BJP which had traditionally a limited electoral influence within the three urban constituencies of Jammu city only increased its space not only in the militancy-infested areas but in the region as a whole. It was the reflection of the extension of its constituency within the region that one could see impressive performance of this party during the 1996 Assembly election. Winning eight seats, its performance was much better than that of the Congress Party. While it registered its victory in eight seats, it was runner-up in eight other constituencies. Of these, in four constituencies its margin of defeat was very small, ranging from 253 to 813 (Chowdhary and Rao 2003, 206). Later, in the 1998–1999 period, it also succeeded in winning one of the two Parliamentary seats the region.

DEMAND FOR REGIONAL AUTONOMY

One of the major implications of the militancy and separatism in Kashmir, as stated above, was the accentuation of the perceptions about the political divergence and, as a consequence, intensification of the regional sentiments in both Jammu and Ladakh regions. By the time the political processes were restored after a gap of seven years in 1996, the 'regional autonomy' had become the most important demand of the region. So much importance had the discourse of autonomy assumed during this time that even the NC that had been opposed to this demand throughout its earlier history incorporated it in its 1996 election manifesto. It raised the issue along with the issue of state autonomy.

The concept of regional autonomy has not been clearly defined by the political parties. The term was initially used by Balraj Puri, a social and political activist from the region. In his opinion, the regional

[4] In another major massacre 22 people were killed in Kulhand and Tharva in 2006.

autonomy for Jammu and Ladakh would be the only solution to the political divergence within the state. He pleaded for the federalization of the internal structure of the state and argued that the concept of the state autonomy as negotiated by the Kashmiri leadership needs to be further evolved to incorporate the autonomy for the regions, and from the regions to the district and panchayat levels. He therefore gave the model of a five-tier federal structure in which besides the Centre and the state, the Region, District and Panchayats would be the other units of the devolution of powers (Puri 1981).

Balraj Puri's model of regional autonomy which acknowledged Article 370 and the special constitutional status of the state, however, was not acceptable to the Hindu rightist organizations like the BJP. As per the ideological stance of this organization, the state needed to be fully integrated with the Indian Union. The demand therefore was for abolition of Article 370. Since acknowledging the demand for regional autonomy would mean acceptance of the state autonomy by default, this party even while seeking to represent the interest of the region did not pursue the demand to begin with.

However, despite the reluctance of the Hindu right organizations to raise the issue of regional autonomy, it started becoming part of the political discourse of the region. During any agitation that was organized to protest 'discrimination of Jammu region', the demand for devolution of power to the region was implicit. What was demanded was greater regional share in governmental structure, devolution of political and administrative powers from state to regional levels, separate allocation of funds for each of the regions and greater share of regions in state resources, employment opportunities, etc.

By the 1990s, this demand came to be more articulated and sharply focused. During the 1996 Assembly election, it was one of the major demands that was raised in Jammu region. Political parties, across the ideological divide, brought this issue in their manifesto in a big way. Even the BJP during this election demanded 'regional councils' for Jammu and Ladakh.

The discourse on regional autonomy became more focused when, after the 1996 Assembly election, the NC government constituted a Regional Autonomy Committee along with the State Autonomy

Committee. The terms of reference of this Committee were to 'evolve instrumentalities like local organs of power to promote better involvement and participation of people in different regions for balanced political, economic, educational, social and cultural development'. It was also expected 'to examine the powers that such organs need to be vested with and to suggest changes in the constitutional structure of the state in this context'. Balraj Puri was appointed as the chairman of this Committee. However, before the Regional Autonomy Committee could submit its report, the government dismissed Puri as the chairman. He, however, submitted an 'unofficial' report recommending autonomy at the regional, district and panchayat levels (Puri 1999).

What brought the debate around regional autonomy to the public space of the region was the controversial official report of the Regional Autonomy Committee. This Report sought to negate the very claims of Jammu and Ladakh as Regions and therefore the very logic of regional autonomy. Using historical, ethnocultural and developmental explanations, it argued that 'Jammu is heterogeneous—culturally, linguistically, ethnically and geographically' and that it never existed as one region. It stated as to how the whole area now claiming to be the Region was segregated into diverse regions, each of which could be considered an independent entity with its 'distinct history, language and cultural identity' (Regional Autonomy Committee Report 1999).

Rather than recommending regional autonomy, the Report recommended reorganization of the region in such a manner that instead of the Jammu region as it exists, there should be three autonomous regions: Jammu (Jammu, Kathua and Udhampur districts, excluding Mahore tehsil); Pir Panjal (Poonch and Rajouri districts) and Chenab Valley (Doda district and Mahore tehsil). Alternatively, it recommended devolution of power straight from the state to the district level.

That the logic of reorganization was clearly communal could be seen from the fact that in underlining the specificity of the three regions, the Report had taken into consideration the factor of religious demography. In practical terms, it meant the separation of the Hindu-majority area of Jammu from the two Muslim-majority belts of Doda and Poonch–Rajouri.

Rather than dealing with the grievances of the region, the Regional Autonomy Committee sharpened the rift between the two major regions of the state. In the wake of this Report, the intensity of the regional sentiments was heightened.

Regional sentiments were also intensified in the wake of the recommendations of the State Autonomy Committee. Since the Report had suggested the reversal to the pre-1953 constitutional position of the state, there was strong opposition to it. The Report was seen to be linked to the history and politics of Kashmir with no connection whatsoever with the political aspirations of Jammu region. Although a reference was made in the Report to the 'mosaic of diversities in its regions, groups and communities', it did not go into the intricacies of the question of diversities. What was worse, the question of regional autonomy was not linked with the question of state autonomy.

The parties such as BJP and Panthers Party reacted very strongly to the contents of the Report. These parties vehemently opposed the idea of pre-1953 position as contrary to the 'national interest'. However, the opposition to the Report came not only from these rightist parties which have been traditionally opposed to the autonomy and special constitutional status of the state, but also from the Centrist parties like the Congress. These parties did not identify with the contents of the Report.

How the people of Jammu perceived the issue of autonomy and regional autonomy gets reflected from the CSDS post-poll survey in 2008. The survey clearly reflected that while people in Jammu in general were more favourable to the idea of regional autonomy, they were either indifferent or opposed to the idea of autonomy of the state. While a large majority of respondents in Kashmir agreed to the proposition that the state should be given greater autonomy (61.4%), only 30.5 per cent respondents agreed to it in Jammu region. Interestingly, a large percentage of respondents (56.5%) had no opinion about it. Similar response was recorded during the 2002 post-poll survey also.[5]

[5] Thus 45.8 per cent responded negatively and 32.2 per cent responded positively.

THE POLITICS OF TRIFURCATION

On the whole, the later years of the decade of the 1990s saw the politics of the two major regions of the state being pushed in opposite directions. The efforts of the NC to radicalize its politics in Kashmir, in the wake of the challenge that it received from the separatist politics, by sharpening the Kashmiri identity increased the gulf between the two regions. It was in this environment that the discourse of 'trifurcation' or division of the state came in vogue. Although it was only on the fringes of the mainstream politics of the region that this politics came to be located, yet it got sufficient media attention.

The idea of division of the state is an old one and has been floated, off and on, since the early 1950s. Initially it was suggested in the form of Dixon Plan in which a suggestion was made to divide the state around the river Chenab. Since the Hindu-majority areas are separated from the Muslim-majority areas by this river, it was seen as a very convenient way to deal with the complex question of social diversity and political divergence. This idea of division of the state on religious lines, however, is quite a far-fetched one since the religious divide in the state does not always necessarily correspond with the political divide.

In the late 1990s, this idea was enthusiastically pursued by the US-based think tank known as the Kashmir Study Group. Headed by an America-based Kashmiri billionaire, Farooq Kathwari, the Group came out with a report titled *Kashmir: A Way Forward*. Following the logic of the Dixon Plan, this Report sought to address the issue of interregional differences by suggesting a five-fold division of the state, largely on the grounds of religion. It recommended 'a separate Muslim state of Kashmir incorporating the Muslim dominated areas of Jammu region like Doda and Poonch–Rajouri. The Hindu dominated districts of Jammu and Buddhist-dominated district of Leh' meanwhile were proposed as autonomous political units (Chowdhary 2000, 2603).

Later, this idea was also pushed through the Regional Autonomy Committee that was constituted by the NC government. The official report of this Committee suggested the division of Jammu and Ladakh regions on communal basis. It not only recommended that the predominantly Hindu districts of the Jammu region be separated from the predominantly Muslim districts (of the Doda and Poonch–Rajouri belts), but also that 'a part of the Muslim-dominated area (Mahore tehsil) be carved out of the rest of the Hindu-dominated districts to fit in the Muslim-dominated area of Doda' (Chowdhary 2000, 2603). It also recommended the separation of Buddhist-majority Leh district from the Muslim-dominated district of Kargil.

It was in the early 1990s that the politics around the demand for division of the state evolved in a rather bigger way in Jammu region. A group of local intellectuals and civil society members came together to form the Jammu Mukti Morcha (JMM). The Morcha, which was led by Professor Virender Gupta, made an argument for separation of Jammu from Kashmir on the ground of the lack of any commonality between the two regions and the reasons of self-sufficiency of this region. Reference was made to the 'domination of Kashmir' not only in terms of political power but also in distribution of resources and availability of opportunities. Thus it was alleged that there was discrimination against Jammu in terms of share of government employees, allocation of funds especially in relation to tourism, location of important offices, etc. It was also pointed out that there was lack of political parity between Kashmir and Jammu regions, in terms of disproportionate and lower representation of Jammu region in the state Assembly, the unfair delimitation process and its poorer share in ministerial births.

The JMM was quite limited in its influence and did not have any real impact on the ground level. It could not mobilize the masses and, on the whole, its politics remained confined to the level of idea that was reflected in media and in the limited intellectual circles.[6]

The idea of the reorganization of the state was given a boost following the support that it got from the RSS. In a conclave of its workers in Kurukshetra, held in June 2002, the RSS passed a resolution in favour of statehood for Jammu region as well as UT status

[6] To quote Behera, 'this organisation was founded by a group of intellectuals whose *modus operandi* remained largely confined to organising processions and strikes and submitting memoranda to the State and Central governments' (Behera 2002).

for Ladakh (Bukhari and Kang 2002). Soon after, the national level leadership of BJP also encouraged the local leaders in their demand for trifurcation of the state. During his speech in the Sindhu Darshan Festival in Leh, Lal Krishna Advani, the then Union Home Minister, spoke in favour of the UT status for Ladakh.[7] However, later the BJP disassociated itself from this idea. This put the local BJP in quite a paradoxical situation, even when the local leaders wanted to openly show their support to the demand for Jammu state but could not take a public position on it.

It was following the passing of the Nagpur resolution by the RSS that Jammu State Morcha (JSM) was formally launched in Jammu (Noorani 2008). Like the JMM, the JSM was also a small organization which comprised civil society members, university teachers, media professionals, advocates and a few traders. Although limited to urban centres of the predominantly Hindu-inhabited towns such as Jammu, Samba, Kathua and Udhampur, this organization had a slightly wider range for its politics. Apart from generating a discourse about the need for Jammu state mainly through wall posters and media debates, it also entered the electoral fray and won one seat during the 2002 Assembly election.

The idea of Jammu state, at this time, was not floated in isolation and was a part of similar kinds of responses in Ladakh and among the Kashmiri Pandits as well. In reality, the Hindu rightist forces in Jammu region were working in tandem with the Panun Kashmir as well as the Ladakh Buddhist Association. What was common in the politics of all these organizations was their demand for reorganisation of the state. Thus, apart from the demand for Jammu state, there was the demand for UT status for Ladakh and that of 'homeland' for Kashmiri Pandits within Kashmir Valley. Although the demand for homeland as articulated by Panun Kashmir was not included in the RSS resolution, yet for the Panun Kashmir leaders like Ajay Crungoo, it was 'a step forward

[7] Though the demand for statehood became more vocal in the late 1990s, it was raised from time to time in Jammu region. Balraj Madhok was the author of this demand in 1947. He formally pleaded for the division of the state on the grounds of national interest. He had written an article to this effect in the Jana Sangh journal, *Organiser* (Kak 2002).

as it accepts the basic principle of internal reorganisation as a means of finding a solution to the crisis in the state' (cited in Kak 2002).[8]

The demand for the Jammu state fizzled out quite soon. In any case, it never took the form of a popular movement. With BJP not being in a position to support the demand, the JSM could not mobilize the masses in its favour. Even otherwise, its sphere of influence was very limited to urban areas of a few towns of Jammu region. Being more of a media campaign rather than a mass movement, its appeal was limited to urban educated middle class only of those parts of Jammu which are predominantly Hindu. It had no presence whatsoever in those areas which had Muslim or even mixed population. It was the RSS support that made it possible for winning one seat during the 2002 Assembly election. However, after the 2002 Assembly election, the JSM lost its visibility. The demand for reorganization of the state of J&K, meanwhile, has continued to be raised once in a while.

As regards the popular response to the idea of trifurcation and the formation of a separate state for Jammu, the CSDS post-poll survey gives some clue. When asked about the opinion around trifurcation, larger number of respondents in Jammu region disagreed with the idea. As against 24.6 per cent respondents who agreed (9.6% agreed and 15.1% strongly agreed) that there should be trifurcation, 64 per cent disagreed (26.2% disagreed and 37.8% strongly disagreed). Similarly, on the question whether there should be a separate state for Jammu, a larger majority disagreed (26.2% disagreed and 26.7% strongly disagreed) and a smaller number at 34.1 per cent agreed (14.2% agreed and 19.9% strongly agreed). Similar was the response on the question whether J&K should be divided into three different states—42.9 per cent fully disagreed and another 3.7 per cent somewhat disagreed, while 3.4 per cent fully agreed and 3.2 per cent somewhat agreed, and a large number at 46.7 per cent here did not have any opinion.

[8] Among the organizations that supported the demand for Jammu state included the VHP. In the opinion of its leaders, the move for demanding the separate state for Jammu was important for protecting the Hindu interests. The VHP committed the role of sadhus in working towards the goal of separating Jammu from Kashmir (Bukhari and Kang 2002).

AMARNATH AGITATION, 2008

In 2008 the region got engulfed in a massive agitation around the Amarnath land row. Despite the 'religious' basis of the agitation, it was the feeling of regional deprivation which was the major driving force of the agitation. To begin with, the agitation had started in Kashmir over a government order related to diversion of 39.88 hectares of forest land in Kashmir to SASB for the purpose of construction of pre-fabricated structures for the pilgrims during the period of pilgrimage. The underlying issue that led to the mobilization of people in Kashmir was the fear of 'demographic change'.

As under the pressure of the agitation in Kashmir the government was forced to withdraw the Order of land transfer, there was a reaction in Jammu region which from the beginning had taken a religious shape. Terming the revocation of the Order as an assault on religious sentiments of the Hindus, various Hindu organizations mobilized enormous support in the region. Various political, social and religious organizations gave a call for complete Jammu Bandh in what they alleged was the 'state's surrender of the claim over the forest land allotted to SASB' and thereby 'hurting the sentiments of millions of Hindus, across the country' (*Kashmir Times* 30 June 2008). Soon the agitation spread to other parts of the region and almost every part of the region got involved in it. A total halt came to all activities with the effect that educational institutions were closed, plying of public transport was stopped, shops were closed and so on. With the involvement of business and trading class, the economic activity was also made fully non-functional. The Bandh was extended even to small shopkeepers and hawkers. The strategy was to impress upon the authorities that there was complete popular support and that there were no dissenting voices. Mass rallies were organized on a daily basis. And on any given day, there were multiple rallies, in fact, waves of rallies. This situation lasted for more than two months.

The agitation had the support of the various Hindu organizations including the VHP, Bajrang Dal and the BJP. BJP, in fact, raised the issue at the national level. A committee named as Shri Amarnath Yatra Sangharsh Samiti (SAYSS) was organized which was a conglomeration of 35 political, social and religious outfits, and included, among others, political parties and organizations such as Lok Jana Shakti Party, Jammu and Kashmir National Panthers Party, Kranti Dal, All Parties Migrants Coordination Committee, Panun Kashmir, and Jammu Kashmir Vichar Manch. Among the organizations which extended the support to SAYSS included the Jammu Bar Council, Federation of Industries, the Jammu Doctors Association, Alliance of Trade and Industries, All J&K Public Sector Employees and Workers Federation, etc.

In the frenzy that was raised and the emotions that were involved, the Amarnath agitation was seen as the agitation of the 'people of Jammu'. Parties other than BJP were soon under pressure to show their solidarity with those agitating 'in the interest of Jammu region'. Not only the Panthers Party came in ready support but the Congress leaders also started defending the agitation. Several of them also expressed their overt support to the Sangharsh Samiti. The common refrain coming from the Congress leaders was that despite their affiliation with the Congress, they were bowing to the popular sentiment of people of the region.

Although it was the religious issue that triggered the agitation in Jammu, however, it clearly came to have regional tones. The revocation of the land order was projected as 'another' example of appeasing the mainstream and separatist leaders of Kashmir and succumbing to their pressures. Jammu's political neglect and discrimination therefore became one of the central points of discourse and the agitation came to be seen as an assertion of the people of Jammu for its political empowerment.

The most serious implication of the land row was the fractured relationship between the two major regions of the state. In an unprecedented manner the two regions were placed in an antagonistic relationship. The issues were articulated in a zero-sum regional relationship leading to mutual acrimony. The situation became extremely difficult when the economic interest of the two regions was placed in a mutually exclusive and contradictory mode—with a call for 'economic blockade of Kashmir' coming from Jammu and the call for 'boycotting the trade through Jammu' came from Kashmir.

What was the most undesirable consequence of the situation was that in both the regions extremist voices came to dominate the political space and the centrist space was fully marginalized. In Kashmir, it was not only the separatists who got the space, but even among the separatists, the most hardliners attained the prominence and it was their politics that set the tone of the agitation. In Jammu meanwhile, the space was acquired by the hardcore Hindu fundamentalist and ultra-chauvinist organizations. While in Kashmir these extreme elements succeeded in generating the fear about demographic change, in Jammu these elements succeeded in generating anti-Kashmir sentiments.

What was worse, the regional confrontation assumed communal direction. Communalization of the protest politics, in fact, was built in the logic of the agitation itself. The emphasis on preserving the 'Muslim majority character of the state' (in Kashmir) was confronted with the assertion to defend the Hindu religious sentiments (in Jammu). For Jammu's multireligious society this was bound to have serious consequences. The region had successfully maintained the tradition of communal amity even in the wake of serious challenges during the peak of militancy. Despite the spate of provocative selective killings of Hindus in the Doda belt of this region, there was no serious incident of communal tension. On the contrary, the region in general and the predominantly Hindu belt of this region in particular became more accommodative and cosmopolitan during this period. Not only the lakhs of Kashmiri Pandits were accommodated here, but the Kashmiri Muslim middle class seeking to escape the traumas of violence and militarization also found Jammu as safe heaven. Due to the relocation of people of all kinds, the city of Jammu, in fact, assumed a cosmopolitan character.

However, during the Amarnath agitation, there was a shade of communal politics that overtook the region. With the religious assertion and the mass frenzy, the situation at times could easily take communal turn and the trivial incidences could lead to localized communal tensions. There were certain cases of skirmishes between the members of the two communities on the issue of complete bandh. While there were Muslim organizations which had openly registered their support to the agitation, there were many others who were either indifferent or not convinced to participate in it.[9] There were also reported incidences of the members of minority being targeted. In many reported cases the stranded vehicles of drivers were targeted. Such incidents were reported on both sides. There were reports of the Jammu drivers being targeted in Kashmir and the Kashmiri drivers being targeted in Jammu.[10]

The kind of regional polarization that had taken place during the Amarnath agitation was unprecedented. Never earlier, the people of the two regions stood so clearly divided on any issue as they were around the issues raised during the agitation. This was clearly reflected in the CSDS 2008 poll survey. On various questions related to the agitation, there was altogether opposite response. For instance, when asked to choose between the two opinions, namely (a) whether the government's decision to give land to SASB was correct and (b) whether the government should not have given land to the SASB, while the larger percentage of respondents in Jammu (64.2%) agreed with the first option, the larger percentage (83.5%) in Kashmir agreed with the second option. On being asked to choose between the two options, namely (a) once the government had given land to the SASB taking it back was wrong and (b) since land belonged to the government, there is nothing wrong in taking it back, in Kashmir

[9] This happened in early July in Bhaderwah where Seri Market became the scene of tension. Here the activists of VHP who were enforcing the Bandh asked all shops to be closed. It was following an argument with one shopkeeper that the people belonging to both the communities started pelting stones at each other. While the police intervened and the mob was dispersed, however, the situation took an ugly turn when a grenade was lobbed (*Kashmir Times* 3 July 2008).

[10] There were voices of concern as well, which sought to restore the intercommunity trust and made appeals from time to time to maintain communal harmony. Of these, one was the voice of Jammu Muslim Federation which sought to work as bridge between the Sangharsh Samiti and the Muslims of Jammu, and while extending support to the agitation also made appeals for communal harmony. Similarly, Pradesh Vishwakarma Sabha appealed people to maintain communal harmony and asked people not to fall prey to exploitation in the name of religious sentiments (*Kashmir Times* 31 July 2008). Similar appeals were issued by Jammu and Kashmir Workers and Employees Joint Action Committee. Appeal was made to uphold the plural and composite culture of the region and the tradition of the secular values of the region.

larger number (78.7%) agreed with the second choice and 60.5 per cent agreed with the first choice.[11]

The Amarnath agitation was an important milestone in the politics of the state that reflected the growing regional divide within. It clearly pointed out a deep sense of political deprivation that has come to characterize the political psyche of the region. The way the people came to be mobilized in favour of the agitation and the way it became a popular movement was more than anything else a reflection of the regional assertion. That there is a domination of 'Kashmir region' in the politics of the state and that Jammu region is 'discriminated against' in the matters of resource distribution and policymaking is the 'common sense' of Jammu region. How deep-rooted is this feeling gets reflected from the CSDS surveys. To a question during the 2002 post-poll survey in which the respondents were asked whether they agreed or disagreed with the statement that the Kashmir leaders have discriminated against the Jammu region larger percentage of respondents agreed to the opinion during the 2002, 2008 and 2014 surveys.

Subregional Identity Politics

Much of the feeling of regional deprivation is shared and pervasive throughout the Jammu region. However, despite this pervasiveness, within the region one can find pockets where discontent prevails both vis-à-vis Kashmir region and the political elite of Jammu region. In these pockets, there remains an inherent feeling that in defining Jammu's political neglect and discrimination, the real pockets of backwardness have not been pinpointed.

[11] On another question when the respondents were asked to suggest ways to resolve the controversy and also suggest whether the government should give all the land back to SASB, or it should not give any land or give some land during the period of pilgrimage, in Kashmir, larger percentage of people (52.6%) were of the second opinion that the government should not give any land. 25.9 per cent were of the third opinion that some land should be given during the period of pilgrimage and only 0.8 per cent were in favour of the first opinion that all land should be given back to the SASB. In Jammu, 47.1 per cent were in favour of the first opinion that the government should give all land back and 13.8 per cent were in favour of the third opinion that some land should be given to be used only during the Yatra. Only 2 per cent respondents were in favour of the second opinion.

This feeling emanates from the way the regional identity politics has been articulated. Since much of this politics has been appropriated by those organizations that seek to speak from the majoritarian perspective, it has failed not only to be inclusive and exhaustive but has also failed to highlight the complex and plural character of the region. To quote Zafar Choudhary:

> What jeopardises the cause of Jammu region is the fact that discrimination discourse in Jammu is mostly city-centric and often lets the religious sentiments to overtake regional issues. For example, the Muslim dominated districts of region—Rajouri, Poonch, Kishtwar, Doda, Ramban and Reasi—often refuse to become party to the cases projected in districts of Jammu, Samba, Kathua etc.— essentially the Hindu dominated districts. With this division within the region, many in Kashmir and elsewhere in the country dub any agitation in Jammu as communal.... (Choudhary 2009, 11)

Much of the discourse of regional deprivation was evolved during the 1952 agitation led by the Praja Parishad and was articulated later by the Bharatiya Jana Sangh/BJP and other rightist organizations. Since the hold of these parties and organizations remains limited to the Hindu-dominated areas of the region, the people of Muslim-dominated belt of Jammu do not identify with this politics. This generates perennial problems for the Muslims of Jammu region. They see themselves as distinct from Kashmiri Muslims and do not identify with the Kashmiri identity politics and yet they do not feel comfortable with the religious tint in the regional identity politics of Jammu region. As Behera argues, 'The Jammu Muslims, for example, do not support the BJP's Hindu politics and the demand for a separate state of Jammu, nor are they willing to be assimilated completely into the Kashmiri Muslim identity' (Behera 2002).

What further complicates the issue is that much of the regional identity politics neglects the real source of backwardness which lies in the peripheral and remote parts of the region. The issues raised in the name of the regional identity politics are more oriented towards the elite interest (for instance, the issues of state employment; admission to professional colleges; opening up of educational institutions such as the universities, professional colleges and the like). The issues concerning the backward areas and sections of society including those related to illiteracy, health, connectivity and infrastructure in remote and far-flung areas have not been paid attention to. Gajendragadkar Commission while recognizing the 'neglect' of the region had also noted that 'within both Jammu and Kashmir regions there are certain pockets which have remained much more backward than the rest of the region' (Gajendragadkar Commission Report 1968).

It is in this context of the regional political discourse that one can refer to the subregional discontent in Jammu region, particularly in the twin districts of Poonch and Rajouri districts, on the one hand, and the erstwhile Doda district (now formed of the three districts of Doda, Kishtwar and Ramban), on the other. On almost all the indices of development, these districts are quite deficit and face peculiar problems. For instance, the twin districts of Poonch and Rajouri form the border area that has faced the maximum brunt of the conflict situation. Quite well-connected before 1947 with Punjab, it became a remote area after the division of the state in 1947 and drawing of the Ceasefire Line. Its remoteness also affected its overall development.

When it was drawn, the Ceasefire Line cut across the villages and divided the families between the Indian and Pakistani side with no legal means of communication. Since the volatility of the borders continued here throughout the post-Partition period, people here have been living here almost in a war-like situation with shelling and mining being the everyday normal. It was only in 2003 that there was some respite to the people as ceasefire was enforced as per an agreement between India and Pakistan. However, this ceasefire could remain in force barely for a decade. In last few years, there have been frequent cases of violation of ceasefire and not only there has been huge loss of lives but there have also been frequent displacements.

Being at the periphery, the development of these districts is quite dismal, facing the problems of low literacy, backward agriculture, not many commercial avenues and no industry at all (Maini 2010, 17–18).

What is peculiar about these two districts is the 'centrist' tradition of politics of the area. Despite the efforts to generate a politics of larger Muslim identity within the state, people have refused to play along. As

Zafar Choudhary notes, 'These districts despite being Muslim majority refuse to be seen as part of a larger Kashmiri identity.' He also notes that these 'two districts have maintained a fair distance from the core separatist politics despite the fact that nearly half of Muslim families there have a sibling in the Pakistan administered Kashmir, militancy too in this region could not take firm roots as it did in Kashmir Valley' (Choudhary 2010a, 5).

The people in Poonch and Rajouri experience as much sense of alienation from Kashmir as from the rest of Jammu region. There is a similar discourse here about the 'Kashmiri domination' vis-à-vis the development of this subregion. However, the sense of discontent here is extended towards the regional elite of Jammu as well. In the context in which the regional discourse of Jammu reflects the urban elite interest and underplays the concerns of the people of this area, there remains a strong sense of alienation vis-à-vis the regional politics of Jammu. This feeling is further intensified when Jammu gets to be represented as the 'Hindu other' of 'Muslim Kashmir'.

It is this sense of alienation that gets reflected in a subregional identity politics that has evolved in the last three decades or so. This is politics based on the demand for a separate Hill Development Council—the Peer Panchal Hill Council. Articulated mainly by the Paharis of the region, this demand emanates from the grievance that people of this subregion are not equal partners to the development process of the region. As Behera notes:

> Pahari grievances touch on familiar subjects in the state: underdevelopment and social and economic backwardness of districts and the dominance of Jammu district in the share of civil services, public sector undertakings, and important institutions. Pahari leaders argue that with a distinct geography, history, language, culture, and socioeconomic conditions, the region is best suited to have its own Autonomous Hill Council. (Behera 2006, 130)

Doda belt comprises another huge geographical chunk of the region, which also faces its peculiar problems of difficult mountainous terrain. Comprised of the three districts of Doda, Kishtwar and Bhaderwah, this area faces severely problems of connectivity, backwardness and poor infrastructure. People here find life to be much more difficult not only due to the terrain and the climate but also due to the lack of resources for employment and livelihood.[12]

One of the major grouses of this area has been that despite being resource-rich, the belt has not been able to reap the advantages of these resources—either these resources have remained untapped or have been utilized without much benefit to the local population. Reference in this connection has made to the large water resources and huge hydroelectric projects which have been developed by the NHPC and are used for the benefit of many states dependent on the northern grid. Despite having huge tourism potential, there is not much governmental attention on investing for the development of tourism in this area.

Due to the overall backwardness of the area, there exists a general feeling that in the context of competitive claims being made between the political elites of Kashmir and Jammu region, this area has remained neglected. The general refrain is that the area is owned neither by the Kashmiri leadership nor by the Jammu's political elite. Even when the Kashmiri leadership seeks to extend its constituency to the area by invoking the religious elements, however, not much energy is used on the development of the region. Similarly, even when the area falls within the Jammu region, the dominant elite of the region does not refer to the backwardness of this belt while referring to the neglect of Jammu region. It is with reference to these problems that demand often is made for Chenab Valley Hill Development Council (CVHDC).[13]

[12] Except for a few pockets of the belt like Baderwah which made great strides in the field of education and also contributed to the first generation of army officials, civil servants and professionals, people in this belt faced acute poverty and backwardness. Migrating in search for lowly jobs in the towns of mainland Jammu has been a tradition of this belt.

[13] A bill was moved by Sheikh Abdul Rehman in the state Legislative Assembly in the year 2002 for constituting the Hill Development Council of region Doda. However, the Bill was referred to select committee and lapsed later when the 2002 elections were announced. Another time a Bill was introduced by Doda MLA Abdul Majeed Wani in 2006, however, the Bill was later withdrawn on the request of CM Ghulam Nabi Azad (Ganai 2009). MLC Khalid Najib Suhrawardy moved a resolution for establishing the CVHDC which was passed by the Upper House on 19 August 2009. The logic that

The subregional politics of both the Poonch–Rajouri districts and the Doda belt reflects the limitation of the regional politics of Jammu. This limitation is defined by the exclusive character of the regional politics which rather than reflecting the concerns of the whole region, somehow, remains confined to the interests of the dominant sections—both in the economic and demographic terms.

REGIONAL POLITICS OF LADAKH

As in Jammu region, the decades of the 1980s and, particularly, the 1990s were defined by assertion of Ladakh's regional identity vis-à-vis Kashmiri identity. In continuity with the politics of the earlier decades, the politics of the post-1980s period was also defined by the demand of UT status for Ladakh. The justification given for this was not only the neglect of Ladakh in the Kashmir-dominated politics of the state but also the distinct identity of Ladakh. As Mona Bhan notes:

> Ladakhis, like other minority groups in the state, did not consider the state of Jammu and Kashmir to be an 'organic political entity', a claim based on their independent cultural and political identity before the British and Dogras annexed Ladakh with Kashmir in 1846, forever altering the course of their political destiny. (Bhan 2014, 13)

Lack of autonomous administrative and political status of Ladakh led to a massive protest in 1980. The major issue raised at this time was related to its being a part of the administrative division of Kashmir. The demand therefore was made that it be given the status of a separate division along with the Kashmir and Jammu divisions. During this agitation a demand for the ST status for people of Ladakh was also made. Demand was also made for the regional autonomy of the area (Puri 1982, 273). Interestingly, it was an all-inclusive agitation

he provided while moving the resolution being: 'Chenab valley, the connecting link between Kashmir and Jammu regions, is the most backward area, highly mountainous with only 5 to 6 percent road connectivity. The area is far behind in the process of development' (Ganai 2009). For the backwardness of the area, the demand was made for formation of a Hill Development Council on the lines of the Ladakh Hill Development Council.

which had a widespread support from all over the region, including the Muslim-majority areas of Kargil.

Ladakh's politics, however, took a different turn in 1989 when it was engulfed in a major anti-Kashmir and anti-Muslim agitation. As Behera (2006, 115) informs, it was a 'minor scuffle between a Buddhist and some Muslim youth in Leh market in July 1989' that took the shape of a major agitation with the demand for UT status of Ladakh. The Ladakh Buddhist Association (LBA) that spearheaded the agitation formed a 'People's Movement for Union Territory Status' (Bhan 2014, 42). Among the many grievances pointed out during the agitation, some major ones related to the Kashmiri Muslims dominating the economy as well as the administration of Ladakh, imposition of Urdu language in school education and neglect of development of Ladakh. Kashmiri Muslims were accused of 'halting development contracts for the construction of buildings, roads, and bridges; of orchestrating the gross underrepresentation of Buddhists in the state services ... and of adopting unrealistic norms for the allocation of plan funds to Ladakh...' (Behera 2006, 116).

The agitation was quite exclusive in nature and emphasized the Buddhist character of the Ladakhi identity (Bhan 2014, 42). The whole discourse of the LBA revolved around the Buddhist culture and history of Ladakh. What contributed to the Buddhist exclusivity was the exclusion of Ladakhi Muslims from the agitation. The LBA initially imposed a social boycott of the Kashmiri Muslims, which was later extended to the Muslims of Ladakh as well. The boycott 'applied both to the personal contacts and to commercial relationships' (Bray n.d., 7). By implications, there was no social interaction between Buddhists and Muslims in Leh. 'Buddhists avoided Muslim-populated areas and did not enter hotels, restaurants, or shops run by Muslims. Farmers were prohibited from exchanging tools. No interreligious marriages were allowed, and meetings among relatives of different faiths were stopped' (Behera 2006, 117). The Buddhist leadership justified the boycott on the ground that there was 'reluctance' on part of Muslims to be part of the agitation. However, scholars observing the situation have noted the communal basis of the strategy of boycott (van Beek 2001, 383).

As the Buddhists avoided any kind of public communication with the Muslims and cut off all traditional relations of mutual dependence and cooperation, the agitation, therefore, saw a complete divide between the Buddhist and the Muslim communities. For instance, the Buddhist dependence on the Kashmiri Muslim butchers and bakers was sought to be done away and replaced by new 'Buddhist shops' which as van Beek suggests were 'run mostly by the natives of Himachal Pradesh' (van Beek 2001, 383). Not only this, there were attempts to clearly demarcate the Buddhist part of the Leh from the Muslim one by using identification marks on the houses, shops and other places. It was in this process that the use of Tibetan script for Muslim shop signs was forbidden by the LBA (Bray 1991, 128–129). Meanwhile, 'Buddhists prayer flags which until now were not so visible, were spotted on Buddhist houses, yellow stickers were pasted on the vehicles of Buddhists' (van Beek 2001, 383).

It was in 1992 with the intervention of the Central Government that the social boycott of the Muslims was lifted by the LBA. However, by this time, the internal cohesion of Ladakhi society was hugely impacted. The gulf that developed between the Buddhists and the Muslims continued to be seen in the later period as well.

One of the major implications of the 1989 agitation was the extension of provision of Ladakh Autonomous Hill Development Council for both the districts of Leh and Kargil. This arrangement was made available in response to the major demand of the agitation—of UT status for Ladakh. As per an agreement between the Central Government, the state government and the LBA leaders, the commitment was given for the Hill Development Council.

The agitation which was exclusive to begin with became inclusive later. It was after the end of the social boycott of the Ladakhi Muslims that the Ladakh Muslim Association (LMA) joined the LBA in raising the demand. 'With the formation of a Joint Coordination Committee drawn from all of the area's communities—Buddhist, Shia and Sunni Muslim, and Christian—the demand for a Hill Council earned support of all the people of Leh' (Behera 2006, 116).

Despite the commitment to provide for the Autonomous Hill Development Councils both for Leh and Kargil, it was only in 1995 that the formal order was passed. To begin with, only the Hill Development Council of Leh became operational since the Kargil leadership refused to accept the proposal for such a Council. It was a gap of a few years before the Kargil Autonomous Hill Development Council also became operational.

Despite the formation of the Hill Development Council of Leh, there remained tensions between the state government and the members of the Hill Development Council. These tensions revolved mainly around the issue of finances and the overlap between administrative sphere of functioning of the Council and the state's bureaucratic officials.

Leh–Kargil Divide

In analysing the politics of Ladakh, it is important to analyse the internal divide that evolved over the years between the Buddhist-dominated district of Leh and the Muslim-dominated district of Kargil. Although Ladakh as a whole suffered from the situation of backwardness, however, this situation of backwardness was initially articulated by the Buddhist leadership located in Leh. And in the process of such articulation, Ladakh was mainly defined from the Buddhist perspective. Although the Buddhist representation of Ladakh mainly sought to emphasize the cultural difference of Ladakh from Kashmir, however, such representation of Ladakh was quite influenced by the religious perspective of Buddhists.

Being more backward than the Leh district, Kargil did not have much voice in the politics of Ladakh to begin with. However, by the late 1970s the political elite of this subregion started asserting their voice. There came a transformation in the politics of Ladakh in general and in the political assertion of Kargil in particular, when the single district of Ladakh was bifurcated between the Buddhist-dominated Leh and Muslim-dominated Kargil, in 1979.

Balraj Puri holds both the Buddhist politics of Ladakh and the NC responsible in creating the divide between Leh and Kargil. As the Buddhists sought to identify with the Centre and sought separation from Kashmir,

> [It] encouraged a consciousness of distinct sub-regional identity among the Muslims of Kargil. Moreover, whatever grievances they may have had

> against Kashmiri leadership, they did not want to opt out of a Muslim-majority state, as the Buddhist leaders were demanding, to become a permanent minority.

He further argues:

> The National Conference was quick to sympathise with the fears of Muslims of Kargil and lent its support for recognition of their identity. The state government went a step further and bifurcated the district of Ladakh into a Buddhist majority district of Leh and a Muslim majority district of Kargil in 1979, both being part of Kashmir division. (Puri 1982, 273)

Right from the time the two districts were created, the political divide between the two districts came to be clearly delineated. While the politics of Leh continued to have its anti-Kashmir bias which reflected in its constant demand for the separation from Kashmir, Kargil's politics saw some kind of dependence on Kashmir's political elite. Although the Muslims of Kargil did not share the political perspectives of Kashmiris and didn't identify in any way with the politics of Kashmir, yet in the process of seeking an assertion of its identity vis-à-vis what was perceived as the 'Leh Buddhist domination', the Kargil's political leadership sought to seek help from Kashmir. What helped in the process was the fact that the NC sought to extend its constituency to Muslims of Ladakh and show its soft corner for Kargil vis-à-vis the district of Leh. The political leadership of Leh meanwhile in its contestation of Kashmir's political leadership sought to see an ally in the Central Government.

However, this relationship could not been seen in a simplistic manner for the reason that due to its backwardness, there was as much resentment in Kargil against the Kashmiri leadership as in Leh district. However, along with this resentment, there was fear of domination by the Buddhist leadership of Leh as well. To quote Mona Bhan:

> Not unlike their Buddhist neighbours in Leh who complain of 'stepmotherly treatment' from the state administration in Kashmir, Kargilis too resent the heavy-handedness of the Kashmiri administration in matters of governance and development. They are also equally troubled by the political machinations of Leh's predominantly Buddhist leadership, which evokes intense distrust and antipathy among the Shia'a Muslim Kargilis. (Bhan 2014, 11)

The political divide between the two districts became quite wide in the 1980s. The first major tension between the two districts came out in the open in 1980 around the issue of generator which had to be shifted to Kargil. This led to agitation in Leh which was headed by Kushok Bakula. Ultimately this led to the parallel demands by All Party Action Committee in Leh for regional autonomy and All Party Action Committee of Kargil for improved communication in Kargil and provincial level status for whole of Ladakh.

The divide was also widened during the 1989 agitation when Buddhists enforced boycott against the Muslims. Being a predominantly Muslim district, it not only distanced itself from the agitation but its leadership also opposed the Buddhist leadership.

Since the formation of the Hill Councils, the two districts have been following their own logic of politics. Leh's politics is still dominated by the Buddhist leadership's demand for the separation of Ladakh from Kashmir in one form or the other. With the onset of militancy this demand came to be raised in more sharpened manner. Like Jammu, the political divergence between Kashmir on the one hand and the politics of Ladakh on the other came to be clearly highlighted since the whole region, including Kargil, remained totally untouched by the militancy or even by separatism.

A peculiar feature of the Ladakh's Buddhist politics during this period was that it operated in tandem with the Hindutva forces operating in Jammu as well as in the Centre. With the BJP taking keen interest in Ladakh, during the early period of its ascendancy in the Centre, there was a mutual ideological linkage between the Buddhist politics of Ladakh and Hindutva politics at the national level. A very significant reflection of the confluence between the Buddhist and Hindutva could be seen with the initiation of Sindhu Darshan Festival by L. K. Advani in 1997. An event which became officially sponsored by the BJP government in the Centre was projected as a part of the 'Hindu nationalist project' seeking to symbolize the religious importance of Indus river in Ladakh and organizing a national and international campaign around it. However, as van Beek notes:

> Despite the participation of local religious and social organisations and the presence of leading officials during the festivities of Sindhu Darshan,

> the spectacle is viewed with mixed feelings by most Ladakhis. As there is no tradition of pilgrimage to rivers in Ladakh, nor in Tibetan Buddhism in general, and the Indus does not enjoy any particularly sacred status in local perception, Sindhu Darshan is regarded above all as a political spectacle. Although local cultural troupes perform during the proceedings and monks play religious music on the margins of actual ritual at the river ... the attitude among the general population for many years was that this was a ceremony of outsiders for outsiders, which brought little or no benefit to Ladakh. (Van Beek 2006, 130)

And even then, the interjection between the Buddhist and Hindutva politics could be seen around the issue of 'trifurcation' of the state. This politics of trifurcation as supported by the RSS suited the political agenda of the Buddhist leadership as their demand for the UT status for Ladakh very much formed a central point of the trifurcation politics.

The politics of trifurcation, however, sharpened the internal divide within Ladakh as the political leadership of Kargil openly disassociated itself from the LBA's demand of UT status for Ladakh and contested the solely Buddhist character of Ladakh. While asserting the Muslim character of the region, a leading Muslim leader of Kargil, Asghar Ali Karbalai, indicated his inclination to identify with the larger Muslim majority of the state (Bose 2003, 92).

The intraregional divide almost on religious basis marked the politics of Ladakh throughout the next few decades. Such divide was reflected through the electoral process as well. During the 2002 Assembly election, so strong was the demand for the UT status for Ladakh that all Leh-based political parties including the Congress, NC and the BJP dissolved themselves to form the Ladakh Union Territory Front (LUTF) and won both the seats of Leh without contest. To show solidarity with the cause, the 'Buddhist ministers in the state government, Rajya Sabha member Thikse Rinpoche, and the two MLAs for Leh district all announced their resignation from their respective political parties' (van Beek 2004, 216). The Kargil leadership, however, did not identify with this politics and clearly articulated their opposition to the demand for the UT status for Ladakh.

Although the LUTF failed to have much impact in post-2002 politics, the demand for UT status continues to dominate the politics of Leh. The political divide between the two districts of Ladakh continues to reflect in one form or the other. The confluence between the Buddhist politics and the Hindutva politics that was reflected in the late 1990s became much more intensified in the recent years. This confluence is clearly manifested in the increased political space for the BJP. The party which did not have much space in the electoral politics of Ladakh till the very recent time succeeded in winning the sole Parliamentary seat of this region during the 2014 Parliamentary election, and also succeeded in registering its victory in both the constituencies of Leh during the Assembly election of the state held the same year.

To Conclude

This chapter focusing on interregional relationship within the state has sought to go beyond the Kashmiri identity politics and to identify the political divergence that exists between the politics of Kashmir region, on the one hand, and that of Jammu and Ladakh, on the other. In both the regions, it is the context of political discontent that has been manifested in the form of agitational politics. With the logic of politics of Kashmir being entirely different from that of these two regions, there remains a constant tension in the interregional relationships.

The tension that exists between Kashmir and Jammu—the two major regions of the state—has various dimensions; however, the most important of these relate to the lack of political parity between these two otherwise almost equal regions. Absence of political parity can be understood both in terms of power politics and in terms of visibility and negotiability of the two regions. Kashmir was seen to be a dominant partner for both the reasons. Until 2002, the power politics continued to be dominated by the Kashmir-based political elite with only a token presence of Jammu region in it. As has been explained, this had much to do with the nature of the party politics which gave the advantage to the Kashmir-based dominant party to control the power politics of the state. With the decline of the dominant party system and fragmentation of the electoral space between two regional parties of Kashmir, there has emerged an intensely competitive party politics in which Jammu has got the advantage of being represented in the power politics almost on the basis of political parity.[14] However, notwithstanding the parity between the two regions in the formation of governments and sharing political power, the deep-rooted psyche of political deprivation continues to prevail in Jammu region.

Much of this psyche is rooted in the way Kashmir region has come to acquire centrality in the politics of the state since the period of Accession. Despite being almost an equal region in terms of its population, Jammu has not attained a sense of partnership. All political arrangements that have come to be formalized vis-à-vis this state have followed the logic of Kashmir's politics. With these political arrangements having become by default the arrangements for the state, there remains the question of negotiability of the political elite of the Jammu region. The conflict situation that has further led to the greater visibility of Kashmir region, therefore, leads to a psyche of political neglect.

References

Behera, Navnita Chadha. 2002, 26 October. 'A Signal from Jammu'. *Frontline* 19 (22). https://www.frontline.in/static/html/fl1922/stories/20021108006002000.htm (accessed on 5 November 2018).

———. 2006. *Demystifying Kashmir*. Washington, D.C.: Brookings Institution Press.

[14] It is in the context of the lack of political parity between the two regions that the issue of 'delimitation' assumes political significance in the regional discourse. There is a strong feeling in Jammu that the region has not been allocated a fair share of Assembly seats, and that given a fair chance the gap between Kashmir and Jammu region can be further reduced. The last delimitation that took place before the 1996 election increased four seats for Kashmir region (42 to 46) and five seats for Jammu region (32 to 37), after which the process of delimitation has been frozen. Jammu-based political parties and organizations often demand fresh delimitation with the plea that a fair process of delimitation can lead to increase the number of Assembly constituencies in favour of Jammu and decrease its gulf from Kashmir. That the perception about the 'unfair delimitation' is quite widespread in Jammu region and that it goes beyond the political parties is reflected in the CSDS post-poll survey of 2002. On the question whether there should be more MLAs in the Assembly from Jammu, around 72 per cent respondents in Jammu agreed (45.7% strongly agreed and 26.9% agreed) and only 6.8 per cent respondents disagreed (1.4% strongly disagreed and 5.4% disagreed).

Behera, Navnita Chadha. 2012. 'Impact on Inter-Provincial Relations'. In *Conflict in Jammu and Kashmir: Impact on Polity, Economy and* Society, edited by V. R. Raghavan. New Delhi: Vij Books.

Bhan, Mona. 2014. *Counterinsurgency, Democracy, and the Politics of Identity in India: From Warfare to Welfare?* London and New York: Routledge.

Bray, John. 1991, November. 'Ladakh History and Indian Nationalism'. *South Asian Research* 2 (2): 115–133.

Bray, John. n.d. 'Old Religions, New Identities and Conflicting Values in Ladakh'. http://www.phil.uni-passau.de/fileadmin/dokumente/lehrstuehle/korff/pdf/conferences/paper_j._bray.pdf p7

Bukhari, Fayaz, and Bhavdeep Kang. 2002, 29 July. 'Slice of Geography'. *Outlook*. http://www.outlookindia.com/magazine/story/slice-of-geography/216656 (accessed on 10 September 2018)

Chandran, D. Suba. 2007, 5 February. 'Declining Militancy in Rajouri and Poonch'. IPCS, #2200. http://www.ipcs.org/comm_select.php?articleNo=2200 Accessed on November 5, 2018

Choudhary, Zafar. 2009, October. 'Look Inwards Also'. *Epilogue* 3 (10): 11.

———. 2010, May. 'Who Patronises Caste Politics in Rajouri, Poonch'. *Epilogue* 4 (5): 14–16.

———. 2010, May. 'Inside the Mind of Pir Panchal'. *Epilogue* 4 (5): 5.

Chowdhary, Rekha. 2009, October. 'The Politics of Regional Identity'. *Epilogue* 3 (10), 16–21.

Daily Excelsior. 2008, 13 June. 'Divided Hurriyat United over SB'.

Gajendragadkar Commission Report. 1968. Jammu: Ranbir Government Press.

Ganai, Naseer A. 2009, 23 August. 'Is Chenab Valley Hill Development Council Making Headway?' *Greater Kashmir*. http://www.greaterkashmir.com/news/news/is-chenab-valley-hill-development-council-making-headway/58892.html (accessed on 10 September 2018).

Kak, M. L. 2002, 13 July. 'Three Is Better than One?' http://www.tribuneindia.com/2002/20020713/windows/main1.htm (accessed on 10 September 2018).

Majid, Zulfiqar Majid. 2008, 14 June. 'Delhi Changing State Demography'. *Greater Kashmir*.

Maini, K. D. 2010, 10 May. 'Rajouri & Poonch: Facing the Challenges Ahead'. *Epilogue* 4 (5): 17–20.

Noorani, A. G. 2008, 13–26 September, 'Why Jammu Erupts'. *Frontline* 25 (19). http://www.frontline.in/static/html/fl2519/stories/20080926251907800.htm (accessed on 9 September 2018).

Pargal, Sanjeev. 2015, 5 July. 'Mufti Rules Out Council, Sets Up Chenab Valley Development Fund'. *Daily Excelsior*. http://www.dailyexcelsior.com/mufti-rules-out-council-sets-up-chenab-valley-development-fund/ (accessed on 9 September 2018).

Praveen Swami, 'Chapnari's Terror,' https://www.frontline.in/static/html/fl1514/15141180.htm (accessed on 5 November 2018).

———. 2006. '"Sons and Daughters of India": Ladakh's Reluctant Tribes'. In *Indigeneity in India*, edited by Bengt G. Karlsson and Tanka B. Subba. London: Kegan Paul.

Puri, Balraj. 1981. *Jammu and Kashmir: Triumph and Tragedy of Indian Federalisation*, New Delhi: Sterling Publishers.

———. 1982, 20 February. 'Route of Ladakh's Integration'. *Economic & Political Weekly* 17 (8): 273–275.

———. 1999. *Jammu & Kashmir Regional Autonomy: A Report*. Jammu: Jay Kay Book House.

Puri, Luv. 2002. 'Insurgency in Jammu Region'. http://www.prembhatiatrust.com/Lov%20puri.pdf (accessed on 9 September 2018).

Regional Autonomy Committee Report. 1999, Government of Jammu and Kashmir, Ranbir Press.

Schofield, Victoria. 2003. *Kashmir in Conflict: India, Pakistan and the Unending War*. London: I.B. Tauris.

Singh, Ajit. 2007. 'Agitational Politics of Jammu Region: An Analysis'. In *Conflict and Politics in Jammu and Kashmir*, edited by Avineet Prashar and Paawan Vivek. Jammu: Saksham Books International.

Swami, Parveen. 1998, 25 April–8 May. 'Divide over Medical Seats'. *Frontline* 15 (9).

———. 1998, 4 July. 'Chapnari's Terror'. *Frontline* 15 (14). http:// www.frontline.in/static/html/fl1514/15141180.htm (accessed on 5 November 2018).

———. 1999, 31 July–13 August. 'Massacres and Cold Facts'. *Frontline* 16 (16). http://www.frontline.in/static/html/fl1616/16160250.htm (accessed on 10 September 2018).

———. 2006, 2 May. 'Politics and Practice of Communal Massacres in Jammu and Kashmir'. *The Hindu*. http://www.thehindu.com/todays-paper/tp-national/politics-and-practice- of-communal-massacres-in-jammu-and-kashmir/article3127583.ece (accessed on 10 September 2018).

Van Beek, Martijn. 2001. 'Public Secrets, Conscious Amnesia, and the Celebration of Autonomy for Ladakh'. In *States of Imagination: Ethnographic Explorations of the Postcolonial State*, edited by Thomas Blom Hansen and Finn Stepputat, 365–390. Durham, NC: Duke University Press.

———. 2004. 'Dangerous Liaisons: Hindu Nationalism and Buddhist Radicalism in Ladakh'. In *Religious Radicalism and Security in South Asia*, edited by Satu P. Limaye, Mohan Malik, and Robert G. Wirsing, 193–218. Honolulu, HI: Asia-Pacific Centre for Security Studies.

9

Democracy and Politics of Separatism in Kashmir

2014 and After

The politics of the state of J&K has been undergoing a very intricate phase since 2014. Despite a massive disaster which inundated large parts of the Valley and killed many people in Jammu region, the state went through one of the most successful democratic exercises—the 2014 Assembly election. The election, on the whole, formed an important moment in the history of the internal politics of the state from various perspectives. For one, for the conflict-ridden politics of Kashmir, it was marked by such intensity of competition and keen involvement of people that it resulted in making the boycott politics of the separatists completely redundant. By the 'normalcy' of the electoral processes one could gauge as to how the democratic politics that had seen a turning point in 2002 had become entrenched by 2014.

Seen from another perspective, the election, throwing up the challenge of the fragmented verdict, generated an unparalleled political situation in which the politically and ideologically divergent forces were forced to come together for the sake of forming the government. The PDP–BJP government that was formed after the election was not only faced with the challenge of contradictory ideological position of the alliance partners but also with the complexity of competitive and clashing logics of the regional politics. The coalition had the possibilities of bridging the regional gap as well as of increasing the regional polarization.

Notwithstanding the success of the 2014 Assembly election, the democratic forces continued to face the challenge of separatist politics and this challenge came into the open soon when the valley of

Kashmir was in the grip of major turbulence in the middle of 2016. This turbulence not only consumed the whole of the summer of 2016 but resulted in an impact that was to be felt for the months to come. With normalcy being completely shattered, the democratic forces were once more pushed on the back foot. It was only towards the middle of the year of 2017 that mainstream political actors could recapture the political space.

It has been rather a difficult time for the state not only with democratic politics facing a constant challenge from the separatist politics, but also the coalition government collapsing in June 2018. It is in the background of these challenges that the present chapter is framed. It is divided in three parts: the first part makes a detailed analysis of the 2014 Assembly election; the second part focuses on the coalition government of PDP–BJP; and the third part deals with 2016 separatist upsurge.

2014 ASSEMBLY ELECTION

PARTICIPATORY NATURE OF ELECTION IN KASHMIR

As stated above, one of the highlights of the 2014 Assembly election was its participatory nature and its rejection of separatists' call for poll boycott. From all angles it could be characterized as a 'normal' election which was intensely competitive and keenly contested. It went through a process of fierce campaigning and generated sufficient interest among the people. The animated electoral scenario was quite different from the one that existed a decade back when rather than electoral politics, it was the boycott politics that had its sway in Kashmir Valley.

Like the 2008 Assembly election, people came out in large numbers to cast their vote. On the whole, the state recorded a poll percentage of 65.91 per cent. In Kashmir, the trend for voting was set during the first phase of election itself when more than 70 per cent voter turnout was recorded in five constituencies of northern Kashmir. As the polling entered into the next few phases, the enthusiasm for voting continued to be reflected. At the end of all the phases of polling in Kashmir, one could note that there were as many as 30 out of the total 46 constituencies in this region where voter turnout was more than 50 per cent; 23 constituencies where it was more than 60 per cent; 13 constituencies with more than 70 per cent; and five constituencies with more than 80 per cent voter turnout. There were certain constituencies in Central Kashmir where the polling percentage was relatively much lower. For instance, in the constituencies of Habbakadal, Amirakadal, Khanyar, Idgah, Zadibal and Hazratbal, there was less than 30 per cent voter turnout. But even here, compared to the 2002 and 2008 Assembly elections, the voter turnout was significantly higher.

That the electoral politics had been entrenched in Kashmir was clearly reflected in the 2014 Assembly election. Despite the fact that the state was still struggling with the flood situation, electoral process was quite competitive and participatory. So upbeat was the electoral environment in the Valley that although the separatists gave a call for boycott, they did not pursue it seriously. As the process of voting started, one could see that rather than the mood for boycott, the general orientation was to exercise the right to franchise.

In terms of the relation between the democratic and separatist politics, there was another context which was symbolic of the expanding democratic space. This was entry of the People's Conference in the electoral process in a rather big way. The party that had shunned its separatist background formally fielded candidates not only in its stronghold in North Kashmir but in many other constituencies of Kashmir. In the end, the party succeeded in registering its victory in two seats with a vote share of 4.23 per cent in the region.

Electoral Outcome: Realignment of Political Forces and Regionally Fractured Mandate

Very keenly contested and highly competitive in nature, the 2014 Assembly election gave a highly fractured mandate (see Table 9.1). With four major political parties, namely the NC, PDP, Congress and BJP, staking a claim to political power and with multi-cornered contests in many constituencies, no political party succeeded in crossing the half-way mark. The largest number of seats that any party could get was 28—that of the PDP. It was followed by the BJP

Table 9.1 *Performance of Political Parties at State Level: 2014 Assembly Election*

Party	*Seats*	*Percentage of Votes*
NC	15	20.8
INC	12	18
PDP	28	22.7
BJP	25	23
People's Conference	2	1.9
Independents and Others	5	13.6

Source: Statistical Report on General ELection, 2014, to Legislative Assembly of Jammu & Kashmir.

which got 25 seats. Among the rest, 15 seats were captured by the NC, 12 by the Congress, 2 by the People's Conference and 5 by the Independents and other parties. The fractured mandate was reflected also in terms of the vote share with 23 per cent votes being polled by BJP, 22.7 per cent by PDP, 20.8 per cent by the NC and 18 per cent by the INC.

Within the power politics, the 2014 Assembly election represented a major change in the way the political parties were positioned in the state. The NC that had already lost its dominance in 2002, also lost its leading position in 2014 (see Table 9.2). Both in 2002 and 2008, it not only held the largest number of seats both at the level of the state and in Kashmir region, but it also had the largest share of votes at both the levels. Although its position was challenged by the presence of PDP in Kashmir region, and multiplicity of parties at the state level, yet it was able to maintain its leading position. However, this time, while the PDP emerged as the largest party of the state in terms of seats, the BJP emerged as the largest party of the state in terms of its share of votes. The NC, getting 15 seats this time, trailed behind the PDP with its 28 seats and BJP with its 25 seats and was placed at the third position. The loss of the electoral space of the NC was reflected in its share of votes as well. Thus from 34.78 per cent votes in its favour at the state level in 1996, its vote share was reduced to 28.23 per cent in 2002 and 23.07 per cent in 2008. It was in Kashmir region that the party faced significant losses. It was beaten by the PDP in terms

Table 9.2 *Performance of NC at the State and Regional Levels: 1996–2014*

	J&K State		Kashmir Region		Jammu Region		Ladakh Region	
	Number of Seats (Total 87)	Percentage Share of Votes	Number of Seats (Total 46)	Percentage Share of Votes	Number of Seats (Total 37)	Percentage Share of votes	Number of Seats (Total 4)	Percentage Share of Votes
1996	57	34.78	40	48.15	14	23.72	3	46.63
2002	28	28.23	18	35.67	9	23.94	1	5.42
2008	28	23.07	20	27.51	6	14.3	2	28.44
2014	15	20.80	12	29.10	3	14.39	0	8.09

Source: ECI, Statistical Report on General Election, 2008, to the Legislative Assembly of Jammu and Kashmir.

of number of seats. Compared to the 25 seats of PDP, it could register its victories only on 12 seats.[1]

Although the NC's decline could be seen mainly in Kashmir region which it dominated till 1996, its electoral space had also been gradually shrinking in other regions of the state as well. Thus in Jammu region the number of seats that the party held was reduced from 14/37 in 1996 to nine in 2002 and six in 2008. In 2014, the number come down to 3. Its share of votes that was registered at around 23 per cent in 1996 and 2002 was reduced to around 14 per cent by 2014. In Ladakh similarly, the party had held three of the four seats in 1996. In 2002, the party had held one seat and in 2008 it had registered its victory in two seats. In 2014, it failed to obtain even one seat. Its share of votes meanwhile was reduced from 46.63 per cent in 1996 to 8.09 per cent in 2014.

For a party that had been dominating the politics of the state in general and the Kashmir region in particular, the 2014 Assembly election reflected a change not merely in terms of shrinking space of this party but also of having to operate within intensely competitive space. Being the ruling party in alliance with the Congress during 2008–2014 period, the party could not overcome the anti-incumbency factor. This factor was clearly reflected during the Parliamentary election held barely few months prior to the Assembly election. In that election, the NC for the first time failed to bag even one seat in the Lok Sabha. (Of the six seats of the state, three were captured by the BJP and the other three by the PDP.)

While the poor performance of the NC in 2014 Assembly election could be partially explained with reference to its incapacity in providing good governance and particularly, its failure to address the issues of employment, corruption, infrastructure including roads and power, there were other reasons for the loss of its electoral space. The party had a difficult beginning after it formed the government at the fag end

[1] Its vote share in this region was registered at 29.10 per cent. This was much lower from its 48.15 per cent vote share in 1996 and 35.67 per cent in 2002. However, as compared to its vote share of 27.51 per cent in 2008, it was able to improve it to 29.10 per cent this time.

of 2008. This was the time when the Valley was undergoing a renewed assertion of separatist politics. Despite the fact that people had come out to participate in large numbers during the 2008 Assembly election, the separatist politics was still in ascendance. This was clearly reflected soon after the formation of the government as Kashmir Valley got caught up in the separatist upsurge. While the whole of 2009 was consumed by the issue of rape and murder of two women in Shopian, there was a massive separatist upsurge in 2010 which lasted for more than five months. The NC government had to face overwhelming resentment for the handling of protests, especially the killing of 120 youth as well as for the detention of a large number of youth (the stone pelters) under the Public Security Act. The NC also faced the public wrath over the handling of hanging of Afzal Guru.[2]

Seen from the perspective of the NC, the 2014 election represents a very significant shift. For an organization that represented the Kashmiri identity politics from the beginning, this election marked the end of an era. Getting defeated to a party that had come into existence only one and a half decades back, one could see the mirror image of the changing times. The Kashmiri identity politics, one could see, had travelled a long way since it was initiated by the charismatic leader of the party, Sheikh Abdullah.

The decline of the NC in Kashmir region had been matched with the ascendancy of PDP there. This party that had made its entry in the politics of the state in 2002 with 16 seats and around 9 per cent votes, it could register its victory in 28 seats with 22.7 per cent votes. In terms of share of seats, it actually emerged as the largest party of the state. In Kashmir, its performance was spectacular as it surpassed the NC as the largest party and pushed it to a poor second position. As against 12 seats and around 29 per cent votes of the NC in Kashmir, this party came to hold 25 seats with around 37 per cent votes.

[2] Although it was a coalition government and the Congress was as much the partner, however, in Kashmir Valley, all resentment was channelled against the NC. The NC was actually seen to be a weaker partner which failed in providing succour to people facing the implications of conflict situation, particularly the militarized approach of the state.

Beyond Kashmir, the PDP had been able to create a space for itself in the Muslim-majority parts of Jammu region. In 2008, the party had won two seats in the predominantly Muslim constituencies of Mendhar and Darhal in the Poonch–Rajouri belt. In 2014, it succeeded in winning three seats from the same belt.

Although predominantly locating itself in Kashmir region, the PDP had started changing its political strategies in the post-2008 period. Understanding the limitations of the region-specific agenda in the context of highly competitive electoral space in Kashmir region, it sought to redefine itself as an all-state party and extend its base in Jammu and Ladakh regions. In the process, it sought to recruit influential opinion-makers in the leadership position from these regions. As a result, the party in 2014 was able to carve some space within the Hindu-majority areas of Jammu region. Not only it won the seat of Rajouri which has a significant population of Hindus, it also emerged as a runner-up in the Hindu-dominated constituencies of Nowshera and R. S. Pura. On the whole, the party has been improving its base in Jammu region. From less than 2 per cent vote share in 2002 and 6.89 per cent in 2008, it increased its vote share to around 11 per cent in 2014. The party also targeted Ladakh during this election. Here the party had no base till 2008 and even in 2014 it failed to win a single seat here, but it registered a vote share of 11.77 per cent (see Table 9.3).

One of the striking features of the 2014 Assembly election of J&K was the unprecedented performance of the BJP. Until the 2008 Assembly elections, the BJP was one of the competing parties in Jammu region. Even after its optimum score of 11 seats in the 2008 Assembly election, it was trailing behind the Congress both in terms of seats share of votes. In what can be termed as a path-breaking outcome of the 2014 Assembly election, this party emerged as the dominant party of this region winning as many as 25 of 37 seats and having a vote share of 40 per cent. It is this position of dominance which made this party a major contender for power at the state level. In any case, at the state level, this party emerged as the largest party in terms of vote share (23%) and in terms of seats its tally was comparable to that of the PDP.

Table 9.3 *Performance of PDP at the State and Regional Levels: 2002–2014*

	State Level Performance of PDP		*Kashmir Region*		*Jammu Region*		*Ladakh Region*	
	Number of Seats (Total 87)	*Percentage Share of Votes*	*Number of Seats (Total 46)*	*Percentage Share of Votes*	*Number of Seats (Total 37)*	*Percentage Share of Votes*	*Number of Seats (4)*	*Percentage Share of Votes*
2002	16	9.04	16	24.51	0	1.76	0	–
2008	21	15.39	19	27.41	2	6.88	0	0.54
2014	28	22.7	25	37.30	3	10.99	0	11.77

Source: ECI, Statistical Reports of Assembly Elections 2002, 2008, 2014.

From any perspective, the rise of BJP in J&K was phenomenal. Its emergence as the dominant party of Jammu region was reflected from its sheer numbers and the weakened position of all other parties (see Table 9.4). The combined strength of all other parties (11) was less than half its numbers. The maximum number of seats that any other party held against its 25 seats was that of Congress (05). Both PDP and NC held three seats each.

Going beyond its traditional constituencies in the Hindu heartland of the region, the party made its presence felt all over the region. For the first time, it entered the Muslim-majority Doda belt constituted of the three districts of Doda, Ramban and Kishtwar, winning four of the six seats, as well as the Rajouri district, winning two of the four seats here. In what can be described as consolidation of the Hindu votes, the party was able to win from any constituency which had a substantial Hindu population. In the Hindu heartland which comprised 21 constituencies across the four districts of Jammu, Samba, Kathua and Udhampur, it actually gained complete control (see Table 9.5). Here the party won all but three seats, of which one went to a rebel candidate from the party and the other two were obtained by the NC. The vote share of the party in this belt was still higher, at 50.23 per cent. In 2008, the party had polled only 26.74 per cent votes here and it had shared the electoral space with many other parties. Thus while it had captured 10 seats, Congress had five seats, Panthers Party had three, NC had one seat and two seats were obtained by independent candidates.

What clearly reflected in the outcome of the elections was the consolidation of Hindu votes not only across the urban–rural divide but also across the caste and subregional divides. One could say this with reference to the total hold of the party in the constituencies reserved for the SCs (see Table 9.6). The party which had held three of the seven reserved constituencies in 2008 now captured all the seven constituencies. Its share of votes was also increased here, from 31.75 per cent to 55.67 per cent. As the trend has been, its share of votes in the reserved constituencies was much higher not only in comparison to its share of votes in the region but also in comparison to the 21 constituencies of the Hindu belt. As against 50.23 per cent vote share of BJP in this belt, in the reserved constituencies it was as high as 55.67 per cent.

Table 9.4 *Party Performance in Jammu Region: 1996–2014*

	1996 Assembly Election		*2002 Assembly Election*		*2008 Assembly Election*		*2014 Assembly Election*	
	Seats	*Percentage of Vote Share*	*Seats*	*Percentage of Vote Share*	*Seats*	*Percentage of Vote Share*	*Seats*	*Percentage of Vote Share*
BJP	8	21.10	1	12.3	11	21.98	25	40.53
Congress	4	20.02	15	29.79	13	22.97	5	20.83
NC	14	23.72	9	23.94	6	19.31	3	14.39
Panthers Party	1	2.55	4	7.02	3	5.69	–	2.55
BSP	4	11.19	1	6.83	–	5.78	–	2.39
Janata Dal	4	7.83	–	–	–	–	–	–
PDP	0	–	–	1.76	2	6.59	3	10.99
Others and Independents	2	13.59	7	18.36	2	17.68	1	8.32

Source: ECI, Statistical Reports of Assembly Elections 1996, 2002, 2008, 2014.

Table 9.5 *Comparative Analysis of Hindu Belt of Jammu Region Comprising 21 Constituencies in Four Districts of Jammu, Samba, Kathua and Udhampur: 2008 and 2014 Assembly Elections*

	2014 Assembly Election		2008 Assembly Election	
	Share of Seats	Percentage Share of Votes	Share of Seats	Percentage Share of Votes
BJP	18	50.23	10	26.74
Congress	0	18.26	5	20.96
PP	0	4.05	3	8.52
BSP	0	3.07	0	8.34
NC	2	16.73	1	12.72
PDP	0	4.80	0	2.37

Source: ECI, Statistical Reports of Assembly Elections 2008 and 2014.

With BJP holding a pre-eminent position in the Jammu region, there are interesting implications for the politics of the state. As already stated, this was not the first time that a party registered its victory in the bulk of seats in Jammu region. In 1983, the Congress had got a large share of seats in the region. However, at that time, the electoral space of Kashmir region was not fragmented and the NC had swept that region. Compared to NC, therefore, the Jammu-based Congress was a smaller party and therefore could not challenge its role. However, what was peculiar about the 2014 Assembly election was the utterly fragmented electoral space of Kashmir region which gave BJP an edge and in the process a greater bargaining power for Jammu region in the power politics.

The fractured mandate of 2014 was in accordance with the pattern that the electoral politics had been following since 2002. However, there was some difference in the way the mandate was fractured this time. For the first time, the mandate besides being fractured on the party lines was also simultaneously fractured on the regional lines. As a result, a different party emerged as dominant in each of the three regions. Thus, while PDP with 25/46 seats emerged as the largest party of Kashmir, BJP dominated the electoral space of Jammu region with 25/37 seats. In Ladakh, it was the Congress Party which won three of the four seats. What was peculiar about the election was that there

Table 9.6 *BJP's Performance in Seven Constituencies Reserved for SC: 1996–2014*

Year of Election	*Share of BJP Votes in Jammu Region*	*Share of BJP Seats in Jammu Region*	*Percentage of Seats*	*Share of BJP Votes in Reserved Constituencies*	*Share of BJP Seats in Reserved Constituencies*	*Percentage of Seats*
1996	21.10	8	21.62	28.40	3	42.85
2002	12.3	1	2.70	11.88	0	0
2008	22.9	11	29.72	31.75	3	42.85
2014	40.53	25	67.56	55.67	7	100

Source: ECI, Statistical Reports of Assembly Elections 1996, 2002, 2008, 2014.

was no one party that had its effective presence in all the three regions. The position of both NC and Congress was quite weakened this time. The NC failed to have any presence in Ladakh and Jammu regions; its number was so reduced that it couldn't play the role of being a bridge between the regions in any manner.

The only party that had its presence in all the three regions was the Congress. But it had on the whole a relatively weak presence in the state. In terms of its total seats, it was placed at number four and trailed behind the PDP, BJP and NC. Hence, its presence, except in the region of Ladakh (where it won three of the four seats), was quite insignificant. In Jammu region, where it had its highest count, it got all the seats from the Muslim-majority constituencies and was not represented in the Hindu belt. The BJP meanwhile dominated the Hindu constituency of Jammu region but had no presence in Kashmir and Ladakh. The PDP similarly dominated the Kashmir region and had a very limited presence in Jammu region, with all the three seats from the Muslim pockets of Poonch–Rajouri belt.

PDP–BJP COALITION GOVERNMENT: CHALLENGES OF IDEOLOGICAL CONTRADICTIONS

One of the major outcomes of the fractured mandate during the 2014 Assembly election was that two such parties emerged as the major claimants of political power which were placed in ideologically opposite position. What further complicated the situation was the fact that the claims of neither of the two parties could be ignored as these were based on their performance on regional basis. Thus while the PDP had emerged as the dominant party of the Kashmir region, the BJP swept the polls in Jammu region. To ignore the claims of any of these two parties would have serious implications for the regional politics of the state.

However, the alliance of the two parties for the sake of forming the government threw lots of challenges. The two parties had not only been holding antagonistic political positions but had been actually representing mutually exclusive constituencies. Their basic differences started with reference to the special constitutional position of the state.

While the BJP had abolition of Article 370 at the core of its politics, the PDP stood for defending this article. In the ongoing context of conflict situation, the PDP recognizing the internal and external dimensions of conflict saw a role for separatists and Pakistan in conflict resolution. This perspective was completely rejected by the BJP as it saw Pakistan and separatists as perpetrators of 'proxy war'. While the PDP critiqued the state for human rights violation and demanded 'demilitarization' and removal of AFSPA, the BJP saw these demands as harming the national interest. BJP had also been opposed to PDP's vision of conflict resolution, especially its framework of 'self-rule' as it perceived it to be challenging the sovereignty of the State.

With PDP joining the BJP in forming the government, there was a lot of scepticism in Kashmir region. This was mainly for the reason that PDP had mobilized the voters during this election by generating anti-BJP emotions. Since BJP had given the slogan of 44 plus seats and sought to enter the electoral arena of Kashmir in a big way, the PDP had sought the mandate in the name of keeping BJP away. With such emotions being raised against the BJP, the PDP's act of joining the BJP in forming the government was seen as an act of betrayal. On the whole, the alliance between the two parties was projected as 'unholy'.

Keeping in view the politically divergent position of the two parties, a formal agenda for alliance was devised. In its form, the agenda was quite dynamic and reflected the flexibility on both the sides. The BJP, on the whole, seemed to have come down from its stated political position and accommodated many issues that were raised by the PDP from the perspective of its core constituency of Kashmiris. While dealing with Article 370, the most controversial issue between the two parties, the agenda stated that 'considering the political and legislative realities, the present position will be maintained on all the constitutional provisions pertaining to J&K including the special status in the Constitution of India'. In the process of negotiating the differences, it was a big leap forward. Going beyond its ideological position, the BJP had not merely pushed back from its commitment of abolition of the Article, but also accepted it as a 'political reality' of the state and agreed to maintain it. Similarly, going beyond the aggressive position of the BJP vis-à-vis the dialogue with Pakistan and Hurriyat, the agenda expressed its commitment to the peace process and further boosting the cross-LoC interactions. Another area where the agenda went much beyond the stated position of the BJP related to AFSPA and DAA. The agenda therefore made reference to the possibility of examining 'the need and desirability of all the special laws being applied to the state in view of the situation which is improving' and the possibility of de-notifying the DAA with a view to enable the Union Government to take a final view on the continuation of the AFSPA in these areas. A commitment was also made about land under the control of the security forces.

Similar flexibility was seen in PDP towards the concerns of the BJP vis-à-vis its constituency in Jammu region. The agenda therefore included the issue of the West Pakistan refugees.[3] It made commitment to 'take measures for sustenance and livelihood' of these refugees. The issue was chalked out as a 'humanitarian' rather than a political one. Various other related concerns included those related to the return of Kashmiri Pandits to the Valley, the issue of POK refugees of various kinds and the issues concerning the people living on the border. The agenda also acknowledged the need for equitable development of all three regions and also referred to the tourist potentials of Jammu region. Among other controversial issues was included the one related to the constitution of a delimitation commission—a long standing demand raised in Jammu region but vehemently opposed in Kashmir region.

The agenda for alliance, however, remained mostly on paper and the contradictory expectations of the constituencies that the two parties

[3] Kashmir-based parties including the NC and PDP are not sympathetic to the problems faced by the West Pakistan refugees. These refugees are the non-state subject residents of the state who got located in the state in the wake of Partition in 1947. Since they have come from West Pakistan, they don't enjoy the rights and privileges meant exclusively for the permanent residents of the state. Thus, they cannot seek jobs in the state services, vote in the state elections including the Assembly, municipal and panchayat elections, and are denied other privileges associated with the permanent residents of the state. The Jammu-based parties including the BJP have been raising the issue of their discrimination and have been demanding the extension of all those rights to them which are enjoyed by the permanent residents of the state.

represented led to recurring tensions between the coalition partners. On the whole the coalition seemed to be quite fragile especially in the initial two years. The first such issue which became a source of tension between the two parties was related to the question of AFSPA. The issue became contentious with Mufti Sayeed showing his keenness to revoke this law from some parts of the state and BJP legislators opposing it both within and outside the Legislative Assembly (Wani and Waza 2015). Among other issues which became contentious between the two parties included those related to location of AIIMS, with PDP wanting it to be located in Kashmir and BJP wanting it in Jammu region. The issue was resolved with the Central Government agreeing to provide AIIMS to both the regions. During the early period of coalition, the issue of flag also became controversial. The issue was triggered with the High Court's directive that the state flag be given equal importance along the national flag, a point to which the BJP was not agreeable. Another issue that became a point of controversy between the two coalition partners followed the High Court decision regarding enforcement of beef ban in the state. The BJP insisted on bringing in a new law on beef ban, while the PDP was opposed to the ban. In the context of politics around the beef ban at the national level, this issue became quite politicized (Chakravarty 2016). The issue of release of Masarat Alam, a separatist of the Geelani camp, as well as the issue of return and resettlement of Kashmiri Pandits also generated tensions between the PDP and BJP.

A major challenge was faced by the coalition government with the passing away of Mufti Sayeed, the patron of the PDP. Mehbooba Mufti, who succeeded her father as the leader of the party, rather than going ahead with taking over the position of CM, kept the BJP waiting for months together before she re-formed the PDP–BJP government. One reason for her reluctance seemed to be the feedback from her Kashmiri constituency. As BJP associates kept on raising issues that seemed to challenge the political position of the PDP, the response of the Kashmiris started becoming more negative about the coalition. On its part, the PDP had its own set of complaints against the BJP. Of these the most important being that there was 'poor headway on the joint agenda' (Ashiq 2016).

The next phase of the PDP–BJP government with Mehbooba Mufti as the CM saw similar tension between the coalition partners. Among various issues that caused such tension was the issue of Article 35A, which was challenged by the BJP associates in the Supreme Court. As per its ideological position, the BJP has been opposed to Article 35A which gives the discretionary power to the state to define the 'permanent residents' of the state and confer them special rights and privileges that go along with it. The PDP is committed to this Article being retained in the form in which it is incorporated in the Constitution.[4]

The 2016 agitation also brought to the surface the differences between the two parties. There were basic differences between the two parties about the handling of stone pelters and mob violence. While the BJP was in favour of strong tactics against the agitators, the PDP was insistent on more sympathetic dealing with the youth on the streets. Among other issues, the issues related to India–Pakistan dialogue and dialogue with the separatists have been the points of continuous discord between the two parties. There were also acute differences between the two parties on the issue of Rohingya refugees in Jammu region with PDP being seen as soft on them and BJP insisting on their 'anti-national' role and seeking their deportation from Jammu. Towards the beginning of 2018, acute differences emerged between the PDP and BJP around the issue of murder and rape of an eight-year-old child in Kathua district. The brutal incident not only pushed the government in two opposite directions but also resulted in generating internal turbulence within the BJP. While two ministers who had attended the rallies of Hindu Ekta Manch, fighting on the side of the accused and demanding CBI rather than the ongoing Crime Branch enquiry, had to resign, the positions of the Speaker and the deputy CM held by this party had to be swapped and the state party president had to be changed. With BJP cadre and leaders showing lack of confidence in the Crime Branch and justifying the demand for CBI enquiry, and PDP cadre and leaders insisting on continuing

[4] How the two parties stood on this question reflected from the controversy created around a remark of the CM that 'If Article 35-A is tinkered with, no one in the State will hold the national flag in Kashmir.' BJP on its part turned the remark as 'shocking and ridiculous' (Newsclick 2017).

with the handling of the case by the Crime Branch, the fragility of the coalition often seemed to be out in the open ultimately leading to the collapse in June 2018.

THE SEPARATIST UPSURGE OF 2016

Despite the fact that the 2014 Assembly election was quite participatory and had given sufficient indications about the expansion of the democratic space, the Valley was shaken by a massive separatist upsurge during the middle of 2016.[5] Although the immediate point for triggering the separatist response was the killing of Burhan Wani, the Hizb commander, however, there were indications of simmering discontent, especially in South Kashmir, right after the formation of PDP–BJP government in early 2015. The year saw an increased frequency of protests and increased incidents of confrontation between the local militants and the security forces. The reports about the young boys from the area joining militancy had triggered the reports about the rise of the 'new wave of militancy' (Geelani 2016). This was a worrying situation for the security forces since militancy had started declining since 2003 and had reached its lowest point by 2014. A report prepared by the State Crime Record Bureau of J&K Crime Branch titled *Crime Gazette 2014* had indicated that militancy had been restricted to Sopore–Handwara belt in North Kashmir and Pulwama–Awantipore belt in South Kashmir. However, in the rest of the Valley, the number of militants was insignificant. Thus, there were 10 such districts where the number of active militants was less than 10.

However, after 2014, the number of militants started increasing.[6] What was particular about this 'new wave of militancy' was that those

[5] After the massive 2010 agitation, there was no major agitation even when there were some reflection of simmering of discontent among the youth. One major event that showed signs of simmering tension was in 2013 when Afzal Guru was hanged. There was an angry response in Kashmir which had to be kept under curfew for a number of days.

[6] As per an information made available in Rajya Sabha by the Minister of State for Home Affairs, Haribhai Parathibhai Chaudhary, while 60 local youth had joined militancy in the year 2014, 79 more had joined in 2015 (*Daily Excelsior* 24 December 2015,

joining militancy were not crossing over to Pakistan to get trained there. But they were self-trained locally. Their local roots made a lot of difference to the linkage they had with the people. Local youth, therefore, strongly identified with them and came to be linked with them via the use of social media.

Although there were a few militant attacks at the time of the 2014 Assembly poll, however, it was in April 2015 that a fresh spate of militant attacks started in Kashmir Valley. The increased militant activity by this time was reflected from the increased number of encounters taking place. As per Riyaz Wani, in a period of around two months (January 2016–10 March 2016), there were intermittent encounters in which as many as 24 militants and seven security personnel were killed. Most of these encounters took place in the four districts of South Kashmir—Anantnag, Shopian, Pulwama and Kulgam (Wani 2016). That this part of the Valley had become the new central point of militancy was something peculiar since traditionally militancy was mainly rooted in the areas around the LoC and in North Kashmir areas such as Baramulla and Kupwara.

Militancy in South Kashmir started quite abruptly. Until the 2014 Assembly election this area was vibrating with electoral activities. The entire South Kashmir, to quote a senior journalist,

> ... was a hub of mainstream activity. Prime Minister Narendra Modi's large size hoardings besides BJP's banners, buntings and flags remained intact for over two months even as the ruling party at the Centre had little fertile ground in the Valley's saffron zone. PDP, NC and Congress conducted hundreds of well-attended rallies before the Valley witnessed arguably the best held and the least controversial Assembly elections (Fayyaz 2015c).

Just in a year's time, there was tremendous change in the situation. The areas around Tral, Awantipora, Pulwama and Shopian became the strongholds of militancy. Despite the fact that the young militants were self-trained and did not have much ammunition, they were

p. 1). By March 2016, the number of militants was reported to be 145 with 'most of them from South Kashmir, with local recruits decisively outnumbering the foreigners' (Wani 2016). While many of these militants were new, a few were also recycled (Geelani 2016). Most of the militants were joining the Hizbul Mujahideen; however, a few were also joining LeT.

highly motivated. That is the reason that they could not give a long fight when they were countered by the security forces and 'died within first hour of the gunfight' (Wani 2016).[7]

The socio-economic background of the militants of this phase was quite distinct. Many of them came from 'families with reasonable socio-economic status' (Geelani 2016). Quite young, either as teenagers or in their early twenties, their decision of joining militancy in most cases was sudden, related to some emergent situation at the ground level. As the newspapers reported, a few of them had consistently good educational record and career ambitions.[8]

One of the features of militancy during this phase was that the militants were popular and locally grounded. Since they were mostly local youth, people identified with them. The use of social media made them specifically popular among the younger people. Their photographs were shared and stories of their 'heroism' were circulated. Most of them were known by their names to the local population. Besides Burhaan Wani who had become an 'icon' because of the use of social media, there were others also whose stories of 'extraordinary feats' were circulated.

It is the popular association with the militants that funeral of militants killed in encounters became a site for youth mobilization. By 2015, it had become a trend for the locals to come in thousands to attend the funeral of the militants.[9] There were also reports of active

[7] In many cases, the militants armed themselves by snatching the weapons from the police personnel. During this period, there were many cases of snatching of weapons from the police force. In almost all of these cases, the militants were involved.

[8] Ishaq Parray, for instance, who 'had an ambition to become a scientist or a doctor, had secured an incredible 98.4% marks in his Matriculation exam. Even in Class 12th, he obtained over 85%. On account of his sharp comprehension of science and mathematics, coupled with his ambition, Ishaq came to be known as "Isaac Newton"' (Fayyaz 2016). Dawood Sheikh, another militant, had an ambition to become an engineer.

[9] Around 3,000–4,000 people were reported to have attended the funeral of Ishaq Parray. Similarly, the funeral of Hizbul Mujahideen militant Dawood Sheikh is reported to have been attended by people from several nearby villages (Wani 2016). Similarly the funeral of LeT Talib Afzal Shah was reported to have been attended by around 8,000 people (Fayyaz 2015a). Funeral of LeT's most wanted militant, Irshad Ganai, was

militants attending the funerals and offering 'gun salute'. The youth would be meanwhile waving Islamic flags and the mosques would be blaring 'pro-freedom' songs. All these indicated that the societal response towards militancy was changing. Unlike the preceding phase of separatism (2000–2014) when militancy had been delegitimized and popular support to the phenomenon had been withdrawn, it had gained new popularity.

That the societal response towards militancy was changing was reflected from another very peculiar phenomenon. Defying the advisory of the police restraining people from being present anywhere near the sites where the security forces would be engaging the militants in encounters, people would gather in large numbers showing their solidarity with the militants. There were incidents after incidents when security forces at the encounter sites were engaged by the demonstrating, sloganeering and stone-pelting local residents with the intension of pressurizing them to call off the operation or to give a chance to the militants to escape from the encounter site.[10] In a large number of cases, such attempts were successful and militants could escape.

Much before the killing of Burhaan Wani, the separatist sentiment in South Kashmir was already getting manifested in various forms. This sentiment was clearly reflected in the public demonstrations or during the religious congregations. While Pakistani flags would be hurled, pro-Pakistan and pro-freedom slogans would be shouted in these rallies. However, after his killing, the separatist sentiment became much more intensified.

attended by a still larger number of people. To quote Ahmed Ali Fayyaz, 'Residents and some separatist leaders claimed that 25,000 to 30,000 people participated in Ganai's funeral. However, independent reports put the number of the participants as 12,000 to 15,000. A J&K Police agency also reported that it was a gathering of 12,000 to 15,000 people' (Fayyaz 2015b).

[10] In one such situation when militants had been holed up in a building in Pampore in February 2016, there were reports of hundreds of women from 20 surrounding villages gathering nearby and singing Kashmiri wedding songs (Bashir 2016). Similarly, during an encounter in Aishmaqam, there was a gathering of around a thousand people who started indulging in sloganeering and stoning. With gathered civilians making it difficult for the security forces to attack the militants, the security forces would often be compelled to use force to disperse people leading to the loss of lives.

With Burhaan Wani militancy acquired a glorified form. Through the use of social media, he presented a romanticized version of militancy which made it attractive for the youth. Besides those who joined militancy, there were those who got ideologically connected with militancy. Separatism that had been earlier facing the challenge of credibility and leadership crisis, thereby gained depth as more and more young people started identifying with militancy. In the six years of his brief stint with militancy, Burhaan Wani's presence resulted in creating a new base for separatist politics both in rural and urban areas. He was a local hero who had replaced all other heroes that the Kashmiri youth followed. What was so special about him was that he represented a new age militancy that was much more rooted in Kashmir. He was a 'local boy' who did not cross border for training but trained locally and raised an impressive team of local boys who were seen as intelligent and coming from comfortable backgrounds. That he and others like him had rejected the option of being educated and following successful careers for militancy gave them an idealized status.

Burhaan was a child of conflict situation, born during the period of conflict. He represented the trauma of growing up in the violent and militarized situation. The story of his joining the militancy because of the harassment that he and his brother faced at the hands of the police sounded familiar for lots of youth. More than identifying with the Hizb, they identified with the circumstances in which he joined militancy.

A few years before his killing, Burhaan started gaining size larger than life, especially after his brother was killed, and he succeeded in evading the police, giving them a really tough time and continuously making his presence felt in the social media. By the time he was killed, he had become a cult figure.

His killing in July 2016 triggered an intense response. Although the youth in the age group of 12–25 were the main actors in the street protests which more than often took the form of stone pelting on the security forces, there was widespread support for the protests. In many ways, the situation was characterized as similar to that of 1990 when the authority of the state had totally collapsed. The normal life had been fully crippled with official curfews or the protest shutdown calls by the separatist leaders. For months together, all business activities, educational institutions and other kinds of activities were fully stalled. With so much anger and defiance on the streets, it was difficult to enforce the writ of the state. With protesters taking to the streets, there was almost no presence of government. It was only after the winter had set in and the government had officially moved to Jammu that it could engage itself in normal governance functions. Throughout the summer months, nothing in the name of government or governance moved.

During the protests in this period, militants dominated the scene with many of them appearing in public and seeking to mobilize support for militancy and separatism. Soon after the killing of Burhaan Wani, a rally was organized in Kareemabad in Pulwama in which Abu Dujana, the topmost LeT commander, along with other militants made appearance. The rally that was attended and addressed by political activists, religious and social leaders had a participation of around 50,000 people[11] (Jameel 2016).

One of the ramifications of the separatist mobilization during this period was the societal involvement in the separatist politics. Echoing the situation of the 1989–1990 period, people seemed to be swayed by the renewed demand for 'self-determination'. There was sufficient pressure on the people representing different walks of life to show their solidarity with the street politics. On the whole, there seemed to be a sense of identification with the separatist sentiment. The expression of the separatist sentiments during this period resulted in more youth involvement in militancy. In a written reply to the question by MLA Mubarak Gul in the State Assembly, CM Mehbooba Mufti stated that in the period of six months (between 9 July when Burhaan Wani was killed and January 2017) as many as 59 youths joined militancy (*Greater Kashmir* 2017).

One peculiar feature of the 2016 upsurge was that it was quite influenced by religious sentiments. Mosques were activated during

[11] Although a number of rallies were organized all over the Valley on 14 August, Pakistan's Independence Day, the biggest rally was held in Kulgam's Redwani village. The rally was addressed by four Hizbul Mujahideen militants (Masood 2016).

the upsurge. After the prayers in the mosques the freedom songs and Pakistan anthems were played.

The 2016 upsurge had serious implications for the democratic politics. In the intensity of separatist upsurge reflected on the streets, not only were the mainstream political leaders forced to withdraw from the scene, but the very legitimacy of the competitive politics was challenged. With the separatists calling for boycott of the mainstream political leaders, it became difficult for these leaders to move around and many of them shifted to Jammu and other places. So challenging was the situation that the process of holding a by-election to fill in a Parliamentary seat in Anantnag in April 2017 was postponed indefinitely. Most difficult was the situation for the PDP which till 2014 Assembly election held its sway in the south of Kashmir. Its alliance with the BJP in forming the government, after the election, had already alienated its political constituency. The reason for this being that it had taken a strong anti-BJP position during the election. The resentment against the PDP for joining hands with a party having an ideologically contradictory position, in fact, was in itself a reason for the extending influence of separatism in the post-2014 phase. During the 2016 separatist upsurge, the PDP further lost its political ground.[12]

To Conclude

This chapter dealing with the situation as it has evolved in the state of J&K since 2014 has reflected on the state of democratic and competitive politics, on the one hand, and the separatist politics, on the

[12] So much ascendant were the separatist sentiments at that time that the legislators of this party lost all contact with the people on the ground. Despite the instructions of Mehbooba Mufti to her party legislators that they remain in touch with people on the ground, the political leaders found it difficult to visit their constituencies or to visit those injured by pellets. So much was the pressure of the protestors on the streets that many mainstream political leaders publicly rejected the mainstream politics and joined the side of protestors. For instance, NC leader Hussain Misgar, who was the party's candidate against CM Mehbooba Mufti in the by-poll elections from Anantnag constituency, quit mainstream politics and joined an anti-India protest outside his residence. Similarly, participating in a debate in the Legislative Council over Kashmir killings, NC MLC Showkat Ganai said, Burhan was a freedom fighter and he attained martyrdom fighting for a cause (*Greater Kashmir* 3 January 2017).

other. These two phenomena, though operating in a parallel manner since 2002, also have been overlapping and cross-cutting each other at many points. The democratic politics of Kashmir, as we have seen in the previous chapters, has expanded in the shadow of separatism which in itself has not remained static but has been changing its form.

The different phases of separatism—the 'militancy' phase, the 'post-militancy' phase and the 'new-age militancy' separatism—have provided different challenges to the democratic politics. Despite the fact that the present phase of separatism is characterized by similar eulogization of militancy as it was in the first phase, unlike that time, it is not the violence and militarization that has thrown the challenge to democracy but the changing popular response to separatism. The post-2014 period has seen a fresh spate of separatist sentiments in the Valley. After the killing of Hizbul Mujahideen militant, Burhaan Wani, the separatist sentiment was further intensified. The situation as it evolved had the impact of denting the democratic space, at least in South Kashmir where the youth not only took to the street politics but also to militancy. The societal involvement in the eulogization of militants and militancy was reflected not only in the presence of a large number of people in funeral of the militants but also in the encounter sites. This has been rather a grim situation, considering the fact that only a decade back people had withdrawn their support to the militancy and its decline was linked to its delegitimacy. From that situation to the one in which the militants acquired the status of heroes leading to more and more young people joining militancy, it has been altogether a different scenario.

Democratic politics, in this scenario, has been struggling to sustain itself. Governance that suffered the most, at least during the summer of 2016, took time to find its feet. It was only by the end of that year that some normalcy could be attained. However, the democratic politics that took the maximum brunt during the period of upsurge has been slow to recover its political space.

The separatist politics, meanwhile, itself has been going through a critical phase. Although there has been a growing sense of scepticism in Kashmir for the last one decade or so, however, the way the anger, bitterness and resentment has been expressed during the last two to three years, indicates a sense of siege—a sense that has been reinforced by the lack of political momentum at any level. It is not only that the political response from the side of the state has been lacking, the separatist leadership itself has been politically paralyzed. With the initiative for sustaining the separatist politics having been shifted to the youth, the leaders have been forced to 'follow' the sentiment on the street. Off and on, questions are raised internally about the direction of the separatist politics and the role of the leaders. In the local newspapers debates are sometime framed around the cost of the separatist assertions, particularly in the context of the increasing loss of youth lives. But as there rises a fresh wave of separatist assertion on the streets, these questions tend to get sidelined.

References

Ashiq, Peerzada. 2016, 31 January. 'PDP, BJP Alliance Reaches Make-or-Break Point'. *The Hindu*. http://www.thehindu.com/news/national/other-states/jammu-and-kashmir-politics-pdp-bjp-alliance-reaches-makeorbreak-point/article8175784.ece (accessed on 7 September 2018).

Bashir, Abid. 2016, 24 February. 'Public Support for Militants Worries Police'. *Greater Kashmir*. http://www.greaterkashmir.com/news/front-page/public-support-for-militants-worries-police/210235.html (accessed on 7 September 2018).

Chakravarty, Ipsita. 2016, 13 January. 'The J&K Challenge: The PDP–BJP Coalition Must Put Their Disagreements Behind Them'. *Scroll.in*. https://scroll.in/article/801770/the-j-k-challenge-the-pdp-bjp-coalition-must-put-their-disagreements-behind-them (accessed on 5 December 2017).

Fayyaz, Ahmed Ali. 2015. 'Over 12000 Attend LeT Militant's Funeral'. http://aafayyaz.blogspot.in/2015/09/over-12000-attend-let-militants-funeral.html (accessed on 6 November 2018).

———. 2015a, 5 June. 'Out of 25 Police Districts in J&K, 11 Are Militancy-Free'. *State Times*. http://news.statetimes.in/out-of-25-police-districts-in-jk-11-are-militancy-free/ (accessed on 7 September 2018).

Fayyaz, Ahmed Ali. 2015b, 8 August. 'Despite "Restrictions," 8,000 Attend Militant's Funeral in PDP Bastion'. *State Times*. http://news.statetimes.in/despite-restrictions-8000-attend-militants-funeral-in-pdp-bastion/ (accessed on 7 September 2018).

———. 2015c, 19 August. 'Fresh Spell of Militancy in Jammu & Kashmir (1) In 23 Police Districts, Only 2 SPs Have Operational Background in Jammu

& Kashmir'. *State Times*. http://news.statetimes.in/fresh-spell-of-militancy-in-jammu-kashmir-1-in-23-police-districts-only-2-sps-have-operational-background-in-jammu-kashmir/ (accessed on 7 September 2018).

———. 2016, 15 February. '2 Civilians Killed in Clash after Militant's Death in Pulwama Encounter'. *State Times*. http://news.statetimes.in/2-civilians-killed-in-clash-after-militants-death-in-pulwama-encounter/ (accessed on 6 November 2018).

———. 2016a, 4 March. '"Isaac Newton" Picked Up Gun 12 Days after PDP and BJP Became Bedfellows in Kashmir'. *State Times*. http://news.statetimes.in/mla-west-reviews-era-pwd-works/ (accessed on 16 October 2016).

Geelani, Gowher. 2016a, 14 March. 'Young and Restless: New Breed of Militants in Kashmir Are Eager to Change the Status Quo'. http://www.catchnews.com/india-news/young-restless-new-breed-of-militants-in-kashmir-are-eager-to-change-the-status-quo-1457966008.html (accessed on 6 November 2018).

Greater Kashmir. 2017, 4 January. '59 Youth Joined Militancy after Killing of Burhan Wani'. http://www.greaterkashmir.com/news/kashmir/story/237786.html (accessed on 7 September 2018).

———. 2017, 3 January. 'Burhan was Freedom Fighter: NC Lawmaker'. http://www.greaterkashmir.com/news/front-page/burhan-was-freedom-fighter-nc-lawmaker/237810.html (accessed on 7 September 2018).

Jameel, Yusuf. 2016, 31 July. 'LeT's "Most Wanted" Abu Dojana Attends Pro-militant Rally in J&K'. *Deccan Chronicle*.

Masood, Bashaarat. 2016, 16 August. 'On Pakistan's Independence Day, Militants Hoist Flags, Address Rallies in Kashmir'. https://indianexpress.com/article/india/india-news-india/on-pakistans-i-day-militants-hoist-flags-address-rallies-in-kashmir-2975787/ (accessed on 7 September 2018).

Newsclick. 2017, 31 July. 'Kashmir's Special Status Faces Legal and Political Challenge'. https://newsclick.in/kashmirs-special-status-faces-legal-and-political-challenge (accessed on 7 September 2018).

Wani, Aijaz Ashraf, and Farooq Ahmad Waza. 2015, 8 August. 'PDP–BJP Coalition Government in J&K: 100 Days of Controversies and Policy Paralysis'. *Mainstream* http://www.mainstreamweekly.net/article5867.html (accessed on 6 December 2017).

Wani, Riyaz. 2016, 10 March. 'When a Militant Dies in Kashmir'. *Tehelka*. http://www.tehelka.com/2016/03/when-a-militant-dies-in-kashmir/ (accessed on 20 November 2016).

INDEX

ABOUT THE SERIES EDITORS AND AUTHOR

Suhas Palshikar taught Politics at Savitribai Phule Pune University and has been associated with Lokniti, Programme on Comparative Democracy of Centre for the Study of Developing Societies (CSDS). He is also the Chief Editor of the journal *Studies in Indian Politics*. He has co-edited two volumes on electoral politics: *Party Competition in Indian States: Electoral Politics in Post-Congress Polity* (2014) and *Electoral Politics in India: Resurgence of Bharatiya Janata Party* (2017). His most recent publication is *Indian Democracy* (2017).

Rajeshwari Deshpande is Professor of Politics at Savitribai Phule Pune University. She is a member of the editorial managing team of the journal *Studies in Indian Politics* and coordinates a forum in the journal on teaching and learning political science in India. She has published over 20 research articles in journals and edited volumes in English as well as in Marathi. She has edited the book *Politics of Welfare: Comparisons across Indian States*, with Louise Tillin and K. K. Kailash (2015).

Rekha Chowdhary served at the University of Jammu as Professor of Political Science till 2013. Since her superannuation, she has been Indian Council of Social Science Research (ICSSR) National Fellow and Fellow of Indian Institute of Advanced Study, Shimla. Earlier, she was a Fulbright Scholar at South Asia Studies, School of Advanced International Studies (SAIS), John Hopkins University, Washington, DC (2005); Commonwealth Fellow at Queen Elizabeth House (QEH), University of Oxford (1997–1998); and Fellow of South Asian Visiting Scholar Programme (SAVSP) at QEH, Oxford (1992–1993). She has been working on Jammu and Kashmir and dealing with issues related to identity politics, ethnicity, nationalism, conflict and peace process, and democratic politics. Following the developments in Jammu and Kashmir in the last three decades, she has been writing extensively about the changing trends in militancy and separatism and the competitive politics in leading national and international journals. Her more recent publications include *Jammu and Kashmir: Politics of Identity and Separatism* (2016) and *Identity Politics in Jammu and Kashmir* (2010).